Understanding Western Culture

Guobin Xu • Yanhui Chen • Lianhua Xu
Editors

Understanding Western Culture

Philosophy, Religion, Literature
and Organizational Culture

palgrave
macmillan

Editors
Guobin Xu
Guangdong University of Foreign
Studies
Guangzhou, China

Yanhui Chen
Guangdong University of Foreign
Studies
Guangzhou, China

Lianhua Xu
Guangdong University of Foreign
Studies
Guangzhou, China

Translators
Kaiju Chen
Guangdong University of Foreign
Studies
Guangzhou, China

Xiyuan Xiong
Sun Yat-sen University Press
Guangzhou, China

Wenquan Wu
Guangdong University of Foreign
Studies
Guangzhou, China

ISBN 978-981-10-8149-1   ISBN 978-981-10-8150-7   (eBook)
https://doi.org/10.1007/978-981-10-8150-7

Library of Congress Control Number: 2018930803

Cover illustration: Alexander Spatari

Printed on acid-free paper

This Palgrave Macmillan imprint is published by Springer Nature
The registered company is Springer Nature Singapore Pte Ltd.
The registered company address is: 152 Beach Road, #21-01/04 Gateway East, Singapore 189721, Singapore

ACKNOWLEDGMENTS

We were approached in 2012 by Professor Xu Guobin, Editor in Chief of the original works *Essentials of Chinese Culture* and *Essentials of Western Culture*, proposing that my research team translate these two books into English and publish them in English-speaking countries. Almost at the same time I was contacted with a publishing proposal by Alisa Pulver, Senior Editor at Palgrave Macmillan. Without the trust and unfailing support of these two parties over the following years, this large translation project—based on the 1.1 million Chinese characters in the original works to be translated for a series of four books, amounting to nearly 400,000 English words—would not have happened so soon after the publication of the original works. The copyright holder, South China University of Technology Press, showed immediate support for our translation project, and our particular gratitude goes to their editors and coordinators: Ms. Qiao Li and Ms. Wu Cuiwei.

Through the six years of painstaking translation and reviewing, we owe our sincere gratitude to the experts in the related areas, whose joint effort has transformed this translation project into the current four books.

Professor Xu Guobin, Chief Editor of the original monographs, always provided support at each stage. In December 2014, on completion of the translation and the first review round, Professor Xu suggested and organized an author–translator symposium, where associate editors Chen Yanhui and Xu Lianhua, together with all the authors of the original works, met with the leading translators, Professor Chen Kaiju, Professor Xiong Xiyuan and Professor Wu Wenquan, together with all the other translators to discuss the key problems encountered in the interpretation of the original texts. Some renowned professors in translation studies in Guangdong—including Mr. Huang Guowen, Mr. Wu Jianguo and Mr. Liang Ruiqing—attended the symposium, offering enthusiastic comment, sincere criticism, and suggestions for improvement.

Professor Mao Sihui always showed his full support for this project and happily agreed to write the preface for the series.

At the review stage, four professors proofread and made invaluable suggestions and corrections: Professor Li Ming proofread *Introduction to Chinese Culture*; Professor Chu Dongwei proofread *Understanding Chinese Culture*; Professor Chen Kaiju proofread *Introduction to Western Culture*; and Professor He Zhigang proofread *Understanding Western Culture*.

Australian translation expert Alex Graeme-Evans reviewed *Introduction to Chinese Culture* and *Understanding Chinese Culture* during the second review round. The leading translators and Ms. Xue Ping carried out the final formal review, wrote the chapter abstracts for each book, and translated all the references.

Our special thanks also go to Sara Crowley Vigneau, Senior Editor, and Connie Li (Yue), Editorial Assistant, of Springer Nature, whose constant help in clarifying all the problems of project management, and format and content organization, were crucial to the finalization of this project.

Last but not least, Guangdong University of Foreign Studies offered us the necessary funds; and many experts and leaders from the College of Continuing Education, the School of Interpretation and Translation Studies, and the School of English for International Business Studies of the University also gave us help throughout the project.

However, due to the scale of the project, the need to shorten the original texts, and stylistic choices made by different translators and reviewers, there may still be problems, which, of course, are the responsibility of the leading translators. We sincerely welcome criticisms and suggestions from readers, critics, and editors so that improvements can be made in later editions.

CONTENTS

CHAPTER 1

Western Philosophy

Philosophy constitutes a fundamental hierarchy of knowledge. It exerts a deep influence on all aspects of Western society, including politics, economy, literature, art, and daily life, encompassing many concepts and a system of knowledge that has profound logical connotations.

1.1   Western Philosophy Before the Modern Age

1.1.1   Greco-Roman Philosophy

1.1.1.1 Outline of Philosophical Ideas
Greco-Roman philosophy emerged in late 600 BC and ended in around AD 500. Regarded as the beginning of Western philosophy, this period was one of the most prosperous periods of ancient European culture, rather similar to the Spring and Autumn period and the Warring States period in ancient China. Various schools and ideas thrived simultaneously, giving rise to different viewpoints.

Three stages of development may be distinguished.

© The Author(s) 2018
G. Xu et al. (eds.), K. Chen et al. (trans.), *Understanding Western Culture*, https://doi.org/10.1007/978-981-10-8150-7_1

1. 600 BC: The focus of philosophy in this period is nature. The earliest materialists are the Milesians represented by Thales, Anaximander, and Anaximenes and the Ephesian School led by Heraclitus. In their opinion, the fundamental ingredients of the world were water, fire, earth, and air. Heraclitus asserted that everything in the world is ever changing. The earliest idealists were the Pythagoreans typified by Pythagoras and the Eleatics headed by Parmenides. The former took abstract numbers as the *arche*, or first principles, of the universe, while the latter defined these principles as Being. All the earliest philosophers discussed the *arche* of the world.

2. 500–400 BC: Philosophers of this period also put an emphasis on social politics, ethics and human beings. Atomism, presented by Democritus and others, represents the greatest achievement of this period. Meanwhile, the Sophists turned the emphasis of philosophical research toward questions of society and human beings, these explicitly bearing the tint of sensationalism, relativism and agnosticism. Plato put forward objective idealism, insisting that the material world was derived from the world of ideas, and that knowledge of human beings was viewed through the world of ideas. Aristotle's philosophy swayed between materialism and idealism. Criticizing Plato's Theory of Ideas, he took ideas as forms that could not be separated from particular substances and existed on their own, and that form was within particular substances. At the same time, he held that matter was passive while form was active. The characteristics of matter were decided by its form, which led to idealism. Aristotle was the first to separate philosophy from other disciplines and make it an independent one.

3. 300 BC–AD 500: The materialist Epicurus inherited and developed Democritus' atomism by introducing the swerve theory of atoms, which overcame the limitation created by denying the existence of contingency as expressed in Democritus' theory. Ethics was the focus of philosophical discussion in this period. As materialists, Lucretius and Lucian insisted on and defended atomism against religious theology and idealism. With their permissive attitude toward reality, their efforts to explain nature and society by teleology, and the popularization of mysticism and asceticism, various forms of idealism became prevalent. These ideas became the sources of Christian theology.

1.1.1.2 Major Figures

Socrates

Socrates and Plato (one of Socrates' students), together with Aristotle (a student of Plato), are hailed as the Big Three ancient Greek philosophers. Socrates was born during the golden age of Athens when it was ruled by Pericles, and died as Athens declined. A historical figure of distinctive personality, controversy and legend, he was Plato's teacher but left behind no written work. His speech and thought can be found in Xenophanes' works. Accused by aristocrats of corrupting the young, Socrates was executed by being forced to drink a cup of poisonous hemlock. As a teacher, he applied a distinctive approach of inspiration and debate in his teaching. In philosophy, he was the founder of Platonism. Stressing the importance of ethics, he was the first in ancient Greece to propose the pursuit of universal ethics through reason and thinking. In founding moral philosophy, his assertion of reason guided by morality justifies the proposition that virtue equals knowledge, taking knowledge as the root of goodness and ignorance that of wrongdoing. The first to suggest idealist teleology, Socrates assumed that everything was created and arranged by God, which demonstrates God's wisdom and *telos* (purpose). With his proposition that "I know that I know nothing," he thought that people were only smart if they forsook the exploration of nature, which is the realm of the gods, and admit their ignorance. People should obey the gods because they have the most knowledge and are the source of knowledge. In logic, according to Aristotle, Socrates was the one who presented inductive arguments, which identify definite arguments based on particular instances emphasize general definitions, thereby precisely explaining concepts. Socrates' philosophical thoughts mainly affirm the existence of criteria for what is good or bad.

Plato

Plato was the founder of objective realism. Born into an Athenian aristocratic family and well educated, he was enthusiastic about politics as were other aristocrats. After becoming a student of Socrates, he revered the thoughts and character of his teacher. In order to realize his idea of an ideal aristocratic state, after the death of Socrates he traveled to various places, such as Egypt, Asia Minor, and southern Italy in order to undertake political activities. In 387 BC he returned to Athens and established an academy named after Academus, a Greek hero, and taught there for forty years until his death. Plato was a prolific writer, whose main thoughts are manifested in *The Republic* and *The Laws*. His Academy was the earliest higher education institution, and it gave its name to future higher scholastic institutions. Besides philosophy, he taught mathematics, astronomy, acoustics, botany, and knowledge of other natural sciences, while philosophy maintained the highest status. The purpose of the Academy was not to impart practical techniques but to focus on theoretical wisdom, with the emphasis on thinking and analysis.

The philosophical system of Platonism is both extensive and profound. From his perspective, the world is composed of the World of Forms and the World of Phenomena. The World of Forms is the real existence of permanence, while the World of Phenomena, which can be felt by human sense organs, is only its faint shadow. Each of these phenomena displays transience and variation owing to the effects of time and space. With this starting point, Plato proposed an epistemology of the Theory of Forms and Recollection, and established this as the philosophical foundation of his teaching theories.

Aristotle

Aristotle is regarded as a universal genius of ancient knowledge. He was born in Stagira; his father was a court physician to the Macedonian king Amyntas and died when Aristotle was very young. Aristotle was sent to Athens aged eighteen, studied in Plato's Academy, and remained there as a teacher. After the death of Plato, he left Athens for Assos to found an academy for teaching and research. Three years later the Persian Empire took the city, and Aristotle escaped to Mytilene on the island of Lesbos. Returning to Athens in 335 BC, he established a new school near the Lyceum stadium next to the Temple of Apollo; for this reason his school was named Lyceum. Compared with Plato's Academy, it put more emphasis on practicality, stressed the importance of questioning, and paid attention to material collection, repeated attempts, and exploration.

Aristotle is universally revered in the history of science because, before the Renaissance in modern Europe in terms of scholarship, no one was comparable to him in their systematic investigation and comprehensive mastery of knowledge, though some attained tremendous achievements in specific fields. One of the intellectual tasks of the early Middle Ages was to assimilate Aristotle's research from incomplete summaries of his works. After his collected works were published, writers of the later Middle Ages made every effort to uncover his original meanings. His works were regarded as the encyclopedia of scholarship in the ancient world. Besides physics and astronomy, he also improved other disciplines that he worked on. In addition, he was the founder of inductive method and the first proponent of organized research. Above all, he is celebrated for his contribution to science and the classification of knowledge. His major works include *Categories, De Interpretatione, Prior Analytics, Posterior Analytics, Topics, Sophistical Refutations*, under the umbrella title of *Organon*, mainly dealing with logic; *Metaphysics*, in which covers general abstract theoretical problems; *Physics, On the Heavens, On Generation and Corruption*, and *On the Soul*, expounding subjects related to natural sciences; *Nicomachean Ethics* and *Eudemian Ethics*, dealing with ethical topics. He also wrote *Politics, Poetics, Rhetoric*, and other works on biology and economics.

1.1.2   Medieval Philosophy

1.1.2.1   Overview of Medieval Philosophy
Medieval philosophy refers to the religious theology of Europe from 500 to 1500, which consists of two stages: patristic philosophy matured into scholastic philosophy in the eleventh century. The existence of God not being doubted, the philosophy of the age took it as its responsibility to comment upon biblical and Christian doctrines, and to justify theology. After the fifth century, feudalism was established in Europe, and Christianity became an international organization with the theology of religion as its only ideology. As the result of the supremacy and monopoly of theology in ideology, philosophy, without any relative independence, was reduced to proving religious doctrines and became the handmaid of theology. However, the sublime nature of God was not able to eliminate struggles within philosophy itself. Scholastic philosophy inevitably declined owing to the centuries-long dispute and opposition between nominalism and realism, the development of science, and the recovery of culture.

The development of medieval philosophy can be divided into early (the fifth to tenth centuries), middle (the eleventh to fourteenth centuries) and late (fifteenth century) stages. Medieval philosophy is an important phase in the history of European philosophy, as its many progressive "heretical" thoughts (as Christianity was dominant in this period, the thought that deviated from the theology of orthodox was dismissed as heretical thought, such as nominalism) inherited and developed the previous materialism and dialectic to some extent. Meanwhile, its mastery of theories exceeded that of its predecessors, making considerable contributions to the development of philosophy.

1.1.2.2 Major Figures

Augustine
Augustine, born in Tagaste, a small town in northern Africa that was part of the Roman Empire, now Algeria, synthesized the essence of patristic philosophy. He was converted to Christianity by his mother but became a follower of Manichaeism (a dualistic religious movement) during his studies in the rhetoric school. After graduation, he taught rhetoric and oratory first in Carthage and then in Rome and Milan. Being influenced by Ambrose, the Archbishop of Milan, he broke away from Manichaeism and became immersed in the works of Platonism and skepticism. The turning point of his eventual conversion to Christianity happened when he was reflecting in a garden. According to his autobiography, *Confessions*, Augustine heard a child's voice urging him to "take up and read! take up and read!" as he was wondering about his beliefs. He hurriedly opened the Bible that was to hand and found himself facing the teachings of St. Paul: "Let us walk honestly, as in the day; not in rioting and drunkenness, not in chambering and wantonness, not in strife and envying. But put ye on the Lord Jesus Christ, and make not provision for the flesh, to fulfil the lusts thereof." This struck him like lightning as Augustine had lived a frivolous life in his youth. "By a light as it were of serenity infused into my heart, all the darkness of doubt vanished away." At Easter in 387 he was baptized by Ambrose and officially converted to Christianity. Later, on his return to his hometown, he was elected a priest of Hippo and promoted to archbishop in 395. During his tenure, Augustine exerted tremendous energy writing, preaching, organizing orders, and refuting pagan beliefs. In his later years he witnessed the invasion of the Vandals, and he died before their occupation of Hippo. After his death, North Africa broke its ties with the Roman Empire and became free of the control of the Roman Church. However, Augustine's works spread to Europe and became the spiritual treasure of Catholicism and Protestantism. Among his prolific works, which are regarded as a theological encyclopedia, *Confessions*, *On the Trinity*, and *The City of God* are his masterpieces, containing considerable philosophical treatises.

Thomas Aquinas
Thomas Aquinas, the most important philosopher in the Middle Ages, was born in Roccasecca, Italy, on the Aquinas family's manor. As a prestigious Lombardic family, the Aquinases were closely connected with the Church and the Holy Roman Empire. Thomas was sent to the celebrated

Monte Cassino Abbey, where he received the necessary training to one day become an abbot, as his parents wished. In 1239, the excommunicated Frederick II sent troops to occupy and close the abbey, forcing Thomas to continue his studies at the University of Naples. There he began to learn Aristotle's works of metaphysics, natural philosophy, and logic, and joined the Dominican Order. On the recommendation of Albertus Magnus, the influential Dominican scholar, Aquinas attended the seminary at the University of Paris and completed his studies in 1256. He wrote extensively, anything up to about 15 million words. Among his works, those containing philosophical views are *On Being and Essence, On the Principles of Nature, On Truth, Commentary on Boethius' On the Trinity.* His masterpieces are *Summa Theologica* and *Summa contra Gentiles.* Aquinas wrote commentaries on Aristotle's works, including *Metaphysics, Physics, Posterior Analytics, De Interpretatione, Politics, Ethics, Sense and Sensibilia, On Memory,* and *On the Soul.*

Applying Aristotle's philosophy to theology, Aquinas created a stupendous scholastic philosophical and theological system; he also made significant contributions to ethics, logic, politics, metaphysics, and epistemology. His famous fivefold proof for the existence of God had a great impact in the future. His philosophical and theological system was authorized by Pope Leo XIII as the official doctrine of Catholicism, called Thomism; it was not only the greatest achievement of scholastic philosophy, but the largest and most comprehensive system of medieval theology.

1.1.3 *Philosophy During the Renaissance*

1.1.3.1 *Overview of Philosophical Thought*
Modern philosophy commenced with the Renaissance at the beginning of the fifteenth century, a significant phase for both the development of Western classical philosophy and the growth of modern philosophy. During this period, scholasticism lost its dominance in ideology, with a massive cultural replacement. Humanism, the cultural movement of the age, stressed the discovery of, respect for, and value of human beings, making dignity and freedom the theme of this period. Human beings were freed from the idea of being created by God. As typical figures, Erasmus attacked the foolishness and madness of believing in Christianity in his masterpiece *The Praise of Folly* which is a satirical attack on superstitions and other traditions of European society as well as on the Western Church, while Leonardo da Vinci maintained that sensory experience is the origin of all knowledge. Philosophers in the Renaissance expressed their thoughts

directly rather than concealing them behind obscure language and rhetoric. Their attack on theology and Christianity was intense. Rationalism and humanism were the major subjects of the period.

The achievement of Renaissance philosophy lies first in its break with the supremacy of feudal theology and its shaking off of the cultural monopoly of Catholicism. Philosophers deliberately tried to break away from the constraint of the Church. Protestantism, which appeared after the Reformation, ended the dominance of Catholicism within Christianity. Second, the legacy of ancient cultures and thought gained importance. Third, human value and dignity were restored. The re-establishment of human beings as the center of a philosophical system paved the way for the development of modern philosophy. Finally, the close connection of new philosophy with natural science began. Despite the cruel persecution of the Church, avant-garde thinkers developed experimental natural sciences, revealing mysteries of the universe and the world, and opening up new frontiers in human knowledge. Philosophers began to contrive their own philosophical systems based on the foundation of natural sciences, initiating a tradition of modern materialist philosophy.

In this transitional period from the Middle Ages to modern times, philosophy demonstrated that it provided a transition between the restrictions of the Church and the preparation for the emergence and development of a new philosophy in the seventeenth and eighteenth centuries.

1.1.3.2   Major Figures

Niccolò Machiavelli

Niccolò Machiavelli, born into a fading aristocratic family in Florence, was an Italian political thinker and historian. In 1494, he joined the uprising against the Medici family. In 1498, taking the office of secretary of the Decemviri, a body for military and foreign affairs, he was in charge of drafting government documents and matters relating to the military defense of Florence, and he served as an envoy, traveling to France, Germany, and Spain. Upon the restoration of the Medici family in 1513, he was arrested and imprisoned. After his release, Machiavelli dedicated himself to writing while living in seclusion. In the hope of being assigned a post, he finally returned to Florence after the exile of the Medicis in 1527, but his request was rejected because of his previous connections with them. The worries and anger caused by this rejection led to illness and his eventual death on June 22, 1527.

As an exponent of the newly rising Italian bourgeoisie in the late Middle Ages, Machiavelli advocated ending political disruption in Italy and establishing a powerful centralized nation. In his masterwork *The Prince* (1513), he proposed the republic as the best form for a country, but contended that a republic would be unable to end the chaos in Italy; only the establishment of a monarchy with absolute power could make its subjects conform and defend themselves against formidable enemies. He justified the tactics of cruelty, cheating, hypocrisy, lies, and betrayal as long as they allowed monarchs to rule. This is called Machiavellianism. His other works include *The Art of War* and *Florentine Histories*.

Martin Luther

Martin Luther, the initiator of the German Reformation and the founder of Lutheranism, was born to a pious Catholic family in Eisleben. His father, a poor yeoman farmer, later worked as a miner and then became the owner of an iron mill. Luther spent his childhood in poverty, but was well educated after his family began to prosper. In 1501, he entered Leipzig University, where he was awarded Bachelor of Arts and in 1505 a master's degree. In May 1505, Luther was preparing to become a lawyer having gained a place at the law school of the University of Erfurt, but in July of that same year he suddenly decided to enter the Augustinian Order and become a monk. Various reasons have been proposed for this, but Luther himself explained it as the result of a loss of self-confidence: this might refer to his experience of nearly being struck by lightning during a thunderstorm, which prompted him to seek God's forgiveness by promising to enter an abbey. Having devoted himself to the monastic system in the abbey, Luther was ordained priest in 1507. In the following year, a bachelor's degree of the University of Wittenburg was conferred on him. In 1517, Luther published the *Disputation of Martin Luther on the Power and Efficacy of Indulgences*, which became known as the *Ninety-Five Theses*. This advanced his opposition to the sale of indulgences by the Church, and in essence started the German Reformation. The strongest argument that Luther proposed is that the supreme authority of Christian was the Bible rather than the Pope. He was the first to translate the Bible into German, which, given the spread of printing, promoted its influence and spread. Soon people began to translate the Bible into other local languages.

1.2   Philosophy in Modern Times

1.2.1   Western European Philosophy from the Sixteenth to Eighteenth Centuries

1.2.1.1   Philosophical Thoughts

The emergence and development of the bourgeois philosophy from the late sixteenth to seventeenth centuries was a revolution of Western classic philosophy, as well as a magnificent era of philosophical development. The bourgeoisie not only needed science to increase productivity, but used it as a spiritual weapon to fight against religious theology. Science gained its independence from philosophy. Progressive philosophers took the knowledge of nature and human beings as their subjects, and made questions about the relation between spirit and material, and the sources of scientific knowledge the themes of philosophy.

From their perspective, the purpose of philosophical research lay in the development of production, the establishment of new social institutions, and helping people to break away from feudal theology to live a liberal and happy life. Questions about human beings became the core and destination of philosophical research. New world views and philosophical systems were built, including modern materialism and idealism, which bore plenteous fruit. In epistemology two opposing factions emerged, empiricism and rationalism. Empiricists and rationalists discussed the source of knowledge, its developmental stages, its methods, and the accuracy and truth of knowledge. Francis Bacon, the forerunner of English empiricism, concluded the inductive method and the empirical methods of scientific experiments. Inheriting Bacon's materialist empiricism, Thomas Hobbes accepted some rationalist factors; meanwhile, there was a tendency toward mechanism in his statement that philosophy was the knowledge of deduction. Baruch Spinoza, the typical figure of rationalism, expressed his philosophical thoughts in *Ethics*, which put the supreme good as the starting point and center.

1.2.1.2   Major Figures

Francis Bacon

Francis Bacon, English philosopher and scientist, was born to an aristocratic family in London in 1561. His father was the Lord Privy Seal to Queen Elizabeth I and his mother was also born into nobility. Bacon began to study at Cambridge University at the age of thirteen but only stayed there for three years. At that time, dominated by scholasticism, Cambridge stressed theology rather than science in order to justify religious doctrines. Bacon left Cambridge with a strong dislike of the intellectual atmosphere there.

In 1620, Bacon summarized his philosophical thoughts in *Novum Organum*, where his viewpoint that "knowledge is power" was voiced. In his opinion, people have to master scientific knowledge in order to control and utilize nature. As a result, he put special emphasis on scientific experiment, through which true knowledge could be obtained. Bacon was not only the most important essayist and philosopher in Britain at the time, but also achieved much in the field of natural sciences. Nevertheless, he experienced hardship on his route to political success. Being ignored by the queen after his father's death, Bacon only gained gradual promotion after James I came to the throne, taking the offices of Attorney General and Lord Chancellor, but in the end his public career ended in disgrace, when he was accused of corruption. After this, he dedicated himself to the study of knowledge, which made him the renowned founder of English materialist philosophy in the Middle Ages.

René Descartes
René Descartes, the famous French philosopher, scientist and mathematician, was born in La Haye and was awarded a bachelor's degree at the Université de Poitiers. Living in an age of intense struggle between the bourgeoisie and feudal lords, and between science and theology, he had a spirit of strong skepticism and criticism, having been resolute in the pursuit of truth since he had begun his education in school. After finishing his doctoral study in law, he served in the Dutch army, traveling and all the while discussing mathematic and scientific questions with his friends. Seeking the right methods, he founded a philosophy that served the needs of practice. Descartes was engaged in the study of knowledge in the Dutch Republic and visited France after leaving the army. His works were either prohibited from being published or were burned both before and after his death, and they were listed in the *Index Librorum Prohibitorum* for many years after he died.

Whether in mathematics, natural science, or in philosophy, Descartes' works created a new age. His *Discourse on the Method* (published in 1637) became a classical philosophical work. The most interesting thing about Descartes' philosophy is his method. He paid particular attention to numerous wrong concepts which were widely accepted, and was determined to start from scratch in order to restore truth. This meant he began to doubt everything: things that were taught by teachers, all the beliefs he held, all common sense, even the existence of the world and his own existence. This naturally led to the question of how doubts could be eliminated so that tenable knowledge could be obtained. Descartes made a series of inferences in metaphysics and came to a conclusion that satisfied himself. Owing to his own existence (Cogito ergo sum/I think therefore I am) God existed, and hence the world existed. This was the starting point of his thinking.

Baruch Spinoza

In parallel with Descartes and Leibniz, Baruch Spinoza is one of the important rationalists in the history of modern Western philosophy. Born to a Jewish family in Amsterdam that had escaped from Spain to the Dutch Republic, Spinoza had the chance to study Hebrew, the Talmud, and Jewish philosophy in the local Jewish theological school as his family was fairly well off thanks to its import and export business. The greatest of his works is *Ethics*, published posthumously. This is written as Euclidean geometry, presenting a set of axioms and formulae, from which propositions, inferences, and explanations are produced. In philosophy, Spinoza was a monist or a pantheist, holding the belief that there was only one entity in the universe: that the universe itself was an integrated object, and God was identical with the universe. This conclusion was based on a series of definitions and axioms, which were inferred by logical reasoning. In Spinoza's idea, God includes the material world as well as the spiritual world, and the wisdom of human beings is part of that of God. God is the inner cause of everything, governing the world through the laws of nature; therefore everything that happens in the world has its inevitability. Meanwhile, only God possesses full freedom, which human beings can never gain despite their ability to eliminate outside constraints. If we recognize the inevitability of what is happening, it is easier to unite ourselves with God. For this reason, Spinoza believed that we should look upon things in terms of eternity. His famous quote goes that "A free man thinks of death least of all things; and his wisdom is a meditation not of death but of life." He practiced this in his lifetime.

John Locke

John Locke, the celebrated English philosopher, was the first writer to expound systematically basic thoughts about constitutional democracy. His thoughts exerted immense influence on the founding fathers of the United States and many philosophers of the French Enlightenment. He spent his college life at Oxford, gaining a bachelor's degree in 1656 and a master's degree in 1658. In his youth he developed a strong interest in science, and was selected to be a member of the Royal Society.

Locke made his name with *An Essay Concerning Human Understanding* (1690), in which he discussed the origin, nature, and limitation of human knowledge. The influence of Francis Bacon and René Descartes on him is obvious, as his viewpoints are basically empiricist. In turn his ideas influenced such philosophers as George Berkeley, David Hume, and Immanuel Kant. Despite the fact that Locke was the founder of English empiricism, he himself did not pursue it consistently. He believed all human thoughts and concepts came from or reflected the sensory experience of human beings. Abandoning Descartes' "Innate Ideas" (the concept that here are ideas such as existence, identity, and infinity that are not derived from the senses and are beyond imagination, but are products of pure reason), he maintained that the mind was like a blank sheet of paper, whose content was provided by experience that could be divided into sensory and reflective ideas. Sense came from the outside world, while reflection originated from the observations of the mind. Unlike rationalists, Locke stressed that these two ideas were the sole source of knowledge. In *Human Understanding*, Locke attempted to explain the origins and nature of nations through natural law. Starting from a natural state, he criticized feudal absolutism, holding firmly to the ideas of the inviolability of private property, the basis of the nation being contract, legislature as supreme, the separation of powers, and the right of people to fight against tyranny.

Gottfried Wilhelm Leibniz

An eminent philosopher, mathematician, logician, historian, and linguist in the German Enlightenment, Gottfried Wilhelm Leibniz is regarded as the last universal genius in German and European history. He was born to an intellectual family in Leipzig. His father, a professor in moral philosophy at Leipzig University, died when his son was only six, leaving behind a collection of books that was much more precious than wealth. His mother, well educated and insightful, sent him to the best school in Leipzig. Leibniz began to formally express his thoughts when he was young, and in 1661 a doctoral degree in law was conferred upon him.

As the first objective idealist in the modern West, Leibniz is famous for the monadic theory of substance. This was the immediate forerunner of German classical idealism and dialectic, and his viewpoints and criticism were succeeded by the Encyclopedists, led by Diderot. His thoughts also made an immense contribution to the establishment of German dialectic thought systems, from Kant to Hegel. His major philosophical works include *Metaphysics*.

David Hume

David Hume, British empiricist philosopher and skeptic, is one of the most important and influential figures in Western philosophy. Unlike those philosophers who were ignored when they were alive and only drew attention after their death, Hume established his philosophical prestige during his life. He was no transitory figure: like Plato, Descartes, Kant, and Hegel, he was a philosopher who had a lasting and profound influence on the development of Western philosophy.

Hume was the last exponent of British empiricism in modern philosophy. Starting from the perspective of empiricism, he reached skepticism in his *A Treatise of Human Nature*. However, this skepticism was mild, disillusioned with the ideal of empiricism. In the history of Western philosophy, he was the first philosopher apart from Aristotle who presented a detailed argument about the theory of causal relationship. Carrying on from empiricism, Hume repeatedly highlighted that people obtained knowledge about causal relationships from experience rather than from transcendental inferences; on the other hand, regarding how causal relationships came into being on the basis of experience and how people extended their experiences to things that they had not experienced, Hume stated that causal relationships were just customary associations in thinking. With the elimination of the substantiality of the causal relationship, Hume turned to idealism. Despite this, his theory exerts a huge influence on logical positivism, and has benefited philosophical thinking.

1.2.2   French Enlightenment Philosophy in the Eighteenth Century

1.2.2.1   Outline of Philosophical Thoughts

The beginning of the eighteenth century witnessed the ferment of an overwhelming revolution in France, where philosophy guided political revolution. With the forthcoming death of feudalism and the gradual maturing of conditions in which a bourgeois revolution could take place, French thinkers vehemently denounced the Catholic Church and absolute rule, holding rationalism to be the sole judge. Thus, the Enlightenment was launched. Directed against the feudal system and Catholic theology, the two most divine authorities of the age, the Enlightenment held rationalism as its guiding principle, and created its own social and political philosophy and a system of mechanical materialism and atheism, with ontology (the philosophical study of the nature of being) at its heart.

Voltaire, Rousseau, and other early Enlightenment thinkers took the lead in the campaign against feudalism and the Church. Their enthusiastic introduction of English philosophy and science to France actively encouraged the emergence and spread of materialism. Meanwhile, they developed the bourgeois theory of society and state, which provided blueprint for bourgeois revolution and the establishment and rule of the state, while exerting a far-reaching influence on bourgeois revolutions in other countries. Enlightenment thinkers observed social problems from the perspective of human beings, inferring the natural rules of the state and making profound progress in the history of human epistemology.

Despite its variety of opinions on some questions, French materialists, centering on the study of ontology, held the same views of atheism and materialism. There were three aspects to this. First, there was the materialist view of nature. French materialists all argued that the world was constituted by a united substance, which was the only existing entity. Diderot explicitly pointed out that it was impossible to presume an entity outside the materialist universe. Holbach maintained that the universe, the aggregation of all existing things, only provides us with material and movement. Second, there was the materialist theory of reflection. French materialists unanimously affirmed that the material world was the only source of the senses and the only object of cognition, and that cognition was the reflection of objective things through human sensory organs. Diderot studied the relationship between sense and thinking, and between perceptual knowledge and conceptual knowledge, on the basis of which he proposed three major methods through which to understand the objective world: observation, thinking, and experiment. The third aspect was militant atheism. Breaking the bounds of deism and revealing the hypocritical nature and reactionary function of religion, atheism was a glorious contribution by French materialists and the peak of modern bourgeois materialist philosophy.

1.2.2.2 Major Figures

Voltaire

Voltaire, French Enlightenment thinker, author, *litterateur*, and philosopher, the forerunner of the French bourgeois Enlightenment in the eighteenth century, is hailed as King of Thought, the conscience of Europe.
An advocate of innate rights, he maintained that all men were born free
and equal, and that everyone had the right to pursue life and happiness, as
these were endowed by God and could not be gainsaid. Born to a middle-
class family in Paris, Voltaire was a son of a lawyer. He gave up studying
law after pursuing this course for some time. Voltaire was witty and versa-
tile, and his works were known for poignancy and sarcasm, which led to
his imprisonment in the Bastille after he was sarcastic about feudal absolutism. He was forbidden to publish his books and was sent into exile on
several occasions. In 1726, he was exiled to Britain, where he developed a
strong interest in English bourgeois politics and culture. He studied the
constitutional monarchy, Locke's materialist empiricism, and Newton's
theory of universal gravitation. After returning to France, Voltaire wrote
his first major philosophical work, *Philosophical Letters*, usually known as
Letters on the English. Published in 1734, it marked the beginning of the
French Enlightenment.

As an eminent leader of the movement, Voltaire created the thinking
that defined the whole Enlightenment. His major philosophical works
include *Philosophical Dictionary*, *Elements of the Philosophy of Newton*, and
Philosophical Letters, his most celebrated piece, which is said to have been
"the first bomb at the old system."

Jean-Jacques Rousseau

Jean-Jacques Rousseau, French Enlightenment thinker, philosopher, educator, and *litterateur*, was born into a watchmaker's family in Geneva,
Switzerland. He was regarded as a pioneer in the thinking behind the
French Revolution, one of the most prominent exponents of Enlightenment
thought. In philosophy, Rousseau argued that senses were the source of
cognition and he insisted on deism. He also stressed the good nature of
humanity and the superiority of belief over rationality. In social affairs, he
persisted in the theory of social contract and advocated the building of a
bourgeois kingdom of rationalism. He stood for liberty and equality and
against private ownership and its oppression. His proposal of natural rights

expressed opposition of absolutism and tyranny. As for education, Rousseau took the cultivation of natural persons to be the purpose of education. Opposing the injury of children and their ignorance, he requested an increase in their role in education, reform of the content and methods of education, an accommodation of children's nature, and the free development of their bodies and minds. His major works include *The Social Contract, Discourse on the Origin and Basis of Inequality among Men, Emile,* and *The Confessions.*

Denis Diderot

Denis Diderot, French materialist philosopher, aesthetician, *littérateur,* and educational theorist of the eighteenth century, was the editor-in-chief of the *Encyclopédie, ou dictionnaire raisonné des sciences, des arts et des métiers* (*Encyclopedia, or a Systematic Dictionary of the Sciences, Arts, and Crafts*), a general encyclopedia that was published between 1751 and 1772, with supplements, revised editions, and translations, and represented Enlightenment thought. Its many writers were known as the Encyclopedists. During his twenty-five years of editing the *Encyclopedia,* Diderot was deeply influenced by Bacon, Hobbes, Locke, and others, but especially Bacon's thoughts about editing encyclopedias. Diderot also wrote many other works, and expressed his materialist thinking in *Philosophical Thoughts* and *Letter on the Blind,* for example. His aesthetic thoughts were clearly conveyed in *Discourse on Drama, Poetry, Paradox on the Actor,* and *Thoughts on Paintings.* His philosophical thoughts both reflect the thinking of metaphysics and dialectical factors. In his *Letter on the Blind* of 1749 he expounded atheism, which extended to theoretical thoughts rather than judging things through the senses. Perceiving the world as a huge system, Diderot argued that there were only time, space, and material. Material itself had a life, which enabled it to move and to participate. Movement was an attribute of material, and its inseparability from material created a colorful and diverse world. The world was united by material, and the unceasing movement of material produced new things. Everything was interconnected, and everything could convert into everything else. But Diderot's idea of nature still had an element of metaphysics. He summarized everything as pure increases in quantity, taking factors in nature to be unchanging. Things that were constituted by factors replaced each other through conversion, which could be defined as recycling.

1.2.3   Classical German Philosophy in the Eighteenth and Nineteenth Centuries

1.2.3.1   Outline of Philosophical Thoughts

Classical German philosophy was the outcome of Western philosophical development for over 2000 years since Ancient Greece, and was the peak of the anti-feudal philosophy of the modern European bourgeoisie. Philosophers since Kant had advocated rationalism and defended liberty. No longer confined to the popularization of Enlightenment thought or the belief that the foundation of social progress laid in the improvement of rationalism, an increase in knowledge, the elimination of mistakes and biases, and formal liberty and equality, they fought against feudal theology using rationalism and freedom, the spirit of Enlightenment being further demonstrated and elevated to a permanent philosophical principle. One of the major achievements of classical German philosophy was the systematic creation of dialectic theory, which was applied to various disciplines to present a universal law of the development of cognition and spiritual culture.

Under the premise of overcoming mechanism and metaphysics, the classical German philosophers united the world on the basis of mind and took the nature of the world to be spiritual. Spirit, self, and subject were the center of their philosophy. Kant admitted the existence of "noumena" beyond people's experience, being the source of sensual experience that could not be perceived.

1.2.3.2   Major Figures

Immanuel Kant

Immanuel Kant was the most important thinker of the Enlightenment and the founder of classical German philosophy. He laid the foundation of what is called materialist dialectic, and drew parallels between this and the Copernican revolution, regarding his new philosophical system as a paradigm shift.

Kant was born in Konigsberg in eastern Prussia to a harness-maker. Brought up in a devout Lutheran family, he received his education in church schools. After 1755, he began to teach in Konigsberg University. During this period, as a teacher and writer, he taught logic, metaphysics, moral philosophy, geography, physics, and mathematics. In the 1760s, he wrote *The Only Possible Ground for a Demonstration of God's Existence* (1763) and other works. His *Dreams of a Ghost Seer* in 1766 inspected the spiritual world from all viewpoints. In 1770, Kant was appointed a professor of logic and metaphysics. In the same year his dissertation, *On the Form and Principles of the Sensible and the Intelligible World*, was published. In the nine years from 1781 he published a series of great works of originality that dealt with matters in diverse fields, such as *The Critique of Pure Reason* (1781), *The Critique of Practical Reason* (1788), and *The Critique of Judgment* (1790), which together brought a revolution in philosophical thought. His *Religion within the Bounds of Reason Alone*, published in 1793, was accused of abusing philosophy, and distorting and being contemptuous of the basic doctrines of Christianity. Because of this, the government censor issued a royal order forbidding Kant from discussing religious matters in his lectures and writings. But after the death of the king in 1797, Kant renewed his discussions in his last important treatise, *The Conflict of the Faculties* (1798). The central theme of Kant's philosophy is identical with that of the Enlightenment: reason, nature, God, and human beings, the relationship between them, and the foundation and methods of natural sciences. In many respects, Kant's philosophy marked the beginning of modern philosophy and was the origin of philosophical schools that were fundamentally opposed to each other. The development of his philosophical thoughts showed the flow of history from natural science to natural philosophy, and thence to metaphysics, finally entering the age of critical philosophy.

Georg Wilhelm Friedrich Hegel

Born into a government official's family in Stuttgart, G.W.F. Hegel studied at the town's middle school. From 1816 to 1817 he was a professor at the University of Heidelberg. In 1818 he became philosophical professor at the University of Berlin and was elected university Rector in 1829. An exponent of modern German objective philosophy and a political philosopher, Hegel made the most systematic and comprehensive exposition of the German bourgeois philosophy of nations.

Hegel regarded Spirit as the *arche* of the world. Spirit was not something that transcended the world. Nature, human society, and spiritual phenomena were all presentations of it at different stages of development. Therefore, the substitution, development, and permanent process of the life of things constituted Spirit itself. The task and purpose of Hegel's philosophy was to demonstrate the Spirit as presented through nature, society, and mind, and to disclose its developmental process and law. It is a discussion about the dialectic relationship between mind and existence, and a display of the dialectic synthesis of the two on the basis of idealism.

Centering on this basic proposition, Hegel established a spectacular system of objective idealism that represents the three developmental stages of the self-evolution of Spirit: logic, natural philosophy, and philosophy of mind. Hegel carried this dialectic principle into arguments about every concept, every object, and the whole system, one of the most daring developments in the history of thinking. Hegel wrote a number of works, including *Phenomenology of Spirit*, *The Science of Logic*, and *Encyclopedia of the Philosophical Sciences*. A symbol of the culmination of the German idealist philosophical movement of the nineteenth century, Hegel's philosophy has exerted a profound influence on ensuing philosophical schools, such as existentialism and Marx's historical materialism.

Ludwig Feuerbach

Born in Bavaria, Ludwig Feuerbach was a German materialist philosopher. At an early age, he studied at the Faculty of Theology in the University of Heidelberg. Later he was engaged in philosophical study, botany, anatomy, and psychology in the University of Berlin, where he received his doctorate and started teaching. His contribution was the restoration of the authority of materialism after the dominance of idealism over German philosophy for decades. A former member of a group known as the Young Hegelians, he criticized Hegel's view that regarded mind and existence as identical, and proposed humanism, which treats human and nature as the only objects of philosophy. He affirmed that nature was the objective reality of material. According to Feuerbach, space, time, and mechanical movement were the forms of material existence; and human beings were the products of nature, the unity of soul and flesh. In addition, he expounded the relation between mind and existence in the materialist way, taking human beings as the subject of cognition, which could achieve unity with the object through the senses. According to his intuitional theory of reflection, nature can be learned by human beings. Feuerbach abandoned Hegel's dialectic, criticizing his idealism. His understanding of humanism was that it was the abstract of natural human beings. Having demonstrated the connection between religion and idealism in nature, he put forward the proposal that idealism was theology remolded by rationality. After denying the religions of the past, Feuerbach attempted to establish a religion without a god to show that love transcended everything. His major works include *The Essence of Christianity*.

1.3 MODERNISM AND POSTMODERNISM

1.3.1 Outline of Philosophical Thoughts

Generally speaking, modern and postmodern philosophies refer to various philosophical schools that have been prevalent in Western capitalist countries since the mid-nineteenth century. The development of modern capitalism promoted the immense progress of science and technology, alongside new social conflicts and crises, all of which are reflected in philosophy. Despite the large number of schools and its diversity, modern Western philosophy can be roughly divided into scientism and humanism. Inheriting the rationalist tradition of European philosophy, scientism takes the nature of science as its object of research, with particular interest in the methods of learning, the truthfulness and certainty of scientific knowledge, the structure of scientific theories, the characteristics of scientific language, the laws of science's development, the relationship between science and society, and so on. The major factions of this ideological trend include positivism, pragmatism, empirical criticism (Machism), logical empiricism, critical rationalism, historicism of science, structuralism, constructivism, and systems philosophy. It is rationalistic in its advocacy of reason, science, criticism, and progress. For instance, positivism highly praises positivity and science. Logical empiricism insists on the principles of verifiability and logical analysis. Humanism, a major tradition in European history, researches the nature of human beings, with their focus on life, instinct, existence, value, dignity, prospects, and the relationship between human and nature. Major schools of this trend include voluntarism, neo-Kantism, philosophy of life, neo-Hegelianism, phenomenology, Freudianism, existentialism, neo-Thomism, personalism, Frankfurt School, hermeneutics, and philosophical anthropology. This trend stands for irrationalism, highlighting mysticism, fideism (exclusive reliance on faith alone), and pessimism. For example, voluntarism claims that the nature of the world is the will, "a blind urge." Freudianism states that libido is the source and basis of motivation for all human behavior and psychological activities. Existentialism claims that the nature of human beings is anguish, abandonment, and despair. Neo-Thomism promotes religious beliefs and God-centered humanism.

In the 1960s and 1970s, as capitalism stepped into a mature phase, an increasing number of phenomena distinct from those in pre-existing society emerged. Some scholars proclaimed the end of the modern era, which had lasted for more than 200 years, and the advent of a new one. Industrial society was turning into post-industrial society, with the postmodern turn of capitalist society; this provoked heated discussions in Western educational circles. In the 1950s, a new postmodern era had already existed. In the 1960s, this postmodern spirit was pushed to centre stage in the field of thought. Scholars held debates about the relationship between modernism and postmodernism in the 1970s and 1980s. By the 1980s, in some scholars' opinion, postmodernism had become the mainstream of Western spiritual culture and postmodern discourse a social trend. Whether these descriptions are appropriate or not, Western spiritual culture has indeed been undergoing profound changes and has exerted increasing influence on various areas in different forms.

Postmodernism is a mentality that has emerged from modern capitalism, a social and cultural trend in thought, and a lifestyle that is dedicated to the reflection, criticism, and transcendence of modernism, which is the existing dominant thinking, culture, and historical tradition that it has inherited from capitalism. With an attempt to recreate the existing culture of human beings and to explore paths of innovation that are as diverse as possible, postmodernism creates an ever-updating, ever-discontented spirit of self-breakthrough and creation that is unconfined by particular forms or the pursuit of fixed outcomes. Postmodernism is more than just an uncentered, nomadic discourse and it is not a systematic theoretical knowledge; it is a cultural appeal, but not just that. Rather, it is practical activities of cultural innovation that transcend traditional discourses and oppose traditional theoretical knowledge. Postmodernism is a historical and social category, a mode of thought and a cultural category, a lifestyle and a new mode of human activity, a method of expression and a strategy of argument, and at the same time a query about and a challenge to the justified ways and procedures of the new society and new culture. It continuously realizes and accomplishes the proof and justification of itself through its own emergence, existence, and continuous criticism, through the challenge and penetration of modern society and culture, and especially through its expansion into the psychological activities and mentality of modern human beings. However, on the other hand, its weaknesses and limitations are also being gradually exposed.

1.3.2   Major Figures

1.3.2.1   Friedrich Wilhelm Nietzsche

A renowned German philosopher, Friedrich Nietzsche was the originator of modern Western philosophy, as well as a distinguished poet and essayist. He had been isolated and sentimental since childhood, and always felt inferior because of his thin and weak body. For this reason, his spent his life in the pursuit of a powerful philosophy to make up for this deep sense of inferiority. Breaking away from the logical development of philosophy, Nietzsche relied on his inspiration to reach a unique understanding, and hence his works are poetic and aphoristic rather than obscure as are those of other philosophers.

Nietzsche dauntlessly opposed the absolute superiority of metaphysics and the vast system of speculation with rationality at its center that had lasted for hundreds of years. His ardent love for life made him an enthusiastic exponent of vitality and willpower. He was a firm believer in the value of human life and society, and regarded nature as the only real world. His philosophy transfused fresh blood into the veins of European classical philosophy and created a brand new era of classical philology. From this perspective, he initiated a new epoch in the history of thinking, which was divided into two phases: pre-Nietzsche and post-Nietzsche. After Nietzsche, traditional philosophy disintegrated, as it converted from non-being to being, returned from heaven to earth, and evoked immense resonance for millions of people rather than remaining in a state of mystery. Influential works by Nietzsche include *The Gay Science, Thus Spoke Zarathustra, Beyond Good and Evil,* and *The Will to Power.* Nietzsche's philosophy had a deep influence on famous thinkers in the following century, such as Jaspers, Heidegger, Rilke, Hesse, Mann, Shaw, Gide, Sartre, and Malraux.

1.3.2.2   John Dewey

John Dewey was an American philosopher, psychologist, and educator. As a pioneer of functional psychology, the founder of the Chicago School of Pragmatism, an exponent of the American Progressive Educational Movement, and one of the co-founders of pragmatic philosophy, he is regarded as one of the most important philosophers in the twentieth century and an influential person in both Western and Eastern cultures. Born into a peasant's family in Burlington, Vermont, Dewey finished his primary and secondary education in his hometown and then attended the University of Vermont from 1875. In 1879, he graduated and began his teaching career, which he had always longed for, and continued to study the history of philosophy. In 1882, his first dissertation was published in the only national philosophical magazine, which was tremendously encouraging for him.

Though his early philosophical opinions drew on Hegel's thoughts, Dewey explained that he abandoned nineteenth-century Hegelian Absolutism because of the impact of biology and the theory of evolution on his thinking. In his opinion, idea is not something fixed or static; it is not absolute; rather, it should be regarded as changeable, dynamic, and instrumental, enabling people to adapt to the external environment more easily. As Dewey took experience and progress as two of his basic concepts, his opinion of knowledge naturally falls on the side of instrumentalism. His works on pragmatic philosophy include *Reconstruction in Philosophy* (1920), *Experience and Nature* (1925), *The Quest for Certainty* (1929), *Logic: The Theory of Inquiry* (1938), and *Knowing and the Known* (1948).

1.3.2.3 *Bertrand Arthur William Russell*

Bertrand Russell, a philosopher, mathematician, sociologist, and Nobel Prize winner, was born to an aristocratic family in Monmouthshire, Wales. He is regarded as the most famous and influential Western scholar and social activist in the twentieth century. Orphaned very young, he was raised by his grandmother. In 1890 he enrolled in Cambridge University to study mathematics, turning to a major in philosophy three years later, and becoming a lecturer in 1908. As a philosopher, his contribution mainly lies in mathematical logic, as he was one of the founders of logical atomism and neo-realism. Modern analytic philosophy, based on Russell's philosophy, plays a significant role in the history of modern Western philosophy. As a social activist, he was an ardent participator in political activities, and he delivered dozens of speeches in support of world peace. During the First World War, he was imprisoned for six months because of his engagement in pacifist activities, but this did not moderate his views. Russell was the focus of the world's attention and controversy at this time, while his main responsibilities remained academic, overseeing research and writing. In the fields of human knowledge and mathematical logic, his innovation and achievement were unprecedented.

Russell was always able to clearly express obscure academic thinking to a non-academic audience; his works are unparalleled even in terms of pure literature. Among the more than sixty books he wrote are *A History of Western Philosophy* (1945), *Human Knowledge: Its Scope and Limits* (1948), *Sceptical Essays* (1928), *Authority and the Individual* (1949), and *My Philosophical Development* (1959). He was awarded the 1950 Nobel Prize "in recognition of his varied and significant writings in which he champions humanitarian ideals and freedom of thought." In 1959, after the publication of *Western Wisdom*, he began writing *The Autobiography of Bertrand Russell*, which he finished aged ninety-five in 1967.

1.3.2.4 Edmund Husserl

Edmund Husserl, the founder of phenomenology, is regarded as one of the most influential philosophers in the twentieth century. His philosophy constitutes the starting point for reflection upon Heidegger, Sartre, Merleau-Ponty, Gadamer, and Derrida. Born into a Jewish family in Proßnitz, then in the Austrian empire and now Prostějov in the Czech Republic, he studied mathematics and physics, and received his doctorate in 1881. From 1883 he became a student of Franz Brentano, German philosopher and psychologist, and studied philosophy. He taught in the universities of Halle, Göttingen, and Freiburg successively, and died in Freiburg in 1938. The development of his philosophy can be divided into three stages: pre-phenomenology (before 1900), early phenomenology (1901–1913), and late phenomenology (after 1913). The first two stages were mainly devoted to criticism of the psychology of various forms of empiricism in the nineteenth century, the development of Brentano's intentionality of consciousness, and the establishment of descriptive phenomenology, which returned from particular individual experiences to the essential structure of experience. Husserl's phenomenology of the late stage eventually evolved to a thorough and subjective transcendental idealism, the objective of which was the return and deepening of phenomenology to the immediate data of consciousness, so that the objectivity or definite nature of knowledge is built up on the basis of pure subjectivity. Through this phenomenological reduction all the empiricist content is excluded, while only absolute consciousness or transcendental consciousness remains. The theme of Husserl's phenomenology in its late stage is the constitution of transcendental consciousness and the world of life, the subject experiences in his visual horizon. Husserl received constant criticism from the school of phenomenology because of his transcendental idealism and the standpoint and perspective of his thorough subjectivism. Among his significant works are *Philosophy of Arithmetic* (1891), *Logical*

Investigation (1900–1901), *Philosophy as Rigorous Science* (1910), *Ideas Pertaining to a Pure Phenomenology and to a Phenomenological Philosophy* (1913), *Formal and Transcendental Logic* (1929), *Cartesian Meditations* (1950), and *The Crisis of European Science and Transcendental Phenomenology* (1954).

1.3.2.5 Martin Heidegger
Martin Heidegger, German philosopher, founder of existentialism, and one of its major exponents, is hailed as the most original thinker and the most prominent ontological scholar and critic of technological society. He became interested in philosophy and began to study Brentano's philosophy at school. Later he attended Freiburg University to study theology and philosophy, and received his doctorate in 1913. After qualifying as a lecturer having passed an exam hosted by Heinrich Rickert, a neo-Kantist, he followed Husserl to teach at Freiburg. In 1927, in order to prepare for his promotion to professorship, Heidegger's unfinished manuscript *Being and Time* was published. It became one of the most significant philosophical works of the twentieth century. In 1928, Heidegger succeeded Husserl as Professor of Philosophy at Freiburg University. After the rise of Nazism, he joined the Nazi Party, and became the University Rector. The connection between Heidegger and the Nazis repeatedly became a heated topic among Western philosophers as well as more generally. However, this his philosophy cannot be described as a reflection of Nazism, and subsequent anti-Nazi existentialists have been inspired by Heidegger's works. This demonstrates that the thought of a great philosopher is far more significant than his political views at certain times. Heidegger's other major works include *What Is Metaphysics?*, *The Basic Problems of Phenomenology*, *On the Essence of Truth*, *Off the Beaten Track*, and *On the Way to Language*.

1.3.2.6 Jean-Paul Sartre
Jean-Paul Sartre is among the most important philosophers in the twentieth century, a major exponent of French atheist existentialism. He was a distinguished writer, dramatist, critic, and social activist as well. Born into a naval officer's family on June 2, 1905, he lost his father at a young age and thereafter lived with his grandfather. At nineteen he attended the École Normale Supérieure to study philosophy, and became a teacher in philosophy in a middle school. In 1933 he studied philosophy in Berlin, accepting Husserl's phenomenology and Heidegger's existentialism. After returning to France, he continued his teaching in the middle school, and

began to publish his first batch of philosophical works: *Imagination: A Psychological Critique*, *The Transcendence of the Ego*, and *Sketch for a Theory of the Emotions*, for example. In the autumn of 1943, Sartre's masterpiece *Being and Nothingness*, which laid the foundation for his philosophical system of atheist existentialism, was published.

Perhaps Sartre's charm lies in his fanatical spirit of worldliness. The famous formula of existentialism is that existence precedes essence. Applying this to his outlook on life, he regarded human involvement in society in the same way that the birth of people was intrinsically haphazard, as it was just the outcome of the broadcast of sperm. Therefore, the existence of human beings was not scheduled in advance to a blueprint, and people should hence be free to be the masters of their own lives and become totally involved in the society they lived in, where fate was determined by behavior. This spirit naturally encouraged him to be critical of the society of the time and supportive of social revolutions. This made him a great social activist and a political idealist of his age.

1.3.2.7 Jean-François Lyotard

Jean-François Lyotard was a typical French postmodernist thinker. It was he who formally presented, expounded, and justified postmodernism, which came into being in the first half of the nineteenth century and developed over the following century into a systematic philosophical theory and methodology in the 1970s. His book *La Condition Post-Moderne*, published in 1979, is regarded as the cornerstone of postmodern theory. At that point, postmodernism officially stepped onto the stage of Western theory and into academia, becoming the most important social trend of the latter part of the twentieth century. The profundity and breadth of its influence gave rise to radical changes in the theory and methodology of Western humanistic and social sciences, as well as in the Western way of life.

1.3.2.8 Jacques Derrida

Jacques Derrida was a renowned French post-structuralist and deconstructionist. Owing to his struggle with and defiance of traditional culture and its basic principles, and his unwillingness to be confined by convention, Derrida would rather act out a vague image of himself. In his opinion, the more indefinite he was, the farther he was away from the range of traditional culture. He repeated that the best trick played by traditional culture was to define someone as having a certain identity so that he could be controlled. According to Derrida, traditional philosophy always stipulates the presence of being and searches for definite foundations and the first cause. Language does not reflect inner experience, as nothing fully exists within signs. We are not only unable to present what we say or write to others, but also to ourselves, because we still need to use signs when we reflect on our own mind or explore our own soul. This means that any communication will be insufficient and not completely successful; therefore knowledge stored and developed by communication is also doubtful.

BIBLIOGRAPHY

He Zhaowu. 2003. *The Spirit of Western Philosophy*. Beijing: Tsinghua University Press.

Liu Fangtong. 2000. *Contemporary Western Philosophy*. Beijing: People's Publishing House.

Miao Litian, and Li Yuzhang. 1990. *The New Introduction to the History of Western Philosophy*. Beijing: People's Publishing House.

Russell, Bertrand. 2003. *A History of Western Philosophy*. Beijing: The Commercial Press.

Zhang Zhicang, and Lin Dan. 2007. *Contemporary Western Philosophy*. Beijing: People's Publishing House.

Zhao Dunhua. 2001a. *A Short History of Western Philosophy*. Beijing: Peking University Press.

———. 2001b. *A Brief History of Modern Western Philosophy*. Beijing: Peking University Press.

Zhong Yuren, and Yu Lichang. 2007. *Critical Biographies of Famous Western Philosophers*. Ji'nan: Shandong People's Publishing House.

WEBSITE

http://baike.baidu.com/view

CHAPTER 2

Political Systems

The political system is part of the social system and structure, and involves polity, structural form, organizational and operating mechanisms, as well as political doctrines that are prescribed by constitutions and laws. It reflects the will of the ruling class and the working principles of the state apparatus.

This chapter deals with the legal design and development of political systems in major Western countries. Initially it outlines the evolution and status quo, and then focuses on political systems in the UK, the USA, France, and Germany.

2.1 Introduction to Western Political Systems

In the seventeenth to nineteenth centuries, capitalist political systems were established successively in Western countries such as the UK, the USA, France, and Germany, and parliaments composed of elected representatives exercised the state's power. This was based on the indirect democracy invented by the European monarchies and aristocracy in the Middle Ages, which was gradually integrated with the democratic system in modern times. The political party system and the interest group are the two key components of the Western political system.

An interest group is a public organization with specific political views that pushes for the formulation, amendment, and implementation of policies and laws in its own interest. Various interest groups were formed in the mid-nineteenth century along with the structural upgrading and

© The Author(s) 2018   29
G. Xu et al. (eds.), K. Chen et al. (trans.), *Understanding Western Culture*, https://doi.org/10.1007/978-981-10-8150-7_2

transformation of industries, changes in social conditions, and the expansion of government functions in capitalist countries. These groups, as the embodiment of political democracy, exert influence on society and politics to protect their own interests and to maintain social stability.

In the West, elections of party politicians in which individuals cannot participate are typically a money game. Raising more funds than rivals is a requisite for winning, and campaigns are vigorous. On account of the limited party membership dues, business conglomerates and consortia are ideal sponsors, being willing to prop up representatives of their interests so that political, economic, and diplomatic policies are made in their favor and so they can gain more legal or illegal profit. Since the economic base determines the superstructure, capitalist private ownership underpins the Western political party system. Essentially, all parties represent the interests of the monopoly capitalist class and preserve, modify, and develop capitalism. Hence the Western multi-party system is just a political method of distributing benefits among the monopoly capitalist class.

2.2   Political Systems in Major Western Countries

2.2.1   *The Political System of the UK*

The UK has been committed to re-establishing its supremacy since decline set in after the two world wars. Britain adopted constitutional monarchy after the modern capitalist revolution, which provided the political foundation for its status as the world's powerhouse. Its political system features two main parties, a permanent civil service, local self-government, and centers on a parliamentary system, which has had a significant impact on the establishment of political systems in other countries.

2.2.1.1 *Evolution*

After the Norman Conquest in 1066, Britain turned into a centralized feudal monarchy, with the king as the most powerful lord who exercised his sovereignty through the king's council. In 1215 aristocrats rose in revolt and forced King John (who ruled from 1199 to 1216) to sign the Great Charter, which acknowledged the privileges of aristocrats and churches and circumscribed the king's powers.

During the reign of the Tudors (1485–1603), Britain was a feudal autocratic monarchy and legislative, administrative, and judicial powers were conferred on the king. Capitalists and a new aristocracy formed an alliance in the mid-seventeenth century and transformed the state from a monarchy to a republic in 1649. In 1653 Cromwell dissolved Parliament and built a military dictatorship, which was overthrown during the restoration of the Stuarts in 1660. After the Glorious Revolution of 1688, the House of Commons exerted the legislative power. From the early eighteenth century, the king no longer attended cabinet meetings and appointed the leader of the majority party in the House of Commons to be the prime minister, who formed the cabinet. In this parliamentary constitutional monarchy, the king was only the titular head while Parliament was the legislative authority, with the cabinet exercising administrative power and answerable to Parliament. The judicial branch, with the Lord Chancellor as its head, exercised jurisdiction, and counties were autonomous. After reforms to parliamentary elections in the nineteenth century, people's democratic rights were expanded and the two-party system and the civil service system were formed. This political system, based on the constitutional convention, evolved and is still in place today.

2.2.1.2 The UK's Sovereign

The sovereign was transformed from a victor in wars, a despot with divine rights, to the titular head of the constitutional monarchy. Centralized imperial power led to revolutions rather than the abolition of the monarchy, and in light of constitutional provisions the king or queen is the hereditary titular head of the state who performs ceremonial roles. The monarch is indispensable to the British political system as a symbol of unity.

2.2.1.3 The Polity

The UK has a cabinet government. According to the principles of parliamentary sovereignty, Parliament has legislative authority and is of supreme power. It comprises the House of Lords, which wields no real power, the House of Commons, and the sovereign. The leader of the majority party in the House of Commons is designated by the sovereign to be the prime minister, forms the cabinet, and assumes joint responsibility for Parliament.

Legislative, administrative, and judicial powers are not separated in Britain. The cabinet controls legislation while the Lord Chancellor, Attorney General and Solicitor General, nominated by the prime minister and appointed by the sovereign, are in charge of judicial administration.

The Lord Chancellor is a member of the cabinet and therefore of the ruling party, responsible for justice, legislation, and administration, and the appointment of all judges. The House of Lords is the highest judicial institution for all civil and criminal cases, except for Scottish criminal cases. Judicial bodies are not given the power of constitutional review and interpretation, yet important judicial precedents have the same legal force as laws. The cabinet is dominant, so much so that there has been a tendency since the Second World War that sovereignty might be transferred from Parliament to the cabinet especially.

2.2.1.4 The Civil Service
In the mid-nineteenth century, the UK was one of the first countries to implement a civil service system that, as a permanent bureaucracy, could implement policy, even while changes took place on account of kings bestowing government posts and two parties taking turns in power. Civil servants are divided into political and administrative officers, with the latter permanently employed. Progressively, appointment, training, assessment, promotion, rewards and punishments, salary, welfare, and the retirement of officers have been institutionalized.

2.2.1.5 The Local Government System
The local government of the UK is partly autonomous, operating either under a single-tier system—unitary authorities, or a two-tier system—county and district councils. There are five types of local authority in England: county councils, district councils, unitary authorities, metropolitan districts, and London boroughs. Local authorities are entitled to make many policy decisions, yet some resolutions passed must be approved by central government departments; consultation is required for legal bills. Management committees appointed by local councils are responsible for the administration of various affairs.

2.2.1.6 The British Constitution
Distinct from most constitutions, this consists of statute law, common law, and conventions. The Great Charter (1215), Habeas Corpus Act (1679), Bill of Rights (1689), the Act of Parliament (1911, 1949), the amended Municipal Corporation Act, and electoral and county council laws are the chief components. There is an independent legal system in Scotland. Under the constitutional monarchy, the sovereign, as head of state and the judiciary, the commander-in-chief of the armed forces, and the Supreme

Governor of the Church of England, is nominally empowered to appoint and remove the prime minister, ministers, senior judges, military officers, governors-general, diplomats, bishops, and Anglican priests of high rank. He or she can convene, prorogue, and dissolve Parliament, approve laws, declare wars, and make peace, but in reality it is the cabinet that wields ultimate power.

Parliament is the supreme judicial and legislative organization. Members of the House of Lords include royal descendants, hereditary and life peers, archbishops and bishops, who join through either political appointment or recommendation. After the reform of November 1999, more than 600 hereditary peers were removed from the House of Lords, with only ninety-two remaining in office. Members of the House of Commons are elected with five-year tenure, based on polls in 650 constituencies with a median total electorate about 72,400 in England, 69,000 in Scotland, 66,800 in Northern Ireland, and 56,800 in Wales (2013 figures).

2.2.1.7 The Judicial System

England and Wales adopt the common law system and the system in Northern Ireland is similar, while a civil law system is adopted in Scotland. Civil and criminal courts constitute the judicial organs. In England and Wales, in a bottom-up approach, institutions for civil trial comprise county and high courts, the civil division of appellate courts, and the Upper House as the court of final appeal, while institutions for criminal trial include local and criminal courts, the criminal division of appellate courts, and the Upper House. The Crown Prosecution Service established in 1986 accepts and hears all criminal cases from English and Welsh police. The Attorney General and Solicitor General serve as counsels of the British government and representatives of the royal family in some national and international cases.

2.2.1.8 The Electoral System

The electoral system is an integral part of the system of civil rights. It is prescribed that every British citizen aged eighteen or over has the right to vote as long as they have lived in the constituency for more than three months (for soldiers more than one month). British citizens aged twenty-one or over have the right to be elected to be a Member of Parliament and are required to pay a deposit of £150. This is turned over to the state treasury unless their votes outnumber one-eighth of the total cast in the constituency. A Member of Parliament is elected directly based on ballots, of which the process follows a majority representation system under a single-member constituency system.

2.2.1.9 *The Political Party System*

The UK is representative of countries that pursue the two-party system. The two major parties developed with Parliament and the cabinet and their competition with each other intensified after the extension of suffrage when the Reform Act of 1832 was passed. They control elections, dominate in Parliament, and the one winning most seats forms the government. With Parliament backing the government, Britain has a more stable cabinet than states that adopt the multi-party system.

The Labour Party

This was founded in 1900 and was initially known as the Labour Representation Committee. At the time of writing, 2017, it had been in power during the periods 1945–1951, 1964–1970, 1974–1979 and 1997–2010. It is the biggest party in the UK with roughly 400,000 members. In recent years, the party has tended to favor the middle class and has become alienated from the unions. The ex-leader Tony Blair put forward the slogan "New Labour, New Britain" and removed Clause Four in the party constitution that concerned public ownership. He proposed to rein in public spending, to maintain steady growth of the macro-economy, and to reduce government intervention in the economy, as well as establishing a modern welfare system. Active international co-operation and European integration were suggested, and the so-called special relationship with the USA was to be maintained.

The Conservative Party

Its predecessor was the Tory Party, founded in 1679 and renamed in 1833; its official name is the Conservative and Unionist Party. It enjoyed a dominant position in politics in the twentieth century and was consecutively in power from 1979 to 1997. Conservative Prime Ministers led governments for 57 years of the twentieth century, including Winston Churchill (1940–1945, 1951–1955), Edward Heath (1965–1975), Margaret Thatcher (1979–1990) and John Major (1990–1997). With more than 300,000 members, supporters of the party are mainly from the affluent classes or business circles; they are in favor of a free market and law and order. They advocate the curbing of inflation by tightening the money supply and cutting public spending, and also limiting the power of the unions.

The party has recently focused on social issues, such as education, medical care, and poverty alleviation on the platform of compassionate conservatism, and there is an emphasis on safeguarding British sovereignty against a federal Europe. It asserts that NATO is the cornerstone of British security and defense.

The Liberal Democrat Party

With roughly 100,000 members, this is the third largest party in the UK, committed to co-operation with the Labour Party and urging the latter to implement the proportional representation system in local and parliamentary elections. It adopts policies that focus on public service, social justice, and environmental protection.

Other British parties include the Scottish National Party, Plaid Cymru, the Ulster Unionist Party, the Democratic Unionist Party, the Social Democratic and Labour Party, and Sinn Fein.

2.2.1.10   The Civil Rights System

The implementation of civil rights system in the UK takes "government by law" as the principle. More stress has been laid on the restrictions of rights, such as the Defamation Law (amendment) of 1888, the Public Meeting Act of 1908, the Sedition Act of 1934, and the Public Order Act of 1936. In 2000, the Human Right Act 1998 came into force with the aim of incorporating into UK law the rights and freedoms contained in the European Convention on Human Rights. In the meantime, personal freedom is secured through the system of habeas corpus—a recourse in law challenging the reasons or conditions of a person's confinement under the color of law.

2.2.1.11   The National Flag, Emblem and Anthem

The National Flag

The Union Jack emerged in 1801. It is a horizontal rectangular flag with a 2:1 length to width ratio. The red cross in the center with white edges stands for the patron saint of England, St. George, while the white cross represents St. Andrew, the patron saint of Scotland, and the other red cross stands for the patron saint of Ireland, St. Patrick. The three overlapping crosses resemble the Chinese character 米 and appear on a dark blue background.

The National Coat of Arms

The British coat of arms is also the coat of arms of the sovereign. The central design is a shield with three golden lions representing England in the upper left and lower right quarters against a red background. The red lion on a golden background in the upper right quarter represents Scotland and the golden harp on a blue background in the lower right quarter symbolizes Ireland. The shield has a lion with a crown, the symbol of England, on its left-hand side and a unicorn, the symbol of Scotland, on the right.

Surrounding the shield is the Garter, with the French maxim "Honi soit qui mal y pense," which means "Shame on him who thinks evil of it." Underneath is a streamer with the words "Dieu et mon droit," which means "God and my right." On top of the shield are a gold and silver helmet, a crown encrusted with jewels, and a lion wearing a crown.

The National Anthem
The anthem is "God Save the Queen," which was composed in the eighteenth century; if a king is on throne, "God Save the King" is sung. There are three verses, all ending with this phrase.

2.2.2   The USA's Political System

After over 200 years of development since the establishment of its federal government in 1789, the USA has become the world's superpower. Its political system is characterized by a combination of Western European democratic ideals and the requirements of modern capitalism; these underpin social stability and growth. As a federal state, the USA forms a presidential government, has adopted the two-party system, and combines separation of three powers and associated checks and balances.

2.2.2.1 Evolution
The USA is the world's first bourgeois republic, and the origins of its political system can be traced back to the colonial times. The Mayflower Compact drawn up in 1620 and the Virginia General Assembly set up in 1619 are referred to by Western scholars as the cornerstone of the US political system. The latter is the first organization that adopted a representative system in the New World, and this became the basic system in all other colonies. The Declaration of Independence passed on June 4, 1776 further laid the theoretical foundations and the Articles of Confederation that came into effect on March 1, 1781 prepared for the implementation of federalism. Eventually the US political system was established after the Constitution of the United States of America had been enacted in 1787.

2.2.2.2 The Polity
The president is head of state and government by virtue of the presidential system. Legislative, executive, and judiciary powers are respectively

exercised by Congress, the president, and the Supreme Court in a balanced way: the president can veto bills passed by Congress, but this veto may be overridden by a two-thirds majority of both houses. The president can nominate senior officials, including the chief justice of the Supreme Court, provided that they are confirmed by Congress, which is authorized to impeach presidents and officials. The chief justice of the US Supreme Court can declare bills passed by Congress unconstitutional and invalid.

Congress
Congress wields the legislative power of the state based on the Constitution and comprises the House of Representatives and the Senate. The two houses consist congressmen and senators representing their constituents and the total electorate.

A) Obligations of Congress

It is prescribed in the US Constitution that Congress has obligations regarding legislation, representation of constituents, supervision, and conflict mediation, among which the first two are of paramount importance.

a. Legislation

Congress is the supreme legislative authority, yet most of the motions are put forward by executive agencies, political parties, and interest groups. After considerable debate and discussion, supporters of the proposals form an alliance to make national policies.

b. Representation

This embraces expressing the thoughts and needs of constituents and representing the interests of the country in a broader sense. Sometimes congressmen and senators perform acts that are against the will of constituents because of political horse-trading among parties, and often they base their positions on constituents' aspirations, even voting against their parties in order to gain re-election. Strictly speaking, congressmen and senators are neither completely the representatives of the state nor of the voters.

c. Serving constituents

Congressmen, senators, and their employees devote much time to individual constituents and help handle affairs that include disputes with governments, local business promotion, and interpretation of proposals.

d. Supervision
Congress ensures that all bills passed are properly enforced by means of holding hearings, investigations, altering departmental budgets, and examining candidates for executive and law enforcement agencies who are nominated by the president.

e. Conflict mediation
Interest groups representing people of different races, ideas, economic organizations, and both genders lobby congressmen and senators to express their dissatisfaction and to influence congressional decisions. Congress has to mediate these views and enact laws that meet diverse demands, especially those of the majority interest groups.

B) Powers of Congress

a. Explicit powers
Article I of the Constitution sets forth most of the powers of Congress, such as tax collection, regulation of interstate and foreign commerce, and the declaration of wars, particularly in Section 8 where explicit powers are enumerated. Other articles delegate powers to Congress that override the president's veto, regulating the Electoral College and interstate relations, defining cases that should be reviewed by the Supreme Court, and proposing amendments to the Constitution. In light of subsequent amendments to the Constitution, Congress can elect the president and vice-president when no candidate gets a majority of votes in a presidential election (the Twelfth Amendment), collect income tax (the Sixteenth Amendment), select an acting president when the president in office is dead or disabled (the Twentieth and Twenty-Fifth Amendments), and govern Washington DC (the Twenty-Third Amendment).

Some powers are conferred on the Senate, for instance ratifying treaties, approving or disapproving presidential appointments of ambassadors, the Supreme Court justices, and officials of executive departments, and trying impeachments of presidents and officials. The House of Representatives is constitutionally empowered to originate financial bills, elect the president and vice-president if is no majority in the Electoral College, and initiate impeachment cases.

b. Necessary and Proper Clause
Congress has implied powers, deriving from the Constitution's Necessary and Proper Clause, to enact laws that are necessary and proper for the execution of the foregoing powers.

c. Limitation of powers
Congress is constitutionally prohibited to define the national guiding ideology or obstruct people's freedom of religion and speech (First Amendment). Besides, Congress cannot pass bills permitting trial default or the expropriation of private property, disfranchising citizens, or the levying of tax and bills that are retrospective. The Supreme Court decides whether congressional actions and laws are constitutional.

C) Congressional election
The electoral process is restricted by the Constitution and relevant federal laws (Section 4, Article I of the Constitution). A senator should be at least thirty years old, a legal resident of the state he or she represents, and a US citizen for over nine years. There are 100 senators (2017) representing fifty states and with six-year tenure. A third of them are re-elected every two years and they may serve for consecutive terms.

Representatives have to be at least twenty-five years old, live in the state they represent, and a US citizen for over seven years. They face re-elections every two years and seats of the House are apportioned among the states by size of population, based on the census that is conducted every ten years; each state is entitled to at least one representative. The District of Columbia and the territories of Guam, the US Virgin Islands, American Samoa, the Northern Mariana Islands, and Puerto Rico are each represented by one non-voting delegate, who may participate in investigations and debates.

a. The Election of Candidates
A primary election is held within the party to nominate the candidates who will campaign in the general election. Candidates usually tend to be radical in order to attract votes in the primary election and moderate in order to win over the middle-of-the-roaders in the general election.

b. Coattail Effect
Most congressmen and senators win re-election, for they are obliged to carry out surveys among voters and are widely covered

in the media. In addition, they help candidates from the same party attract votes in the election to strengthen their positions in constituencies; this is called the coattail effect. However, constituents may change their votes in the midterm election in light of the president's performance.

Constituencies are divided according to their population density. The Congressional majority proposes redistribution plans on the basis of the census conducted every ten years. Though the Supreme Court protects constituents' rights to vote, parties still attempt to draw electoral district boundaries to their advantage, for instance by designing with the aid of computers contiguous districts that pack opponents into as few districts as possible.

D) The Structure of Congress

Under the Constitution, the vice-president is the ex officio President of the Senate authorized to preside over Senate sessions, though he or she can vote only to break a tie. Senior senators of the majority party are customarily elected by the Senate to serve as President *pro tempore* to preside in the vice-president's absence.

The Senate party leaders and whips elected by the caucus have the real power, and the majority leader acts as spokesman. The House of Representatives resembles the Senate in structure, with the Speaker of the House presiding over the chamber having similar powers to his or her counterpart in the Senate. The majority leader subordinate to the Speaker serves as the spokesman of the party.

Most legislative work is carried out by committees and subcommittees. Proposals are passed to special committees for review and put to a vote afterwards.

E) Legislation

Congress and executive agencies subordinate to the president can bring in bills that are usually concurrently proposed to both houses, except those concerning only one House, such as fiscal plans and treaties. The proposals are passed to special committees where experts hold hearings and debates in order to improve them. When committees report to the houses, the Senate majority leader or the House Rules Committee will settle on a date for public debates. A bill becomes a law if the president signs it; otherwise Congress may offer revisions to gain the president's favor or override his veto with a two-thirds majority (abstention is not allowed). If there are fewer than ten days left for the congressional session when the bill reaches the president and he fails to sign it within the time limit, it will be tabled and invalid but may be put forward again in the next session. It is required that provided over one-fifth of the congressmen and senators are present for voting on bills, their votes and names should be announced in the proceedings of the houses for their constituents' oversight.

F) Budget
Congress is empowered by the Constitution to collect tax, but motions of tax and appropriation are proposed by the House. The president is required to submit the budget for the next fiscal year, which begins in October every year. The Office of Management and Budget is responsible for checking budgets submitted by all departments eighteen months ahead of schedule and for organizing the president's budget to be presented to Congress each February. Congress is supposed to approve budgets before the new fiscal year starts; however, the deadline is often missed, in which case it has to enact temporary legislations to allow the normal operation of the government.

The US President
The president is head of the state and government of the USA. He leads the executive branch of the federal government and is the commander-in-chief of the armed forces. The presidency is framed in the US Constitution, which was passed in 1788: the first president took office in 1789. In light of the Twenty-Second Amendment, the term of service for presidents is four years and they can serve two terms at most.

US presidents are hugely powerful and influential as the supreme leader of the world's superpower. Traditionally, the wife of a president is referred to as "the first lady" and his family "the first family." An African American's election as the forty-fourth president was a breakthrough, for all ex-presidents have been white males.

A president must be at least thirty-five years old, born as a citizen of the USA (a precondition for presidential and vice-presidential candidates) and a permanent resident in the USA for at least fourteen years. The official presidential residence is the White House in Washington DC. The radio calls for the airplane and helicopter that the president is aboard are respectively Air Force One and Marine One.

A) The Election of the President

The president is elected indirectly by the Electoral College, all electors from each state to choose a slate of electors who are pledged to vote for a particular party's candidate, their number being equal to the size of the state's delegation in both houses (the combined total of senators and representatives). The party to which the candidate who wins a majority vote in a state belongs can choose the electors who vote in the Electoral College.

B) Powers of the President

The USA has adopted a presidential system. According to Article II of the Constitution, the president is delegated to take care that laws be faithfully executed. The president leads the executive branch with over 4 million staff, which includes more than 1 million military personnel on active service, and has some legislative and judicial powers.

a. Administrative powers

Members of the cabinet and federal judges are appointed by the president with the approval of the Senate. A president may make up to 6000 appointments each year, including heads of executive agencies, bureaus, and departments, with confirmation of the Senate, and hundreds of other high-ranking officials in the federal government. He is empowered to deal with national and federal affairs and issue government decrees. The president can summon the National Guard and declare wars even without congressional authorization. During wars and emergencies, Congress may delegate greater powers to him.

b. Legislative powers

A bill does not become a law if the president vetoes it unless the houses override the veto by a two-thirds vote. The president can propose legislations in the form of reports, including the State of the Union Message, the budget, and economic and special messages. In addition, the president has delegated legislative power, which indicates he can not only re-organize existing executive agencies but also set up new ones.

c. Judicial Powers

The president can appoint supreme judicial officials and federal judges, and even Supreme Court Justices with the Senate's approval. The president can grant complete or conditional amnesty to anyone who has broken federal laws unless he or she is impeached.

d. Foreign Affairs Powers

The president is the principal official for foreign affairs: he appoints ambassadors, envoys, and consuls with the confirmation of the Senate and receives foreign ambassadors and officials. The president can conclude treaties with foreign countries under senatorial approval by a two-thirds vote; yet he can always sign executive agreements instead, as these do not require authorization from the Senate.

The US Supreme Court

This is the highest federal court of the USA and was established in 1790 in Washington DC in accordance with the Constitution. The Supreme Court consists of the Chief Justice and eight associate justices based on the congressional decree of 1869. Justices are appointed by the president with the approval of the Senate and have life tenure; they cannot be removed without congressional impeachment. If they have been in office for more than ten years and are seventy years old and above or have been in office for more than fifteen years and are sixty-five years old and above, they may voluntarily retire.

It is prescribed in the Constitution that the Supreme Court exercises original jurisdiction in cases affecting ambassadors, envoys, and consuls or in which a state is a party. It can review cases that have been heard by state supreme courts or federal appellate courts, grant writs seeking judicial review on cases from lower federal or state courts and has the power of judicial review on the constitutionality of federal and state legislative and administrative acts. Any judgment of the Supreme Court is final. It is in session from the first Monday of October to mid-June the following year. Judgments are given on the basis of the majority votes of justices and the views of all parties are listed in the verdict.

2.2.2.3 The Structural Form of the USA

This was established as federalism in the Constitution that was drawn up in 1787. The states have their own written constitutions, laws, and governments while the federation as the main route for international communication sets up supreme legislative, executive, and judicial organs under unified laws. When state constitutions and laws contradict those of the federation, the latter are superior.

The federal government, as stipulated in the Constitution, can collect taxes, contract loans, mint coins, have armies, deal with foreign affairs, and regulate interstate and international commerce. Under the Constitution, all powers not granted to the federal government nor prohibited by it are reserved to the state governments, which are responsible for state affairs, such as collecting local taxes, governing intrastate industries and labor, organizing security forces, and preserving order, for example. Jurisdictions for the federation and the states have changed over the past 200 years.

2.2.2.4 *The Electoral System*
Constituents in each state elect electors in equal number to the number of the state congressmen and senators. Electors then vote for the presidency and vice-presidency concurrently in the state capital cities, this being referred to as indirect election. Both congressmen and senators are directly elected in light of the Seventeenth Amendment of the Constitution and governors, justices of some states, and executive officials for key positions are directly elected by constituents. Systems of single-member constituency and majority representation underpin the dominance of the two major parties in elections at all levels.

2.2.2.5 *The Political Party System*
The two-party system is an important and influential component of the US political system, through which the monopoly capitalist class controls national political institutions and politics. Members of the two parties, the Democratic Party and the Republican Party, are the primary candidates in elections, especially in presidential elections, and one or the other rules, despite the existence of other parties.

Evolution
After the federal government was founded in 1789, serious disagreements arose between the two parties regarding the interpretation of the Constitution, jurisdiction of the federation and the states, government bonds, and the establishment of the state bank. Gradually, the two factions developed into national political parties: the anti-federalists formed the Republican Party with Secretary of State Thomas Jefferson as the leader, whose power expanded after European wars broke out in 1792; Jefferson won the presidential election in 1800.

In the 1820s, the Republicans split into two groups, of which the Democratic-Republican Party which supported Andrew Jackson was renamed the Democratic Party at the third national convention in 1840. With the Whigs, a league against the Jackson regime was founded in 1834, and this joined the new Republican Party formed in July 1854 in Jefferson City, Michigan. The Republicans became the arch-rivals of the Democrats and the two-party system was established. After the Civil War, the USA transformed from a laissez-faire capitalist country to a monopoly capitalist one, and the two parties both serve the interests of monopoly capitalists.

Other parties are called third parties, and the first of their kind was a labor party that emerged with the rise of working-class and socialist movements. The increasing number of workers boosted its campaigns and national workers' organizations were set up. Yet without specific political programs and a stable leading nucleus, the party declined, disintegrating at the end of the nineteenth century.

The third parties also include those that were born for presidential elections, such as the Green Party, the Civic Party, and the Democratic Socialist Organization.

Characteristics
Since the establishment of the two-party system, the Democrats and Republicans have been in office in turns and their common features are:

- There are no fixed programs, ultimate aims, or long-term purposes. All they have are programs for the general election.
- Members are not confined to their parties and do not have to pay dues.
- They both have a four-tier structure: national, state, county, and constituency committees.
- Government officials including the president, governors, mayors, congressmen, and senators are mainly from the two parties.
- Presidential candidates are nominated in the two parties' national conventions and the ruling party is the one led by the candidate who wins the presidential election.
- The majority or minority party is distinguished by the number of seats obtained in congressional elections. A ruling party is not always the majority party, since the president is elected by the Electoral College rather than Congress.

Major Parties

a) The Democratic Party

In 1933, when the USA was deeply involved in the global economic crisis, the Democrat Franklin D. Roosevelt was elected to the presidency and enacted the programs of the New Deal. The government's intervention in the economy promoted the development of state monopoly capitalism. He was elected for four consecutive terms, with the Democrats being in office for twenty years. During its period in office, the party implemented the Fair Deal, New Frontier, and Great Society policies, and advocated expansionism. The Democratic National Convention is the party's ultimate authority and this is held every four years, during which members select candidates for the presidency and vice-presidency and set out election platforms. The Democratic National Committee, a standing body of the party with a four-year tenure, is responsible for arranging national conventions and presiding over campaigns. State committees are in charge of state elections. The party mascot is a donkey.

b) The Republican Party

Founded in 1854, the party rose to prominence in 1860 with the election of Abraham Lincoln. It had been in office for twenty consecutive years since the Civil War, during which period it led the north to quash the revolt by southern slave owners, abolish slavery, and defend the unity of the federation. From 1969 to 1976, the Republican President Richard Nixon was in office: he visited China in February 1972 and issued the Joint Communiqué of the People's Republic of China and the United States of America with Premier Zhou Enlai. In 1981, President Ronald Reagan proposed an economic recovery plan that consisted of cutting tax and government expenditure, reducing government intervention, controlling the money supply, and pushing forward tax reforms. He also proposed the Strategic Defense Initiative, better known as the Star Wars Program. The Republican National Convention is the highest authority of the party and is held in the summer of the election year. Members nominate candidates for the presidency and vice-presidency and set out election platforms. The Republican National Committee, a standing body of the party with a four-year tenure, assumes similar responsibilities to its counterpart in the Democratic Party. State committees are in charge of state elections. The party mascot is an elephant.

c) Socialist Party of America

This was a coalition of the Hillquit group of the Socialist Labor Party and some other labor parties, and it was formed in 1901. It asserted social improvement and focused on a parliamentary struggle and winning votes. During the First World War, the right wing of the party was in favor of imperialist policies, whereas the left wing was against them; this caused the party to split.

d) The Communist Party USA

Founded in January 1919, this developed into the United Communist Party, having allied with the Communist Labor Party in May 1920. After a coalition with the Labor Party in April 1923, it was renamed the Communist Party USA in 1930. After the Second World War, the party was weakened because of governmental suppression. It proposed the embodiment of people's rights in government at all levels, controlling economic lifelines and nationalization.

2.2.2.6 The System of Civil Rights
It is stipulated in the Constitution and in legal provisions that governmental power is not absolute; it is from the people, for the people, and limited by laws. Congress cannot enact laws to obstruct the exercise of citizens' individual freedom of speech, press, assembly, and religion, their rights to vote and petition, private property rights, and habeas corpus. Citizens and their residences, documents, and property cannot be searched or detained illegally and they cannot be deprived of their lives, liberty, and property without the due process of law.

2.2.3   The Political System of France
In modern times, France is a single unitary centralized state that has alternately adopted the parliamentary, presidential, and semi-presidential systems.

2.2.3.1 Evolution
In the second century BC, the Roman Empire conquered the ancestors of the French, the Gauls, and set up a slavery province there. In the fifth century, France was gradually transformed into a feudal state and in the

fourteenth century the king enhanced his power by suppressing churches, collecting new taxes, and convening the Estate General with the participation of monks, aristocrats, and citizens; a hierarchical monarchy that combined the monarchy with a hierarchical representation system was formed. With the economic development and formation of the unified state in the sixteenth century, the king governed all the territory and replaced the Estate General with the imperial conference. Henceforth France became highly centralized, as can be seen from the remark of King Louis XIV "l'état, c'est moi" (I am the state). The absolute monarchy culminated in the second half of the seventeenth century and triggered the French Revolution (1789), which overthrew feudalism and established the modern capitalist system. Yet the bourgeois republic was not founded until the establishment of the Third Republic in 1875 owing to the regime changes from constitutional monarchy to autocratic monarchy and republicanism in the twentieth century. After the Second World War, the Fourth and Fifth Republics were established and the capitalist political system underwent further development.

The Political System of the French First Republic

In 1791, the constituent assembly was convened, in which the constitution and constitutional monarchy were established, conferring great powers on the king. But shortly afterwards in 1792 the monarchy was abolished by the National Convention and the First Republic was founded. In 1793, the Jacobins promulgated a new constitution, prescribing that France was a parliamentary republic with the executive, legislative, and judicial powers separated. Though the constitution was not implemented owing to the unstable political situation, the foundation of the First Republic marked the establishment of the modern capitalist political system.

In July 1794, the Jacobin government was overturned in the Thermidor reaction; universal suffrage and the direct election and unicameral systems were abolished in the constitution passed by the bourgeoisie in 1795. Napoleon Bonaparte assumed power after a military coup in 1799 and set up the First Empire in 1804.

The Political System of the French Second Republic

The July Revolution broke out in 1830 in Paris and led to the fall of the Bourbons and the establishment of the July monarchy, which was overturned in the February Revolution in 1848 and replaced by the Second Republic.

The Republic adopted the presidential system, with the president who won the general election serving as head of state and government with a four-year tenure. He led the army and government and was empowered to appoint and remove prime ministers and officials, yet the president had to be authorized by the parliament to sign treaties. The unicameral parliament could make laws, declare wars, make peace, and ratify treaties, and couldn't be supervised or dissolved. Citizens also enjoyed extensive democratic rights. In 1848 Louis Bonaparte became the president, proclaimed himself emperor in 1852, and established the Second Empire in 1852, which brought an end to the Second Republic.

The Political System of the French Third Republic
The French people overthrew the Second Empire after its defeat in the Franco-Prussian War in 1870 and founded the Third Republic, yet the bourgeoisie usurped power and signed treaties to cede territory and pay indemnities to Germany. The people of Paris were indignant and seized power in an armed uprising on March 18, 1871 and established the Paris Commune. By the time the commune was overturned by bourgeois reactionaries, the French people had long been fighting, republicans against royalists. Eventually the new constitution was passed in the National Assembly in 1875 and a multi-party parliamentary system was built.
The new parliament comprised the Chamber of Deputies and the Senate. Deputies assumed office through a general election and held legislative and supervisory powers, while senators were indirectly elected and authorized to veto the deputies' resolutions. The president was head of state, elected indirectly with seven-year tenure, and could be re-elected. Presidents could appoint cabinet members and military and political officials, put forward bills, and dissolve the parliament. The Third Republic was a product of compromise between republicanism and monarchism. The powers of the president, parliament, and cabinet were balanced. When German fascists invaded France in May 1940, the era of the Third Republic was over.

The Political System of the French Fourth Republic
After the Second World War, the left wing predominated, and under the influence of democratic tendencies the National Assembly drew up a new constitution that was passed after a referendum in 1946: thus the Fourth French Republic was set up. A multi-party parliamentary system was introduced and the National Assembly became the locus of power, which was

empowered to make laws, supervise public finance, as well as approve treaties, the formation of the government, and administrative programs. Powers of the Senate and president were limited while civil rights were expanded. Besides the rights enumerated in the Declaration of the Rights of Man and of the Citizen, citizens had economic and social rights such as the rights of social security and poverty relief, the right to strike, and women's rights to vote and enter politics. The Fourth Republic also established a relatively complete civil service system, yet it only existed for twelve years with twenty-four sessions of governments, each of which lasted for less than six months.

The Political System of the French Fifth Republic

To accommodate the economic, political, and social situations of the 1950s, the De Gaulle administration established a new constitution in 1958 to consolidate presidential and executive powers. This was passed in a referendum that September. The era of the Fifth Republic began.

2.2.3.2 *The Polity*

France adopted a semi-presidential system, which falls in between the presidential and parliamentary systems and is characterized by:

a) The president, directly elected by universal suffrage, is the locus of state power with seven year tenure and cannot serve more than two consecutive terms. He is constitutionally delegated to ensure the proper functioning of authorities and the continuity of the country by his arbitration. Besides the powers of naming senior officials, signing decrees, and commanding armies and powers in foreign affairs, the president can appoint the prime minister, organize the government, dissolve the National Assembly, hold a referendum, and declare a state of emergency.

b) The government is the supreme executive authority answerable to parliament. Its status has been greatly improved and it is empowered to direct and decide national policies, administer executive agencies, direct the actions of armed forces, implement domestic and foreign policies, and issue orders. The prime minister leads the government and is responsible for national defense and law enforcement, and assists and takes orders from the president. All members of the government are nominated by the president on the advice of the prime minister.

c) The parliament comprises the National Assembly and the Senate, and cannot intervene in the presidential election or the appointment of the prime minister.

2.2.3.3 *The Local Government System*
France was once highly centralized, whereas the powers were devolved after regions were set up in the 1980s. There are now three tiers of local governments: regions, provinces, and towns. Local councils have been more autonomous since the reform.

2.2.3.4 *The Civil Service System*
The Fifth Republic has improved the Fourth Republic's civil service and has drawn up special regulations which combine examinations and the recruitment and training of civil servants. The civil service is an integral part of the political system, and is about examinations, recruitment, appointment, assessment, promotion, training, salary, welfare, retirement, rewards and punishments, job classification, and administration. By definition, civil servants are regular employees who serve in public administration and public administrative establishments, and they are not elected to these positions.

Evolution
In the sixteenth century the centralized monarchy was set up and officials were appointed by the king. The French Revolution (1789) specified the basic essence of the modern civil service system. However, for more than a century there was no uniform system and administrations could decide their own qualifications for civil servants. In October 1945, the General Administration of Public Service (later renamed the Directorate General of Administration and Public Service) and the National School of Administration were founded, and a uniform system of recruitment, training, and appointment of senior civil servants was set up, with the General Statue of Civil Servants adopted the following year. Gradually a complete civil service system has been formed.

Content
The civil service system involves the following aspects.

a) Rights, Obligations, and Punishments

It is enumerated in the General Statue of Civil Servants and other relevant legislation that civil servants have freedom of religion and speech, and the freedom to strike and to join labor unions, as well as rights of training, remuneration, leisure, life, hygiene, and health. Full commitment to their professional activities, hierarchical obedience, and professional discretion constitute their obligations. When civil servants cannot fulfill their statutory duties or violate criminal laws, they are put on trial in criminal courts, and those who break administrative laws are tried in administrative courts. In cases of a breach of discipline, civil servants are punished by the executive branch; they may be warned, reprimanded, demoted, transferred, dismissed, or temporarily removed from office.

b) The Job Classification

After the Second World War, civil servants were divided into corps, which are grouped in three categories (formerly four) named A to C in decreasing order of seniority and qualifications. Each category is divided into different classes, based on job description, recruitment, profession, and method of promotion. Each class is further divided into various ranks and subdivided into grades on account of workload, complexity of job, and responsibilities. Different grades have differing working standards, responsibilities, and pay, these differences providing the criteria for recruitment, assessment, promotion, pay, retirement, and budgeting.

c) Recruitment

Civil servants are recruited internally or externally under the principles of equal opportunity, open competition, and selection made on the basis of qualification. An independent examination board holds the tests, except those for senior civil servants (category A) who are recruited through the entrance exams of the National School of Administration. Examinees are appraised by test performance and are on probation before they are officially employed.

d) Training

France attaches great importance to the education and training of civil servants. Ministerial deputies in charge of personnel and administrative reforms in the chancellery lead this nationwide, with executive branches responsible for training within the branches. There are pre- and in-service types. The former may last from three months to three years, with its funds accounting for 70% of the total training budget.

e) Appraisal and Promotion

Civil servants are appraised by their chief executives annually in the following aspects: physical condition, professional knowledge, competence, punctuality, neatness, team spirit, spirit of service, initiative, efficiency, working method, insight, and organizational, oversight, and investigating capabilities. Promotion includes a rise in rank and pay. A civil servant is given a rise in rank on account of performance and competence and by means of selection, examination, or evaluation.

f) Salary and Welfare

These principles are followed: (a) the principle of indexation: salaries for civil servants of all levels are the products of base pay multiplied by an index that is directly linked to ranks and prices; (b) the principle of bridging the gaps; (c) the principle of negotiation; (d) the principle of balancing the state's ability to pay with salary levels in private companies. Civil servants enjoy quarterly allowances as well as base pay, for instance a housing allowance.

g) Retirement

The government stipulates the retirement age for resident civil servants as sixty and fifty-five for those who travel a lot. The maximum retirement age can be up to sixty-eight. Generally, civil servants receive pensions after they have served for more than fifteen years and paid 6% of their salaries as retirement savings for at least fifteen years. The amount of pension they receive depends on length of service.

Administrations of Civil Servants
Heads of the government and department are the leaders for national and departmental personnel administration. Executive civil service agencies include the Directorate General of Administration and Public Service, the Supreme Committee of Public Service, administrative courts, and local and departmental personnel administrations.

Characteristics

The French civil service system is characterized by:

a) Personnel agencies are set up within administrations to take charge of recruitment, appointment, assessment, promotion, training, salaries, welfare, retirement, rewards, and punishments.
b) The self-management of civil servants is emphasized.
c) There is a set of relatively complete written laws and regulations for the management of the civil service.
d) Except for highly professional or junior administrative posts, civil servants are recruited through competitive examinations and strict assessment. A complete training system has been built.
e) Hierarchical management under a unified command. Regions, provinces, and cities are fairly autonomous in personnel matters.

2.2.3.5 *The Political Party System*

France is representative of modern capitalist nations that implement the multi-party system, and all its governments have been formed by one party or a coalition of parties since 1944.

Evolution

The history of French parties can be traced back to two centuries ago and divided into five phases.

a) The Early Phase (1789–1870)

This phase includes seven periods: bourgeois revolution, the First Republic (1792–1804), the First Empire (1804–1814, 1815), Bourbon Restoration (1814–1830), July Monarchy (1830–1848), the Second Republic (1848–1851), and the Second Empire (1852–1870).

Centering on the vital political issues in each period, there emerged party factions such as the Jacobins, Girondins, republicans, and radicals, which laid the foundation for the establishment of subsequent parties.

b) The Third Republic Phase (1870–1940)

Parties were set up successively at this time. With the development of the labor movement and the spreading of socialist ideas, the first party of the working class, the French Labor Party, was founded in October 1879.

Then the Socialist Party of France (1902) and the socialist French Section of the Workers' International were founded on the basis of the splitting, merger, and reorganization of labor parties and socialist organizations. The ruling party in the Third Republic were the Republican, Radical, and Radical-Socialist Parties, established by capitalists in 1901.

c) The Second World War Phase

The Vichy regime gave in to the German fascists who invaded France in June 1940. Consequently parties, except ultra-right-wing parties such as the French Socialist Party and the French People's Party, were driven underground. Meanwhile, guerrillas organized by the French Communist Party rose up in arms against the invaders, making the party much more influential and powerful.

d) The Fourth Republic Phase (1946–1958)

Numerous parties were founded or rebuilt after the Second World War. The cabinet-styled parliamentary government of the Fourth Republic was held accountable to the parliament. However, the proportional representation system parliamentary elections that followed prevented the emergence of a majority party. With loose coalitions of parties taking turns in power, there were twenty-five governments in twelve years.

e) The Fifth Republic Phase (1958–)

In June 1958, De Gaulle reformed the government and electoral systems to consolidate presidential power and relegate the parliament to a back seat. There have been significant changes in parties. (a) From 1958 to 1986 and after June 1988, there has existed a presidential majority in the National Assembly and the three vital positions of president, prime minister, and President of the National Assembly have all been held by candidates from the same party or alliance of parties. (b) Parties began to polarize. After thirty years of development, up to the early 1980s, two party groups (left and right wing) and four major parties (the French Communist Party, Socialist Party, Rally for the Republic, and Union for French Democracy) were formed. In 2006, Emmanuel Macron, a former Minister of Economy, Industry and Digital Affairs founded La République

En Marche! (frequently abbreviated REM, LRM, or LREM; officially LaREM). Observers and political commentators have described the party as being both socially and economically liberal in ideology, as well as being a party of the radical center. By winning an absolute majority in the National Assembly in the second round of the legislative elections on 18 June 2017, La République En Marche! became France's party of power in support of the President, Emmanuel Macron.

Characteristics
(a) Diversity. There have been more than 400 parties since the establishment of republicanism in 1875. By the 1980s, there were still over forty parties playing an active role in French politics. (b) Instability. It is common for parties to be split, consolidated, reorganized, or rebuilt. (c) Socialist and communist parties have a longer history than the other existing parties.

Major Parties

a) The Socialist Party

This is the largest and long-ruling party of the French centre-left. Influenced by chauvinism, the party entered politics during the First World War and disintegrated during the Second World War. It was rebuilt in 1943 and took part in the anti-fascist movement. During the Fourth Republic, it promoted the nationalization of France and European Union (EU) integration. In May 1981, its candidate Mitterrand was elected President of France and appointed the prime minister in June; the party achieved a governing majority in the National Assembly. The party's guiding principles are: solidarity inside the party, implementation of moderate and realistic policies, opposing racism, and advocating pacifism and north–south dialogue. The party journal is *Solidarity* (a weekly).

b) The French Communist Party

Founded in December 1920 by the majority faction of the socialist French Section of Workers' International, it is the largest French left-wing party. In 1941, it participated in the anti-fascist movement and was among the governing alliance for five sessions of coalition governments after September 1944. In 1946, it became the biggest party in the general election, but was excluded from the government in May 1947 owing to concerns over communist influence, and the number of members dropped off henceforth. During the 1960s and 1970s, the communist formulations of a dictatorship of the proletariat and Marxism-Leninism shifted toward building French socialism as part of Eurocommunism. In 1981 it was allotted a minor share in the left-wing coalition government, resigning in 1984. The party journal is *Humanity* (daily).

c) Rally for the Republic

As a Gaullist Party, this was once the major ruling party of the Fifth Republic, originating from the Rally of the French People founded by De Gaulle. This party pursues Gaullism, maintains the political system of the Fifth Republic, and defends the national independence of France. Since the 1980s, it has been committed to the privatization of state-owned enterprises.

d) Union for French Democracy

This was set up as an electoral alliance in June 1978 with the founding parties being Giscard's Republican Party, the Center of Social Democrats, the Radical Party, the Social Democratic Party, and the Perspectives and Realities Clubs. From March 1986 to May 1988, it participated in the government. The alliance aims to coordinate the actions of member parties, organizations, and individual participants; it is devoted to national unity, justice, and the economic and political integration of the EU.

e) Front National

This is one of the ultra-right-wing parties, founded in October 1972. Its predecessor was the banned fascist New Order Party. Since the 1980s, it has won an increasing number of votes in European Parliament elections and indeed French parliaments at all levels. Front National advocates nationalism, exclusionism, and racism, and is influential among unemployed youths.

2.2.3.6 The System of Civil Rights

Besides the rights enumerated in the Declaration of the Rights of Man and of the Citizen, citizens enjoy the right to work, join unions, and receive social security.

2.2.4   The Political System of Germany

2.2.4.1 Evolution

In 1867 Prussia established the North German Confederation. The German Empire was founded in 1871, uniting all parts of Germany; it provoked the First World War and collapsed in 1918 after its defeat. In 1933, Adolf Hitler took office and waged the Second World War from 1939. Germany was under dictatorial rule until Hitler was vanquished on May 8, 1945. In light of the Yalta and Potsdam agreements, Berlin and the other parts of German territory were partitioned into four military occupation zones by the Allies. The western sectors, controlled by the USA, UK, and France were merged on May 23, 1949 to found the Federal Republic of Germany. The German Democratic Republic was formed in the Soviet zone on October 7, 1949. On October 3, 1989, Germany regained full sovereignty and was reunified after forty years of division. The constitution, the People's Chamber, and the government of the German Democratic Republic were abolished, and the former fourteen districts were redivided into five federal states that conformed to the organizational system of the Federal Republic of Germany.

2.2.4.2 Basic Law for the Federal Republic of Germany

This came into force in May 1949 and lays out the framework of the political system, based on which Germany is a federal parliamentary democratic republic with the president as head of the state. The federation administers diplomacy, national defense, currency, customs, aviation, the postal system, and telecommunications. The parliament comprises the Bundestag (the lower house) and Bundesrat (the upper house). The former, with a term of four years, is authorized to elect the chancellor and to exercise legislative power and the oversight of law enforcement and the government. Members of the Bundestag from various parties form their own parliamentary groups.

2.2.4.3 The Bundesrat
Participating in legislation, it can exert an influence on administration. Three to six members of state governments are appointed in proportion to their populations to form the Bundesrat. There are altogether sixty-nine members. The post of the President of Bundesrat rotates annually among the minister-president of each federal state. The chancellor and other ministers organize the government, with the former serving as head of the government.

2.2.4.4 The Federal Constitutional Court
This is the supreme judicial body and is mainly in charge of the interpretation of Basic Law and judicial review. The sixteen judges with twelve-year tenure are elected by the Bundestag and Bundesrat and appointed by the president.

2.2.4.5 German Parties
Germany has adopted the multi-party system, with the main parties being the Social Democratic Party of Germany, Christian Democratic Union of Germany, Christian Social Union of Bavaria, Alliance 90/The Greens, Free Democratic Party, and Social Democratic Party of Germany.

2.2.4.6 The Administrative Division
Germany is divided into sixteen federal states, which are further subdivided into several government districts.

2.2.4.7 The National Flag, Emblem and Anthem

The National Flag
Germany's rectangular flag has a 5:3 length-to-width ratio and is composed of three horizontal equal rectangles in black, red, and yellow. The tricolor flag can be seen in airports and hotels and at special occasions, while governments or German embassies in foreign countries hang the national flag that features a black eagle.

The National Emblem
This is a golden coat of arms with a black eagle. With red claws and beak and wings spread, the eagle symbolizes strength and courage.

The National Anthem

The national anthem is "Das Deutschlandlied" (the Song of Germany, the third verse), composed by Joseph Haydn (1732–1809) with words by August H.H. von Fallersleben (1789–1874).

BIBLIOGRAPHY

Hu Kangda. 2000. *Relations Between the Central and Local Authorities of Major EU Countries*. Beijing: China Social Sciences Press.

Huan Qingzhi. 2001. Western Theory of Party System: A Comparative Perspective. *Journal of Shandong University* 5: 91–98.

Jiang Jingsong. 2002. Relations Between Parliament and Parties in the Six Countries: America, the UK, France, Germany, Switzerland and Israel. *People's Congress Studying* 6: 45–46.

Liu Yu'e, and Shi Yongyi. 2002. *Western Political Systems*. Beijing: China Renmin University Press.

Ma Xiaoyuan. 2000. *A History of Western Political Systems*. Beijing: Higher Education Press.

Mao Shoulong, et al. 1998. *Governance Reform of Western Governments*. Beijing: China Renmin University Press.

Shen Yongdong. 2008. Understanding Western Political System from the Perspective of Interest Groups and Parties'. *The Science Education Article Collects* 7: 117–117.

Xu Guangchun. 1998. Similarities and Differences Between the Political Systems of the UK and America and the Historical Origin. *Local Government Administration* S1: 64–69.

Zhang Dinghe. 1998. *The Origin and Evolution of the American Political System*. Beijing: China Social Sciences Press.

WEBSITES

http://usa.bytravel.cn/art/mgd/mgdzzzd/
http://www.hudong.com/wiki/
https://en.wikipedia.org/wiki/La_R%C3%A9publique_En_Marche!

CHAPTER 3

Economic Systems of the West

3.1 Economic Systems of the European Union

After its sixth enlargement, in January 2007, the European Union (EU) has become the most economically powerful and integrated state coalition in the world, covering twenty-seven countries with a population of more than 480 million.

3.1.1 Establishment of the European Community

The European Atomic Energy Community (EAEC) was a new undertaking for the six Western European countries, namely France, Germany, Italy, Holland, Belgium, and Luxembourg, aiming to extend the application of the Paris Treaty to other fields. In 1967, the EAEC merged with European Economic Community (EEC) and the European Coal and Steel Community to form the European Community (EC), but the EAEC was still an independent legal entity.

It was decided by the EEC, the European Common Market, to found the European Investment Bank in order to implement common investment policies and new industrial plans, and to assist economic development in backward areas of individual member countries.

© The Author(s) 2018   61
G. Xu et al. (eds.), K. Chen et al. (trans.), *Understanding Western Culture*, https://doi.org/10.1007/978-981-10-8150-7_3

The Common Market and the cooperation regarding tariffs and agricultural policies between the six countries showed that the EC was protectionist, but was sure to play an important role in the global economy and in politics.

3.1.2   Development from EC to EU

After ten other countries (Cyprus, the Czech Republic, Estonia, Hungary, Latvia, Lithuania, Malta, Poland, Slovakia, and Slovenia) joined the EU on May 1, 2004 and Bulgaria and Romania joined on January 1, 2007, it became the largest regional economic integration organization in the world, with twenty-seven member countries.

3.1.2.1   The First Enlargement of the EC

After long-term negotiations, the UK, Denmark, and Ireland were admitted as new members of the EC on January 1, 1973. The arrival of the UK elevated the EC's status in Europe and in the world, promoted its economic development, and helped redress the balance between America, the Soviet Union, and Europe, and maintain the independence of the EC.

3.1.2.2   The Second Enlargement of the EC

On January 1, 1981, Greece became the tenth member state after years of negotiations lasting from its application in June 1975 to its formal acceptance in April 1979. Based on this agreement, Greece has enjoyed full membership of the EC since January 1, 1981 and has all due rights and obligations. In the five-year transition period, EC regulations came into effect by stages and Greek monetary policy was one part of the European currency basket thereafter.

In 1987, the gross domestic product (GDP) per capita of Greece increased to $4728, compared with $476 in 1961, $2590 in 1976 and $3366 in 1985. The economy of the EC was further strengthened after the admission of Greece.

3.1.2.3   The Third Enlargement of the EC

On January 1, 1986, the two comparatively economic backward states Spain and Portugal joined the EC because of non-economic reasons. Their admission indicated that unification was the mainstream for Western European countries despite economic conflicts. Yet new problems were introduced by this: the economic gap was widened among member countries; it was more difficult to carry out common agricultural policies; conflicts escalated in discussions about the EC budget. For example, there were disagreements between the UK and other members about its share of the budget. In the long run, though, however severe the economic situation became, this aggrandizement was significant for every member state.

3.1.2.4 The Fourth Enlargement of the EC

During the 1990s, owing to changing political and economic circumstances in Europe, countries in northern, central, and eastern Europe, and even some Mediterranean countries were applying for membership of the EC. This was extended to fifteen states after Austria, Sweden, and Finland were admitted.

Urged on by French president François Mitterrand, the European Bank was founded on April 9, 1990 with the special purpose of aiding Eastern European countries and Russia. The EC and its member states held 51% of the stock. On December 11, 1991, a treaty was signed in Maastricht, the Netherlands, by EC members, and it was resolved to establish political, economic, and monetary alliances.

3.1.2.5 The Establishment of the EU

The Maastricht Treaty came into effect on November 1, 1993 after being approved by parliaments of member states and referenda, and the EC was renamed the EU. The core of the treaty was establishing European Monetary Union. There were four criteria for economic convergence, regarding inflation rate, public deficit, government bonds, and the stability of the exchange rate. In 1994, the European Monetary Institute was set up, and this laid a technical and legal foundation for the establishment of European Monetary Union. By the end of that year, 90% of EU directives had become laws in member states.

By January 1, 1995, the membership of the EU had expanded to fifteen countries. In December of the same year, members agreed to launch a single currency—the euro—on January 1, 1999 and the first eleven states agreeing to adopt this were France, Germany, Holland, Belgium, Luxembourg, Italy, Ireland, Spain, Portugal, Austria, and Finland. In 1998, member countries stepped up their preparations and publicity around the establishment of the European Central Bank. This and the circulation of the euro challenged the European Monetary Union of these eleven countries, yet facilitated the development of capital and a trade market with the single currency.

The accession of ten more countries (listed in Section 3.1.2) was resolved at the council of foreign ministers on November 18, 2002 and accomplished on May 1, 2004; this was the fifth and also the greatest enlargement of the EU. Romania and Bulgaria's admission in January 2007 marked the sixth enlargement and made the EU the most economically powerful and integrated state coalition in the world, covering twenty-seven countries that have a population of more than 480 million.

3.1.3   The EC and Its Economy

The prime objective of the EC is to strengthen its economy and to contend with other great powers through economic integration and united development. Common policies have been made to co-ordinate member states' efforts.

3.1.3.1 Customs Union

Tariffs were eliminated progressively from the six countries of the EC from January 1, 1958 to July 1, 1968, and a single customs system was adopted. The Customs Union was then established, its major principles falling into the following areas:

- Internal tariffs. Within the framework of the Rome Treaty, tariff cuts among member states were carried out in three stages from January 1, 1958 to January 1, 1970, and then it was accelerated by the EC council and completed by July 1, 1968.
- Trade volume. Stipulations on trade limits were stretched during the transition period and finally abolished in 1961.
- External tariff. After negotiations of the six countries within the framework of Rome Treaty, a common external tariff was adopted gradually, based on the arithmetic mean of tariffs levied on January 1, 1957 in the four different tax zones, France, Italy, Germany and the other members such as Holland, Belgium, and Luxembourg. By January 1995, the Customs Union had expanded to fifteen countries.

Domestic markets within the union were combined and commodities of member countries circulated freely in the integrated market. The common external tariff protected producers and consumers against competitions from other countries and the development of EC was indissolubly linked with the Customs Union that played an active role in the following aspects:

- First, it boosted the growth of EC foreign trade comprising the trade among member states and trade between a member state and other states. After its establishment, trade among member countries accounted for 51.7% of total EC foreign trade in 1972, compared with 30% in 1958. In terms of trade with non-members, the volume increased owing to increasing imports at lower costs than domestic commodities in countries such as France and the UK that experienced a tariff cut.
- Second, it promoted the internal division of labor and the specialization of production. Member states cultivated their own competitive edges.
- Third, it stimulated economic development. In an integrated market with safe competition, with production and capital concentrated, fixed capital investment from member countries increased at a higher speed even than in the USA, which pushed forward equipment upgrading and the adoption of new technology. Labor productivity was also enhanced and the economy grew faster.
- Fourth, it provided funds for the EC. Members reached the consensus that 50% of their tariffs should be transferred to EC from January 1, 1971 and progressively up to January 1, 1975, 90% of tariffs were turned over to the EC, with only 10% left as commissions.

The Customs Union also had negative effects on the EC economy. It led to the improper allocation of resources and impaired social welfare. It slowed down industrial restructuring and accounted for the stagnation of the EC economy from the 1970s to the 1980s, during which period the EC lagged behind the USA and Japan in high technology owing to different technical norms, complex formalities, and restraints in multi-national businesses. There also existed barriers to economic integration, and many foreign commodities were rejected by domestic markets.

The integrated form of the EC was transformed from the Customs Union into the European Common Market after a complete single market was achieved on January 1, 1993. On January 1, 1994, the EC amalgamated with most of the member states of the European Free Trade Association and a new economic zone was established with free circulation of commodities, services, personnel, and capital. On January 1, 2002, the euro came into circulation and the individual currencies of participating member states were removed from circulation on February 28, 2002, when the great plan of European Monetary Union was completed.

3.1.3.2 Common Agricultural Policies
Agriculture is the foundation of the national economies, yet with low labor productivity and a low degree of self-sufficiency EC agriculture was underdeveloped and there was a strong urge toward the implementation of common agricultural policies.

The Background to Common Agricultural Policies
After the Second World War, the six EC founding states had sustained low labor productivity and a small production scale. The ratio of the agricultural labor force to the whole workforce and the GDP from agriculture indicated that farmers had much lower incomes than workers in other industries. The EC was not self-sufficient in agricultural produce. Plunder from the numerous overseas colonies before the Second World War had led to an imbalance between the development of industry and agriculture in member states. Common agricultural policies consolidated European integration, and were necessary for dealing with varied situations in different countries that had impeded competition on an equal footing. Moreover, common policies helped to reform agricultural structures in member states.

The Basic Content of Common Policies
It is prescribed in the Rome Treaty that for the operation and development of a common agricultural market, there must be common agricultural policies among member states, the fundamental objectives of which are promoting agricultural labor productivity, securing fair incomes for farmers, stabilizing the produce market, ensuring a sufficient supply of farm produce, and allowing reasonable prices for consumers. The Rome Treaty provided a basic framework for EC agricultural policies, which comprised price and market management mechanisms.

   a) Price mechanism. The price system included target price, intervention price, and threshold price. Target price was the ceiling price decided at the council of ministers at the beginning of each marketing year and was the highest price that farmers received. Intervention price, also known as shore up price or protective price, was the floor price in the market fixed by the council of ministers annually. Threshold price was the floor price set for foreign produce reaching EC ports (the prices at Rotterdam were referred to as the standard) to control imports.

b) Management of price supports and external protection constituted the market management mechanism, in which the former ensured the stability of produce prices through EC intervention and the mechanism included intervention purchasing, storage subsidy, withdrawal price, and so on.

Intervention purchasing was made by EC intervention organizations when produce prices fell to intervention prices in the common market. Storage subsidy was given to producers or merchants who stored produce in season and delayed sales to avoid price fluctuation. Withdrawal price was another kind of subsidy that was granted by the EC for seasonal farm produce (especially vegetables and fruits) that exited from the market to stabilize prices. The above three methods were adopted when supply exceeded demand. In contrary circumstances, produce in storage was sold to bridge the price gap between export and domestic produce or export duty was collected to increase supply so that prices fell below the target price.

Management of external protection included collection of a variable levy for foreign farm produce besides imposing duties and quota restriction, and export subsidies and duties, subsidizing EC agricultural exports when the market price was above the international average price, or when the EC market price fell below that and farm produce flew out, and especially when the target price was reached, export duties were collected.

Market management mechanism also included market organization management by means of support price, intervention, external protection, direct support, and interest-free loans.

Monetary Mechanisms of Common Agricultural Policies

In 1962, a special accounting unit for the common prices of farm produce—the Agricultural Unit of Account (AUA)—was established to unify prices given the different currencies in member states. The EC set common prices in AUA annually and members converted them into their domestic currencies based on the price parity. The European currency unit (ECU) replaced AUA after the establishment of the European Currency System in 1979.

The price parity between AUA and currencies in member states was called the green rate. When it changed, farm produce prices were adjusted in conformity to the common price; for example, when currencies devalued, prices were raised, and vice versa.

Monetary Compensatory Amounts (MCA) were used to reduce from the impact of discord between the green rate and market rate and the consequent speculation. It adjusted prices indirectly by collecting transit tolls or giving out subsidies, instead of compelling member states with currency changes to modify prices.

Effects of Common Agricultural Policies

These policies led to great changes in West European agriculture in three decades. The agriculturally employed population accounted for 7.5% of the whole workforce yet supported 400 million people in West Europe and contributed to 3% of GDP, making the EC the second biggest agricultural exporter internationally, behind America. The agricultural population in each member country was decreasing while farms were expanding and modernizing. Agriculture became a vital part of the West European economy.

Yet there were problems in the EC agricultural common policies, such as excessive farm produce, heavy financial burdens, and trade friction with non-EC members.

Reforms of EU Common Agricultural Policies and Effects

Since 1990, there had been several great reforms to the common agricultural policies. The MacSharry Reform was initiated on May 21, 1992, touching upon a number of aspects. In terms of society and economy, the EU planned to rein in the excessive growth in agricultural production and budget and provide direct subsidies to farmers. In terms of environment, land management and environmental protection took place. Sustainable farming and afforestation were encouraged to develop rural economies.

The reform touched the core of EU common agricultural policies—the price support mechanism—and marked the launch of the biggest policy intervention and protection in the agricultural market.

Another reform, Agenda 2000, was carried out in March 1999. With regard to the social economy, support prices were further decreased and direct payment was made to compensate for the decline in farmers' incomes. For environmental protection, the EU attached importance to the environment and rural development. The importance of policies in rural development as well as the multi-functionality and sustainability of agriculture were emphasized.

The third reform was the Preizler Reform, which was implemented in June 2003. The main measures were:

a) Cutting the agricultural budget. After 2006, agricultural expenditure was to be equivalent to that of 2000–2006 with a slight annual increase.

b) Introducing Green box policies (domestic or trade policies that are deemed to be minimally trade-distorting) and adopting the Single Farm Payment (SFP).

c) Applying the policy of direct subsidies. Certain member states could give out direct subsidies to prevent farmers from abandoning farmland.

d) Setting new standards for subsidies: agricultural subsidies were linked with environmental protection, food safety, and animal welfare.

e) Establishing farm auditing systems and reducing subsidies to large farms.

f) Specifying subsidies for new member countries.

In 2007, the European Commission proposed a new round of reforms to agricultural subsidies, which involved disconnecting them from output and using them for rural development; reducing subsidies to large farms and enhancing support for small farmers; progressively calling off protective prices for most farm produce and export subsidies; abolishing a fallow system that had been implemented for more than a decade; and relaxing restrictions on milk production quotas, and by 2015 canceling them.

3.1.4   Fiscal Systems of EC and EU

A common finance system for the EC was established based on the internationalization of production and capital and the supranational alliance.

3.1.4.1   Establishment of Common Fiscal System

On November 1 and 2, 1969, EC members restructured financial revenue and expenditure at the Hague Conference. The new fiscal system defined three internal resources of revenue: export variable levy and sugar tax on farm produce, duties collected according to common tariffs, and value added taxes from member states. The European Social Fund, Development Fund, and Overseas Territory Development Fund were founded to coordinate the economic activities of member states.

3.1.4.2   Nature of Common Finance

Obligations of members were prescribed through the formation of laws. It was required that all members should abide by the regulations of revenue and expenditure or the European Court would interfere. In addition, there were independent sources of revenue and the common fiscal expenditure was distinctive. With most of the expenditure transferred to member states, only 4–5% was used for administration, while in ordinary international organizations the ratio was 95–100%.

3.1.4.3 Fiscal Revenue and Expenditure

There were mainly three sources of EC fiscal revenue in light of the Hague Conference. These were import duty on industrial products, where common duties collected were to be turned into common finance and the EC had the priority in tariff revenue; variable import levies on agricultural produce, which was imposed owing to the gap between the lowest cost, insurance, and freight price and threshold price; and value added taxes proportionally from member states. All members turned in 21% of their value added taxes to the common finance.

The expenditure of common finance underpinned the EC's functioning as a super-state and fell into four groups: expenditure on agriculture, development of backward areas, foreign aid, and science.

3.1.4.4 New Development in EC Finance

In the early 1990s, financial impediments (including barriers in the free flow of commodities, capital, and personnel owing to divergent tax systems and subsidies in member states) were eliminated. The EC developed into the European Common Market and then into the EU as integration speeded up. The euro was circulated as the single currency.

On March 20, 2005, a modification of common financial policies was approved, based on which member states were punished by the European Commission if fiscal deficits exceeded 3% of GDP. These policies demonstrated a higher level of flexibility.

3.2   ECONOMIC SYSTEMS OF MAJOR EUROPEAN COUNTRIES

3.2.1   Germany

3.2.1.1   An Overview of German Economy

Economic System

The existing system gradually took shape after the Second World War and is referred to by German economists as a social market economic system, in which the state regulates the market through macroscopic readjustments instead of intervening directly in prices and salaries.

The major characteristics of this system are:

a) The market system functions adequately. Full competition of all commodities is encouraged and protected and spontaneous vicious competition is restricted.
b) Economic administration strengthens macro-control and concentrates investments in basic industries.
c) As one of the first countries in Europe to implement welfarism, Germany attaches much importance and devotes above 25% of GDP to it.
d) The system stabilizes the monetary system and curbs inflation by virtue of Deutsche Bank, the state bank directly answerable to parliament, and its lack of regulation by the government ensures the independence and consistency of policy implementation.

A Brief History of Economic Development

Germany is a newly developed country, and the seed of capitalist production relations emerged in around the late fifteenth and early sixteenth centuries. In the 1830s, when the British industrial revolution had come to fruition, Germany had just started industrialization. At that time, three-quarters of the residents lived in rural areas and the economy was lagging far behind the UK and France.

The rise of Prussian militarism boosted the development of industry, particularly heavy industry. During the years from 1850 to 1870, industrial production doubled and the proportion of industrial output rose from 21% to 28% in terms of GDP. In 1870, German industrial production accounted for 13.2% of that of the world, surpassing France yet still falling behind the UK and the USA.

By the end of the 1870s and the early 1880s, Germany had completed an industrial revolution in its main aspects, and at the beginning of the twentieth century it was industrialized. In 1913, industrial production accounted for 45% of GDP with agricultural product reduced to 23%. Heavy industry had supplanted light industry, and dominated industry production. Germany had set up a relatively integrated industrial system on the basis of up-to-date technology and became the strongest capitalist country in Europe, with gross industrial production higher than that of the UK.

According to the Yalta and Potsdam agreements, after Germany's defeat in the Second World War in May 1945, Germany was divided and occupied by the USA, UK, France, and the Soviet Union. In May 1949, the Federal Republic of Germany (Federal Germany or West Germany) was founded in the incorporated areas occupied by the USA, UK, and France, and in October, the German Democratic Republic (Democratic Germany or East Germany) was set up in the eastern Soviet Union-occupied area. On October 3, 1990, the two Germanies merged, reunified after forty years.

3.2.1.2   The Economy of Federal Germany from 1945 to 1990

In the early post-war period, the economy was dislocated by hyperinflation, a rampant black market, and a sharp decline in foreign trade. Industrial and agricultural production were backward and industrial production in 1946 was only 22.9% of that of 1938. Despite the havoc caused by the Second World War, West Germany witnessed a swift recovery from the recession on account of the strong reserve force of technology, skilled workers, and production management organizations. Besides, it enjoyed a concentrated monopoly of capital and a developed economy, as well as support from the USA.

Main Characteristics of Post-War Economy in West Germany

The main characteristics of the post-war economy in West Germany were:

a) The national economy grew rapidly and steadily. After a short-term recovery, the German economy that had once been on the verge of collapse returned to prewar levels and developed at a much higher speed than other major Western capitalist countries. The average annual growth rate of GDP was above 5% during 1950 to 1980.

b) Germany was one of the most economically dependent states on foreign countries among the seven Western industrialized countries, next to Canada and the UK.

c) Germany became the European economic giant and the world's third greatest economy. It grew into the biggest power in Western Europe in 1960.

Economic and Industrial Structure Before Reunification

The industrial structure of Germany changed remarkably in the fifty years after the Second World War: agriculture and industry shrunk in GDP with each passing year and tertiary industry (including commerce, transportation, and services) expanded.

There were also internal structural changes. By the end of the 1990s, sectors such as automobile manufacturing, electrical, electronic and chemical equipment, machinery, food, and construction made up 31% of the GDP and became the leading force in the economy.

3.2.1.3 Post-war Economy of East Germany

The division of Germany cut off metal-processing industries from steel and coal bases and ravaged the national economic framework and uniform market, which posed enormous difficulties for the recovery and development of the economy. In the early post-war period, East Germany nationalized means of production, public utilities and enterprises such as banks, transportation, postal services, and telecommunications, and confiscated property, mines and factories belonging to war criminals and monopoly capitalists. Meanwhile land reform was carried out and the industrial structure was altered: the proportion of industry increased from 42.2% in 1949 to 67% in 1989 and that of agriculture and forestry decreased correspondingly from 30.8% to 9.9%; the proportions of commerce and service industries also rose. Democratic Germany was a fairly industrialized socialist country before reunification.

3.2.1.4 Economy of Germany After Reunification

Within the framework of Reunification Treaty signed on August 31, 1990, five eastern states were incorporated into West Germany on October 3 and Germany was reunified. In contrast to some developed countries in recession, examples being the USA and the UK, Germany boasted a dynamic economy, with the GDP annual growth rate hitting 1.4% during the years from 1995 to 2006, allowing it to grow into one of the greatest economic powers among the capitalist countries.

Reunification began with the formation of monetary union and the adoption of a common currency—the Deutsche Mark. Meanwhile price controls of commodities were lifted and merchandise was circulated freely across the borders, entering the international market. Moreover, the federal government increased taxes and borrowing in the West to aid the East and to subsidize investments there. In the East an employment and social security system was established and the government set up a special trustee bureau to privatize state-owned enterprises, on which most attention had been focused since reunification.

Micro-electronics, chemical industries, and automobile industries were the highlights in the growth of the East, whereas it lagged far behind the West in infrastructure, capital market, technology and management, and environmental protection. The East could not adapt to the new economic system and competitive market owing to the few divisions of labor based on specialization and the obsolete industrial structure. Consequently, its GDP dropped by 30% between 1990 and 1991 and from 1989 to 1991, exports declined by 59%, as the disintegration of the Soviet Union had deprived it of the Eastern European market and exposed it to the competition of high-quality Western products. After reunification in 1998, the overall unemployed population totaled 5 million and the unemployment rate averaged 12.8% throughout the country. In light of official statistics, the unemployment rate in the east reached 21.1%, with the actual figure estimated to be 30 to 35%. The internal cause of the economic stagnation was the so-called "German disease," because of the extensive inputs into revitalizing the economy of the East. External reasons included the recession in the US economy since 2001, the bursting bubbles in the fields of communications and technology, sluggish world trade, a deceleration in international economic growth, and fluctuations in the petroleum price.

Along with the robust recovery of the world economy, Germany witnessed a moderate growth of 1.8% in 2004, yet the economic resurgence was unbalanced because private consumption and domestic investment didn't improve.

3.2.1.5   Major Industrial Sectors of Germany

The Automobile Industry
With the first car invented there in 1886, Germany is one of the birthplaces of the automobile industry. Calculated by turnover, this is the biggest industry nationally. In 2006, the output of German automobiles ranked the fourth in the world, next to Japan, the USA and China. The biggest car-making center, Wolfsburg, is also known as the Motor City of Germany, and it is where the headquarters of Volkswagen is located.

The Machinery Manufacturing Industry
This is the third major industry in Germany, with German-made machinery taking up 19.1% of the world market share. Machine building is the biggest and most traditional industry, with the longest history in Germany. Products that are made in Germany have an international reputation for reliability, sound engineering, and excellent service. For years, Germany

has been ranked number one in patent registration and machinery export, with the USA and Japan placed second and third.

Chemical Industry

The German chemical industry plays a vital role thanks to large-scale and advanced scientific research and technology. Expenditure on research and development (R&D) amounted to 6.3% of total turnover, ranking first among countries with the same industry (Japan was placed second with R&D expenditure taking up to 5.9% of turnover).

Electronic and Electrical Industry

This is second only to Japan, with around 100,000 types of product. Siemens is a principal player in this industry, and has an important position in the fields of computers, communication apparatus, energy, domestic appliances, industrial control, and electrical and medical equipment. The core business lies in infrastructure construction and industrial solutions, and Siemens currently offers roughly 400,000 jobs, creating a profit of 72.4 billion euro according to 2007 statistics.

Steel Industry

Germany is a major producing and trading nation in steel, and about 50% of total production is for export. On account of the increasing demand for steel products and the recovery of Germany's economy, as well as the growth of industries such as automobile and machinery manufacturing, and environmental protection, the industry has entered a new phase of development. In 2006, the export volume of crude steel reached 29 million tonnes, ranking fifth worldwide.

3.2.1.6 Economic Policies of the German Government

The social market economic system of Germany is built on free competition and appropriate state regulation. Macro-control gives full play to the positive functions of the market economy and promotes economic development in a virtuous circle by correcting market deviations and preserving competition.

Distinctive Monetary Policies

The ultimate goals of macro-economic policies in the West are price stability, full employment, moderate economic growth, and a balance of international payments, which are described as Rubik's cube corners thanks to

the difficulty of achieving them simultaneously. These goals can be summarized as: economic growth and currency stabilization, which seems
contradictory and leaves policymakers in a dilemma as they can realize
only one at a time. Yet currency stabilization has always been the priority
in Germany, and its monetary policies are constantly against inflation.

Fiscal Policies

Fiscal policies are an important means for the government to intervene in
the economy. In 1998, Gerhard Schröder was appointed prime minister,
and faced with an economic downturn and serious unemployment, he
gave a high priority to cutting government expenditure and the balanced
development of the society. In 2003, Schröder took the most forceful
measures since his assumption of duty and proceeded to cut welfare, ease
burdens on enterprises and the state, and implement measures to boost
employment.

When Angela Merkel was appointed prime minister in 2005, the economic problems of Germany not only became a domestic issue but also
affected EU integration and enlargement. She made the employment law
more flexible, decreased unemployment insurance to reduce the fringe
costs of incomes, and levied taxes on the rich. By 2006, the economy had
improved, with a declining unemployment rate, and Germany had
regained its position as top exporter in the world.

3.2.2   France

3.2.2.1   An Overview of the French Economy

Economic System
In general, France has adopted a modern market economic system that has
its own features despite similarities to systems in other Western countries.

a) The state-owned economy plays an important role in the national
   economy. After long periods of nationalization, state-owned enterprises have become the mainstay in monopolizing industries such as
   energy, transportation, finance, and insurance, and hold a dominant
   position in such competitive industries as computers, aviation, electronics, chemistry, steel, and machine manufacturing.

b) The government bases planned regulation on the dominance of the market mechanism. After the Second World War, France combined market adjustment with a guiding planning system and started extensive and thorough intervention in its national economy.

c) The intervention in national economic operation is supposed to be the strongest among Western market economies. The French government controls the redistribution of national income and amasses income equivalent to above 40% of its GDP, by virtue of which it directly invests in infrastructure and emerging industries and affects the overall economy.

A Brief History of Economic Development

France was one of the first countries to develop capitalism. Its capitalistic economy had grown rapidly since the French Revolution broke out in 1789. In the 1820s, an industrial revolution was initiated, which was fifty years later than that in the UK, and until the 1860s the value of French industrial output was ranked the second in the world, behind only the UK. By 1914, the French colonies had covered an area of 10.6 million square kilometers, which was eighteen times larger than the metropolitan territory.

After the First World War, France regained Alsace and Lorraine and obtained huge reparations from Germany as well as mining rights over the Saar coalfield by means of international management, which contributed to the economic boom in the post-war period. Yet the Second World War again caused havoc with its economy with losses totaling 4893 billion francs according to 1945 prices. Owing to the effective measures that were taken during five years of adjustment and recovery, the economy was restored to its prewar state in 1949.

3.2.2.2 *French Economy After the Second World War*

After the end of the 1950s, France witnessed rapid and sustained economic development owing to European economic integration, and was fully modernized in fifteen years. From 1959 to 1974, its GDP annual average growth rate was 5.7%, higher than that of the USA (3.9%), the UK (3%), and West Germany (4.7%). From 1985 to 1990, the GDP annual growth rate averaged 3%, yet declined again in the early 1990s because of the impact of the global economic recession. The figure dropped from 2.3% in 2004 to 1.2% in 2005, then rebounded to 2% in 2006.

Features of French Economy

a) France is a developed industrial and agricultural state, the fourth greatest economic power among the capitalist countries, next to the USA, Japan, and Germany. Its industrial production and foreign trade both take the fourth place internationally and are second in Europe.

b) France has been Europe's biggest agricultural producer and exporter and the second biggest exporter of farm products and food globally since 1979, next to the USA, with agricultural exports taking one fifth of the total. Industry and agriculture are of equal importance in its economy, similar to the world's leading power, the USA.

c) France is highly industrialized and has created 7% of the world's industrial output. Manufactured goods occupy three-quarters of the general exports.

d) The French economy is mainly controlled by big monopolies, and production and capital are increasingly centralized on account of developed state monopoly capitalism. Two banks among the world's top ten and four industrial giants among the world's top fifty are state monopolies. Up to the 1990s, French state monopoly economic sectors outnumbered those in other developed capitalist countries. Meanwhile, agricultural production was quickly concentrated in very few hands after the war. Small and medium-sized enterprises play a very important part in the economy.

e) The industrial structure has undergone significant changes after fifty years of development in the post-war period. In light of statistics from the French national statistics bureau (INSEE), from 1990 to 2004 the ratio of agriculture and building industry trended downward in gross added value in the national economy while that of industry and tertiary industry increased.

Major Industrial Sectors

A) Agriculture
Agriculture not only dominates the national economy but labor productivity is high, ranking the third in the world. France is the biggest EU agricultural state, with 3.4% of the total labor force agriculturally employed, creating 4% of GDP. Features of agricultural production include:

a. Superior labor productivity, which is further raised by virtue of the complete range of agricultural machinery and a high level of automatization;
b. Diversification and comprehensive development; crop farming, animal husbandry, forestry and fishery, and agricultural processing industries are all thriving;
c. Farms have decreased in number but increased in scale;
d. High level of specialization, which is an inexorable trend of modern agriculture. After agricultural mechanization, France pushed ahead with specialized operation, including regional specialization, and the specialization of farms and production;
e. Integration of agriculture, industry, and commerce.

B) Industry
France is the world's fourth greatest industrial nation. One-fifth of the working population is industrially employed and creates one quarter of GDP; roughly one-quarter of the manufactured goods are for export. Sectors such as astronavigation, automobile and land transportation facilities, communication apparatus, nuclear energy, munitions, and agri-food processing are competitive in the international market and the main force earning foreign exchange. Because of the lack of mineral resources, particularly energy, industry has shifted to be knowledge-intensive so as to save energy and raw materials.

The automobile industry as the backbone of French industry grew rapidly after the Second World War and is placed the fourth in the world, next to the USA, Japan, and Germany. In 2006, the total output of cars was 3.17 million, with 70% of the aggregate output value from export. Renault-Nissan and PSA were respectively the third and ninth biggest automakers globally in the first half year of 2017.

Aerospace is the third greatest French industry after automobile manufacturing and the electronics industry, and ranks the third in the world after the USA and Russia. At present, France boasts manufacturing for military and civil airplanes and many models of tactical missile. Moreover, it excels at the development and production of man-made satellites, aerospace equipment, and strategic missiles. In 2006, the aerospace turnover amounted to more than 30 billion euro, with exports contributing to three-quarters of that: half of the export value was from the Airbus project.

Owing to the shortage of conventional energy such as coal and oil, much importance is attached to developing nuclear power. As an industry, this has a development history of more than thirty years and is an international leader. France is also a major exporter of nuclear power equipment and technology (its development of the neutron breeder reactor is placed the first in the world and nuclear waste treatment technology is similarly advanced). Complete sets of equipment for nuclear power plants are exported to countries such as Korea, Belgium, Spain, South Africa, and China.

Nowadays the USA, France, and Japan top the list in the world's nuclear power industry. There are fifty-nine French nuclear power plants in operation with an aggregate installed capacity of 63,363 megawatts, which are 14% and 17.6% respectively of the global totals, second only to America internationally. Nuclear power comprises 78% of the gross power generation in France, ranking first among major industrial countries.

3.2.2.3 Economic Policies of the French Government

After the Second World War, France pursued Keynesianism and intensified economic intervention. When faced with the stagflation that was pervasive in Western countries in the mid-1970s, the former president Giscard d'Éstaing advocated the rationalization and reduction of government intervention, proposing production be regulated by the market and that the austerity package be adopted to curb inflation. In May 1981 the Socialist Party led by Mitterrand came into office, and there were three stages in policy evolution during the fourteen years of his reign:

- Stage one: from 1981 to May 1982, the party pursued an inflationary policy and unveiled a series of loose fiscal and monetary policies to stimulate consumption and demand. By means of increasing public expenditure, minimum wage, and social welfare, the fiscal deficit and investment in enterprises were raised so that demand, employment, and economy were boosted. Those measures spurred economic development but worsened unemployment, and foreign debts soared.
- Stage Two: from June 1982 to 1986, policies shifted to control aggregate demand and curb inflation to stabilize the economy. Promoting productive investment replaced boosting consumption and anti-inflation took priority over anti-unemployment. These deflation policies produced marked effects.

- Stage Three: since 1986, the government has endeavored to build a free economic regime to invigorate the economy and facilitate its growth. Meanwhile, reforms in the macro-economic management system further deepened, with the purpose of reducing state intervention and strengthening market discipline.

The political strongman Nicolas Sarkozy won the election in 2007. In light of defects in the economic system, he urged the establishment of a free market economy by reforming the existing welfare and labor system. As for people's dependence on the generous national welfare system, Sarkozy reiterated the value of work and emphasized more pay for more work. He proposed to ease the burdens of social welfare and tax on enterprises, thereby stimulating the economy and reducing unemployment. Measures were also taken in education and society to speed up economic development and enhance global competitiveness.

3.2.3   UK

3.2.3.1   An Overview of the British Economy

Economic System

After 200 years of development, the UK established a typical hybrid market economic system with the following features:

a) The distinctive property right system. After the Second World War, hundreds of large state-owned enterprises were privatized in sectors such as gas, petroleum, electricity supply, coal, astronavigation, automobiles, and telecommunications. Business lines of state-owned enterprises covered the postal service, municipal transportation, nuclear fuel industry and civil aviation. Though the proportion of state-owned economy decreases, public and private economies still co-exist in the UK.

b) A hybrid free-enterprise system; it forms the micro-foundation for the British market economic system, in which as long as they register in accordance with laws and pay taxes, everyone has the right to establish and manage new enterprises that operate independently, assuming full financial responsibility and risks.

c) A hybrid mechanism of resource allocation; the flexible market system provides the primary means for resource allocation and the government mainly adjusts aggregate demand and supply by the requisite macro and indirect regulation and control.
d) A fully functional market system, especially a labor market with a high level of employment and the financial market, are prominent for complete and perfect functioning.

A Brief History of Economic Development
From the 1750s to the 1850s, the UK's industrial revolution took place, and it transformed from an agricultural country to an industrial one. It became the most advanced state and the workshop of the world, with production, trade, and merchant tonnage topping the world. By virtue of a strong shipping industry, the UK acquired cheap raw materials worldwide, traded, and obtained substantial profits. London grew into the international financial center.

By the 1870s, a great colonial empire, the British Empire, was formed. Up to 1914, the colonies covered an area of 33.5 million square kilometers, which was 110 times the metropolitan territory, with a population of 390 million. Despite its victory in the First World War, the UK was drained of strength and lost the edge in shipbuilding, foreign trade, shipping, and finance. As its economy declined, the Empire was on the verge of collapse.

3.2.3.2   British Economy After the Second World War

An Overview of British Economy After the War
During the Second World War, the collapse of the colonial empire and damage to industry and finance undermined British hegemony. Enormous military expenditure and the attempt to control the Commonwealth nations made it draw upon production funds. Consequential huge deficits in the national budget led to the alternation or concurrence of financial crisis and economic stagnation after the war.

In 1979, the Conservative administration headed by Margaret Thatcher adopted a series of measures that successfully reduced the deficit and money supply. The inflation rate dropped from the record high of 22% in May 1980 to 3.9% in 1986. The impetus for sustained economic growth was increasing real personal disposable income and improving consumer confidence. After 1996, the British economy grew steadily with low inflation.

Based on survey data from the Organisation for Economic Co-operation and Development (OECD) and the International Monetary Fund (IMF), during the decade from 1997 to 2006 the UK's annual economic growth rate was 2.7%, while GDP per capita rose from $22,781 in 1997 to $39,213 in 2006.

Major Industrial Sectors

Tertiary industry is the British economic mainstay, and in terms of economic value added, the shares of various industries in British economy are: tertiary industry (including finance, wholesale and retail, and real estate) 72%, manufacturing and construction industries 23%, energy and natural resource 4%, agriculture, fishery, and forestry 1%.

a) Financial Service Industry

The modern financial system originated in the UK. Besides the six financial trading centers nationwide, Edinburgh, Manchester, Cardiff, Liverpool, Leeds, and Glasgow, London is among the world's three greatest financial centers. In 2007 London edged out New York and became the biggest international financial center, with major financial markets being foreign exchange, banking, gold, and insurance.

b) Industry

This covers extensive fields and is mainly divided into manufacturing, energy, and water supply as well as construction industries. The UK takes the lead in making and exporting an array of commodities such as machinery, power equipment, radio, airplanes, engines, chemical products and fertilizer, artificial fibers, and textiles. About 80% of the exports are manufactured and semi-manufactured goods.

UK boasts the world's third most complete aerospace industry (next to the USA and Russia) and the most diversified electronics industry in Europe. The government invests 70% of its total aerospace expenditure in European aerospace projects. There are 3000 companies engaged in the industry creating an annual revenue of £17 billion, 10% of the gross revenue of engineering manufacturing.

The UK is the sixth greatest producer of chemicals worldwide. The chemical industry is the biggest sector in the manufacturing industry, placed second in Western Europe. The major products are organic and inorganic chemical products, plastic goods, and fertilizer. Recently, the industry has been restructured and is more specialized and distinctive in terms of an internationalized market, advanced technology, high added value, and full production process control.

The UK is a major supplier and market for mechanical and electrical products that are imported in large quantities from Germany, America, Japan, and France to meet growing domestic demands. Blessed with rich resources, the UK is a major producer of petroleum, gas, and coal, and the world's fifth and eighth greatest producer of gas and oil respectively. Since 2004, it has become a net energy importer with the volume reaching 52.4 million tonnes of standard oil in 2006. In the future round of economic development, the UK will be faced with severe tests by the energy crisis.

An Overview of British Economic Policies

At the end of the 1990s, Tony Blair was elected prime minister for his proposal of "the third way," and the recession was curbed on account of institutional and technological innovation. He made a huge contribution to shaping domestic economic policies.

a) Monetary policies and an interest rate lever were adopted to regulate the economy, and the power of adjustment was conferred on the British Central Bank—the Bank of England.

b) Fiscal means, such as tax cuts and expenditure increase, were used to ensure economic growth. It has been recognized that the Blair government invested massively in education, medical care, and infrastructure, set a minimum wage, and offered training to the unemployed. The unemployment rate was kept below 4%.

Economic policies toward the EU were typical: on one hand, the UK never accepted EU economic integration policies entirely; on the other hand, it was unwilling to withdraw from the EU. Consequently, it maintained a special status and opted out of the common currency. It withdrew from the European Exchange Rate Mechanism and refused negotiation and co-operation with other member states in some important political fields.

During the ten years while Blair was at the helm, the UK was the world's fifth greatest economy with low inflation and low interest and unemployment rates. In 2007, the Chancellor of the Exchequer Gordon Brown assumed the office of prime minister, and proposed tax cuts to pep up demand and foster sustained economic growth.

3.2.4   Russia

3.2.4.1   Russian Economic Structure

The main sectors are industry, agriculture, commerce, communication, transportation, post and telecommunications, and other service industries, among which agriculture and industry, comprising heavy and light industries, are of paramount importance. In the Soviet Union, the development of heavy industry was granted top priority and agriculture and light industry were disregarded, causing a shortage of consumer goods and affecting living standards. Russia's independence in 1991 didn't help to improve an unbalanced economic structure due to political instability. After the failure of shock therapy and a financial crisis in 1998, the Russian economy did not improve until Putin came into office in 2000.

In light of data released by the Russian Federal Service of State Statistics, in 2004 the proportion of product manufacture in GDP dropped to 41% while that of the service industry reached 59%. Currently the main features of Russia's industrial structure are the energy industry, which is the pillar, and military and heavy machinery industries; civilian industry is still backward.

3.2.4.2   An Overview of Russian Economic Policies

In May 1990, President Yeltsin put forward shock therapy tactics to reform the economy with such guiding principles as price liberalization, privatization, and land reforms. The objective was to establish a complete market economy; but this scheme ended in failure.

Putin's inauguration in 2000 was the signal for new reforms, and he was to build a social market economy characterized by mixed ownership, limited intervention, and social equity and security, which was described as a third way in contrast to the former planned economic system and Western radical economic reform. With respect to the micro-economic system, he advocated the strengthening of administration of enterprises and state-owned assets on the basis of the Yeltsin-era privatization to improve economic performance; he was against renationalization. As for the macro-economic system, Putin proposed to establish an effective financial system, adopted a proactive fiscal policy, and opposed a minimal public finance policy that embodied economic liberalism. He adjusted the existing financial system, drew lessons from the financial crisis, and dealt with the aftermath. In the new era, remaining on Putin's reform path, Russia is shifting from an economy based on energy to innovation.

3.3   ECONOMIC SYSTEM OF THE USA

3.3.1   *An Overview of the US Economy*

3.3.1.1   *Economic System*

The USA is a highly developed free-market economy. The essence of its economy is that there are few restrictions, responsibilities, or obligations among the four main economic entities: families, enterprises, banks, and governments.

Main Characteristics of the Market Economic System

a) Private monopoly dominates the mixed economy. Less than one-tenth of the US economy is nationalized and what is left belongs to private owners.

b) There are few government interventions in the economy and markets. The role of market forces to boost economic development is stressed and the government takes a back seat. Without nationwide economic planning, the administration tends to impact economy through government procurement.

c) The consumer-oriented market economy means that the administration often regulates the economy in the interest of consumers instead of producers.

d) On mechanisms of social economy, market competition is the basic means of regulation, yet orderly competition is favored, which requires direct legislation as well as efforts from the government.

e) In the free enterprise system there are three primary forms of firms: individual proprietorship, partnership, and corporations, among which the third has proven to be the most effective in accumulating capital for project investment.

f) With respect to the trends and prospects of social economy, freedom is stressed rather than social welfare.

Strengths and Weaknesses of the US Economic Model

The major strengths are: a highly flexible workforce and product market, low tax, fierce competition, and shareholder capitalism, which refers to the exerting of pressure by shareholders on managers to maximize profits. The weaknesses are a wide income gap, poor welfare, low-quality public services, such as elementary and secondary education, public services out of proportion to social wealth, and low investment and saving rates. This model is also known as "Anglo-Saxon" or "laissez-faire" capitalism.

3.3.1.2 A Brief History of American Economy

Since the foundation of the USA in 1776, the favorable natural conditions, foreign advanced technology, capital, and the labor force have underpinned its economic boom. Business tycoons and great financiers monopolized the economy in the latter half of the nineteenth century. With the advent of corporations, technicians—high-salaried professional managers—replaced big bosses. To meet the demands of the emerging middle class for government regulation over business and those of farmers and labors for conciliation, the administration began to intervene more in the economy, and many regulators were established, examples being the Food and Drug Administration and the Federal Trade Commission.

During the First World War, as the neutral state, the USA amassed fabulous wealth by providing munitions for the warring parties and loans for the Entente countries. After the war it turned into a creditor country with $10 billion lent, and became the richest state in the world. During the Second World War, military needs pushed forward the technological development of the USA and the dollar ascended to become the dominant currency equivalent to gold. In the post-war period, the country's economy has been very prosperous, and it tops the world, a status the USA is always committed to consolidate.

3.3.2   The US Economy After the War

3.3.2.1 Economic Development After the War

An Overview of the US Economy After the War

The economy witnessed sustained growth after its transition from wartime to peace. Until the middle of the 1950s, more than half of the world's commodities were made in the USA. From 1945 to the early 1970s, GDP tripled and industrial production increased by 290%, with an annual average growth rate of 3.6% and 4.3% respectively, and this is known as the golden age in US history.

Yet in the 1970s the economy entered a recession, even with a trade deficit. As the gold reserve gradually decreased, the dollar devalued until the Bretton Woods System collapsed. After 1975, like other major capital-

ist countries, the USA was beset with stagflation reflected in stagnant production, inflation, high unemployment, rising prices, and a slowdown in
foreign trade growth.

In the 1980s, its contention for hegemony with the Soviet Union
intensified, leaving the country heavily in debt for the development of
high-tech military industry. Then the government adjusted policies and
gradually reversed the declining tendency. In the 1990s, to retain the
USA's supremacy in the multi-polar world, President Clinton furthered
the reforms and focused on the development of up-to-date technology,
especially the information industry. Since March 1991, new features such
as high growth and income and low inflation and unemployment rate
were present in the booming economy. Another golden age for economic
progress, also known as the new economy, emerged.

After ten years of sustained development, in March 2001, the economy
sunk into a cyclical recession, experiencing a robust recovery in March
2002. From 2002 to 2005, the annual growth rate averaged 2.9% and in
2006, the US economy maintained a rapid growth of 3.4%.

Main Features of the Economy After the War

a) The economy grew steadily, with the center of economic gravity
   shifting westward and southward.
b) The economic crisis was less severe after the war.
c) Modern multinational corporations sprang up and grew in leaps and
   bounds.

The Economic and Industrial Structure

In 1975, tertiary industry accounted for 65.5% of the gross output value,
and in particular the information industry contributed to 50%. Under the
influence of new technological revolutions, characteristics of the US
industrial structure are the center of national economy shifting to tertiary
industry—that is so-called deindustrialization, the center of manufacturing transferring to high-tech industry, and cutting-edge technology being
adopted to upgrade existing equipment.

3.3.2.2 Main Industrial Sectors

The Steel Industry

This rose in prominence in the second half of the eighteenth century and
was one of the three US economic pillars, together with the automobile

and building industries. In 1890, the steel output reached 4.8 million tons, exceeding that of the UK and ranking first globally. Yet the industry began to decline on account of increasing production costs, obsolete equipment, and the improvement in competitiveness of Japan and Western Europe. In the early 1980s, large-scale technical innovation and restructuring began, and since the twenty-first century US steel output has remained at 11% of the world's total.

The Automotive Industry
In 1893, automobiles went into mass production and humans entered a new era. The traditional automotive industry was concentrated in Detroit and the surrounding states in the Great Lakes Region, and the Big Three automakers are located there. They are General Motors, Ford, and Chrysler. In 2006, they sold 9.058 million cars in total, decreasing by 8% compared with the sales volume of the previous year.

Building Industry
This is recognized as the US economic barometer and nationally consumes 10% of metallurgical products, 70% of cement, glass, and tiles, 40% of wood, and 50% of paint, while 8% of the transportation capacity serves it. The industry mainly deals with housing construction. In 2005, it created 5.1% of GDP, while real estate and relevant rental services contributed to 10.1% of GDP.

The High-Tech Industry
In contrast to the general downturn in traditional industries, the high-tech industry is vibrant, this comprising micro-electronic technology, computer software, robots, communications equipment, computer-aided design, fiber-optic techniques, superconductivity research, bioengineering, and aerospace technology. According to estimates by the OECD, the USA takes the lead in high-tech sectors such as computer technology, electronics and telecommunications, bioengineering, chemistry, and aerospace, and is second only to Japan in terms of industrial robots, computer chips, and synthetic metal.

The USA predominates in the production of commercial airplanes, helicopters, aero engines and components, satellites, carrier rockets, space station technology, space shuttles, and space science experimental devices. The Boeing Company keeps ahead internationally in aircraft output, sales and export volume, profits, and technology.

The Machine Building Industry

With respect to numerically controlled machine tools and industrial robots the USA faces great challenges from Japan, and foreign products have seized 75% of its market share.

Energy Industry

This is the biggest industrial sector, including the petroleum, natural gas, coal, water, electric, and nuclear industries, with the first two being the principal ones. Above 50% of the national coal output is from the core producing area around the Appalachians.

Apart from conventional energy, such as oil and coal, new energy, for instance tidal and solar energy as well as synthetic fuel, is being vigorously exploited. By December 2007, the USA had built the most nuclear power stations (104) globally, which produced 19% of the national gross generation, according to statistics released by the International Atomic Energy Agency.

3.3.2.3   Economic Policies

The USA is a developed capitalist country with a fully fledged market economy. It adopts laissez-faire and moderate policies especially toward domestic large enterprises. These policies actually guide what appears to be a free economy.

US Monetary Policy and Its Evolution

1) Monetary Policy

It is prescribed in the Federal Reserve Act that the objective of monetary policies is to curb inflation, promote full employment, and create a relatively stable financial environment. For a long time, the Central Bank of America, the Federal Reserve System (FRS) has been committed to making and implementing monetary policies to regulate the federal funds rate, that is the interbank rate, and above all the overnight rate.

2) Evolution of the U.S. Monetary Policy

In the 1960s, a cheap money policy was carried out. The increasing money supply and easy monetary and fiscal policies added up to an ever-rising inflation rate and stagflation in the 1970s, when monetary aggregates were the intermediate target of FRS regulation. In light of the growth rate, the tight monetary policy adopted by the FRS led to the economic crisis in 1979.

The FRS shifted to a stable rate policy after inflation was restrained. In the early 1990s, when the economy sank into recession, the FRS reduced the interest rate seventeen times between July 1990 and September 1992 and the short-term interest rate dropped from 8% to 3%, which promoted investment, consumption, and overall economic development. From 1994 to July 1995 the FRS raised the federal funds rate seven consecutive times, and the overheated economy achieved a soft landing.

In 2001, to stimulate economic growth, the FRS cut the interest rate for six times in succession between January and the end of June. At the end of June 2001, the US federal funds rate and discount rate were 3.75% and 3.5% respectively, a record low in the last seven years starting from the third quarter of 1994.

US Fiscal Policy and Its Evolution

a) Fiscal Policy

This refers to principles and measures set to accomplish certain economic objectives through the regulation of fiscal revenue and expenditure. By means of altering policies on taxation, budget outlays, transfer payment, fiscal subsidies, and government procurement, the aggregate social demand is adjusted and therefore the macro-economy is regulated. Fiscal policies are mainly drafted by the Treasury and the White House Office of Management, and the Office of Management and Budget also participates in making policies on budget, tax, and finance.

b) Evolution of Fiscal Policy

Before the Great Depression, the US federal government pursued Smith's fiscal theory of cheap government with a tight and balanced budget. From the early 1930s to the early 1970s, compensatory and expansionary fiscal policies were adopted for aggregate demand management. Roosevelt's New Deal was typical of this, in view of measures such as government expenditure expansion and the initiation of government projects to revitalize the economy.

In the 1970s, the economy sustained stagflation with high unemployment and inflation rate, huge deficits, and low growth. Under such circumstances, Ronald Reagan proposed cutting tax and non-defense expenditure, increase defense spending, reduce government intervention in the economy, and endorse the FRS's tight money policy. In the 1990s, supply and demand were equally stressed and bills were passed by Congress to raise taxes.

After George W. Bush assumed office in 2001, economic policies centered on tax cuts to boost employment and economy. Yet a budget surplus turned into huge deficits owing to substantial military expenditure in the Iraq war and the global war on terrorism, mass unemployment, and the ballooning social welfare costs for the retired population reaching their peak.

BIBLIOGRAPHY

Chen Baosen. 2007. *U.S. Economy and Governmental Policies: From Roosevelt to Regan.* Beijing: Social Sciences Academic Press.

Cheng Xinxuan. 2003. *The Changes in the Economic Policy Coordination System in the EU.* Beijing: China Financial & Economic Publishing House.

Chryssochoou, Dimitris, et al. 2003. *Theory and Reform in the European Union.* Manchester: Manchester University Press.

Dobbin, Frank. 2008. *Forging Industrial Policy: The United States, Britain and France in the Railway Age.* Shanghai: Shanghai People's Publishing House.

Feng Shaolei. 2007. *Russia in the 20th Century.* Shanghai: SDX Joint Publishing Company.

Lan Tian. 2006. *Mode of the EU Economic Integration.* Beijing: China Social Sciences Press.

Laurent Beduneau-Wang. 2007. *Financial System in France.* Beijing: Economy & Management Publishing House.

Liu Ningning. 2006. *A Study of the European Economic and Monetary Union Policy Coordination System.* Beijing: Economic Science Press.

Qiu Yuanlun. 2003. Reform of the EU Common Agricultural Policies. *QIUSHI* 8: 57–59.

Song Jian. 2003. *Economy and Market in Deutschland.* Beijing: China Commerce and Trade Press.

Wang He. 2002. *European Economic and Monetary Union.* Beijing: Social Sciences Academic Press.

Wiener, Antje, and Thomas, Diez. 2004. *European Integration Theory.* Oxford: Oxford University Press.

Zhang Jianxiong. 2006. *An Introduction to Economic Policies of the European Union.* Beijing: China Social Sciences Press.

Zheng Bingwen. 2002. *Annual Development Report of Europe (2001–2002)-Euro and European Reform.* Beijing: Social Sciences Academic Press.

Zhou Nianli. 2008. *A Study of Fiscal Constraint to the European Economic and Monetary Union.* Wuhan: Wuhan University Press.

Zhu Xinmin. 2000. *Introduction to Economy of the European Union.* Chengdu: Sichuan University Press.

CHAPTER 4

Western Military Culture

Military culture includes military theories, art, technologies, institutions, and education created by military practice, military equipment and installations that involve cultural elements, as well as the unique psychological state, morality, and cultural awareness possessed by soldiers. Elements such as the evaluation of soldiers, legal issues around military operations, army morale, non-war operations, coordination and combined operations in the military field, gender and racial equality, service personnels' quality of life, and military education are taken by Western scholars to be the primary components of military culture.

There are many ways in which military culture can be analyzed. Divided by form, it involves military ideas, systems, behavior and technologies; divided by discipline, it involves military philosophy, politics, economics, sociology, ethics, psychology, and history; divided by region, it involves Eastern and Western military culture; divided by location, it involves barrack, academy, and community military culture; divided by time, it involves ancient, modern, and contemporary military culture. Military practice, the basis for the development of military technologies, culture, and thoughts, also tests the vitality of military culture. Accordingly, this chapter focuses on an analysis of the development of Western military culture from the perspectives of practice, technologies, and thoughts.

© The Author(s) 2018
G. Xu et al. (eds.), K. Chen et al. (trans.), *Understanding Western Culture*, https://doi.org/10.1007/978-981-10-8150-7_4

4.1   Western Military Practice

The development of human civilization has failed to eliminate war, whose enlarging scale and increasing damage deepen the threats for the human race. Many inventions and applications of Western new technology take place on battlefields, and in the past military revolutions have brought changes to the forms of war.

4.1.1   Changes in Forms of War in the West

War may be defined as fierce military confrontation that is organized by opposing forces for political and economic purposes. It is the final way in which conflicts may be solved between classes, nations, or political groups, allows the continuation of politics through violence, and is the basic model for the enforcement of state will. People have been engaged in wars for thousands of years, attempting to discover how to prepare and prevent wars. To distinguish the features of current wars from previous wars, a new concept, "war forms," has been introduced. There are three standards: social productivity, military technology, and operation method. According to these standards, there are four types of war.

4.1.1.1 Cold Weapon Warfare

Before the invention of gunpowder, there was the cold weapon age, when important technical innovations such as the use of metals and the emergence of metallurgical techniques appeared. Initially weapons were basically instruments that could be easily produced for daily use, whilst in late primitive society specialist war weapons appeared, including bayonets and throwing weapons, with clubs and stones being the earliest representatives. As methods that allowed the use of metals developed, spears, bows, crossbows, swords, and shields were produced. Infantry were used to construct phalanxes; cavalry were used on plains; in ancient Greece heavily armed hoplites, or foot soldiers, engaged in set-piece battles; and sailors used wooden boats as their basis for attack.

It was a long time before clubs and stones were replaced by metal weapons. The focus of war changed from simple fighting to formations. This has been called the first generation of war, because weapons were simple and people's physical power was the main element of battle effectiveness. Operational commands such as choosing battlefields and keeping in formation were very simple, and these included gesture, semaphore, gong and drum, and smoke signals. Commanders were also combatants who fought from the center of formations, standing up high or sitting on horseback.

4.1.1.2 Hot Weapon Warfare

The invention and application of gunpowder was an important revolution in military technology. The displacement of spears and swords by muskets marked the beginning of the hot weapon age. Mercenaries, supported and led by individual nations, appeared in large numbers, breeding a new military system. With the quick exit of heavy cavalry from battlefields, the infantry became the leading actors, and artillery was increasingly valued. A new linear formation was favored by military strategists, and in naval battles boarding was replaced by firing, with intensive shelling becoming the way in which to triumph. Fighting often began with hot weapons and ended with cold weapons, with the combination of infantry and artillery. Commanders spent a large amount of energy on strategy, and decision-making did not simply rely on commanders; in other words, reconnaissance became more important. Assisting professionals, institutions, advisers, and agents gradually came into being. War form had changed little by the eighteenth century and can be called the early stage of hot weapon age.

The late eighteenth to the early nineteenth century was the post-hot weapon age. In this period, the form of war changed, with the use of rifled firearms that possessed long range, the ability to fire frequently, and high precision. The adoption of rifling and breech-loading bullets increased weapons' lethal nature, and wooden sailing ships were replaced by steel steamships, which were equipped with broadside cannon. In this period, as social productivity increased, many states built giant armies and navies. During the military revolution that was triggered by the second scientific and technological wave, a bourgeois national army took the place of the feudal mercenary army, and compulsory military service began to be implemented. Complex armies including infantry, cavalry, and artillery came into existence. A mobile strategy was replaced by decisive strategy, and inflexible linear tactics gave way to decentralized skirmishing from trenches. The books *The Art of War* (1834) by Antoine-Henri Jomini and *Principles of War* (1812) and the later *On War* (1832) by Carl von Clausewitz, as well as the proletariat military theory proposed by Marx and Engels were the significant military works of this period.

4.1.1.3 Mechanized Warfare

Mechanized war is war that involves the use of such weapons as tanks and airplanes, and it was the basic form of war in the industrial era. Because of the second scientific and technological wave and its wide application, the third and fourth military revolutions arose rapidly one after another. At the beginning of the Franco-Prussian war, the third military revolution swept across Europe, North America, and East Asia, in which breech-loading rifling cannon replaced muzzle loading weapons; smokeless powder replaced black powder; steamships replaced wooden sailing ships. Decentralized skirmishing and linear fighting became the basic formation, and railroads were used for military purposes, so that strategic maneuverability was greatly improved. Telegraphs and telephones facilitated military communication; the navy entered the dreadnought era; and the General Staff Headquarters became the supreme military commander agency. The fourth military revolution developed in the early twentieth century, characterized by the use of new weapons and the replacement of trench attrition by blitzkrieg ("lightning war," whereby an attacking force uses overwhelming power, speed, and surprise to defeat the enemy). In this period, the world witnessed the existence of two hostile social systems. New weapons such as tanks, artillery, rocket launchers, airplanes, submarines, aircraft carriers, and chemical weapons were used on battlefields. Air defense forces, armored forces, engineering corps, and marines subsequently appeared. The scale of armies increased unprecedentedly, with the number of troops in some countries increasing to 10% or even 20% of the total population and the total number of soldiers in several countries reaching tens of millions.

Mechanized war includes such features as challenging goals, tremendous firepower, impressive maneuverability, operation over large areas, and the considerable consumption of resources. In this period, with intensive armed struggles and a high casualty ratio, there were more than 500 wars and large-scale armed conflicts that depended on a tremendous input of human resources, weapons, military technical equipment, and ammunition. New operational patterns such as air and ground, infantry and artillery, infantry and tank co-ordination, and blitzkriegs emerged. On the sea, there were aircraft carriers, submarines, and anti-submarine weapons. Battlefields changed from two dimensions to three dimensions with the development of air force. The main goals of war included improving the domestic economy and political regime, and affecting these aspects of the enemy. In military theory, concepts such as "air force winning theory," "armor winning theory," "total war," and "grand strategy" were developed and elaborated upon, one after another.

4.1.1.4 Nuclear Weapon Warfare

The appearance of the atomic bomb in the 1940s ushered in the nuclear era. Because of their immense destructiveness and lethal nature, nuclear weapons soon incurred strong opposition throughout the world. Rocket nuclear weapons were the basis of nuclear war, and a strategic nuclear weapons became a new part of military power. By their use, there were changes in both the organizational and operational structure of conventional forces. Resistance to nuclear, chemical, and biological weapons (the so-called "three-resistances") became a requirement and an important part of training and research tactics. In military thought, there emerged new concepts such as nuclear war and nuclear deterrence. The primary targets to be destroyed in the nuclear war involve not only armed forces, but also important targets and all the residents in the territories of the warring parties.

Toward the end of the Second World War, the USA dropped two atomic bombs on Japan; this is the only time that nuclear weapons have actually been used. These bombs were dropped on Hiroshima and Nagasaki on August 6 and August 9, 1945. In Hiroshima, which had a population of 300,000 people, about 15,000 tons of TNT were released. There were about 144,000 casualties, of whom about 68,000 were killed; and 67% of the city's buildings were destroyed. In Nagasaki, which had a population of 200,000 people, about 20,000 tons of TNT were released. There were about 59,000 casualties, of whom about 38,000 were killed; and 40% of the city's buildings were destroyed.

The long-time nuclear confrontation led to a "Cold War" between the two hostile systems.

4.1.1.5 Information Warfare

In the 1970s, the third technological revolution, which had information technology at its core, led to a new military revolution in most countries. The basic form of war in the information age is that either one or both sides chooses an information army as its main fighting force. It is generally agreed that the Gulf War of 1990 was the beginning of this new military revolution, and it is expected that the revolution will reach its peak in the mid-twenty-first century.

The wide use of information technology and other new materials and technologies in the military field led to the changes in forms of war, which also brought upheaval to the scale of armies, organizational establishment systems, military theories, strategies, and tactics, and military service systems. At the end of the twentieth century, major regional wars and military conflicts showed some new features. First, the operational goal was not to crush the opposing armed forces, but to destroy the other side's economy, military facilities, and command and control system. Second, the aim was to paralyze the other side quickly. Wars were brief, tight, and quick. Third, operations were more precise and miniaturized, and the controllability of fighting improved. Fourth, the battlefield was varied, including ground, sea, air, and space. There was a high degree of integrated joint operations but combat power was deployed on a small scale and with higher transparency. The number of combat casualties was smaller than in fourth-generation wars, but consumption of resources and their losses increased. Fifth, the method used was strong information assault followed by intensive real assaults with all kinds of long-, medium-, and short-range high-precision weapons used without contact (an example being the use of drones). Although the Gulf War, the Kosovo War, the war in Afghanistan, the Iraq War, and other main military conflicts at the end of the 20th century showed some features of information war, they could not be counted as information wars per se. It is generally believed that no world state has completely built an information army.

4.1.2   Western Military Revolution

In the early times, owing to the isolation of states, military revolution in a nation or region rarely had universal significance. By modern times, because of the development of science and technology and convenient information exchange, the whole world can be affected by a military revolution in an individual region.

4.1.2.1 Overview of the Western Military Revolution

Ancient Western city-states and countries implemented a citizen-soldier system, by which military service was not only a civil right but an obligation. The Athenian and Roman citizen-soldiers were divided into different ranks according to the amount of property they had. There were four ranks in Athens and five ranks in Rome. Cavalry and heavy and light infantry were selected from different ranks of citizens. Before the decline and disintegration of city states, there was no regular army or mercenary system. After the Peloponnesian War, owing to the development of slavery and increased social division in Greece, many small producers went bankrupt and became vagrants, and some chose to become mercenaries.

After the military revolution (107–101 BC) that began to implement the mercenary system, Rome established formal regular army at the beginning of Augustus Principate (27 BC). In the ancient West, the navy was more important than the land army for some coastal countries. For instance, Athens established a strong navy which was a major strength in wars. The first large-scale naval campaign, which was the famous Trojan War at the end of the Mycenaean civilization (in the early twelfth century BC), occurred in Greece: it is said that there were 1200 ships involved this campaign. Rome defeated the powerful Mediterranean nation Carthage with its strong navy and achieved victory in the Punic War (264–146 BC), and the Roman navy became the most powerful in the ancient world. In strategy and tactics, the ancient Westerners were particularly fond of phalanxes and later three-line legion. In the Mediterranean area, there were formations such as Assyria, Persian, Spartan, Theban, Macedonian, and Roman legion phalanxes, among which the Roman legions' phalanx was the most powerful in the Western cold weapon age.

The Macedonian phalanx, which was formed by sixteen × sixteen infantry with spears and shields, was created by Philip II (Philip II of Macedon), and was well known at the time, becoming an unbeatable powerful force. Alexander the Great (356–323 BC, whose name means the guardian of human beings) often used it to co-ordinate with cavalry: this was called the drilling hammer tactic. As the King of Macedonia, Alexander kept the Greek city states unified, and conquered Persia and other kingdoms, reaching the border with India. But the Greek–Macedonian phalanx was not suitable for fighting in complex terrains. In the fourth century BC, Rome narrowly escaped a devastating blow in the Gallic Wars, so Romans decided to give up the foreign Greek–Macedonian phalanx and replaced it with the Roman legion. The basic unit of the Roman legion was a small unit called a maniple composed of two centuries, each of which consisted of sixty to eighty soldiers. Three of these small units formed a big unit called a cohort with about 450–570 people. A big unit contained about 120–160 junior soldiers, 120–160 young soldiers, 120–160 middle-aged soldiers, sixty to eighty adult soldiers and a unit of thirty cavalry. Ten big units composed a Roman legion, which usually contained 4500–6000 people. The legion had an affiliated legion that was composed of 600 cavalrymen. Two Roman legions and two associated legions together constituted a group army, which was commanded by a consul. A Roman legion was organized with twenty people per row and six people per column, with a distance of 1.8–2 meters between two people. The maniples were small enough to permit tactical movement of individual infantry units on the battlefield within the framework of the greater army. The maniples were typically deployed into three discrete lines (Latin: *triplex acies*). The first line were young soldiers, who when at a distance of 20 yards from the enemy threw heavy javelins. After several minutes, the second line, composed of middle-aged soldiers, replaced those in the first line, who were held back to have a rest. The light infantry was composed of junior soldiers who were responsible for covering both wings and the back of the legion. Meanwhile, usable javelins were needed to supplement the first row. A battle usually involved several rounds of substitutions. Adult soldiers served as the reserve team for legions. Since Roman legions' tactics were flexible and adaptable to all kinds of terrain, they outperformed the Macedonian phalanx in wars.

The fief system was popular in medieval European countries. When feudal lords enfeoffed land, they provided the feoffees with the peasants on it as well, and in return, feoffees were to fulfill obligations that included fighting for feudal lords. This was the prevalent system in Europe, having associations with and differences from the citizen-soldier system. The system of enfeoffment had an economic base, and cavalry was the main source of service. It was created by the Frankish statesman and military leader Charles Martel (686–741) in the early eighth century, who noticed the important role of cavalry in wars when fighting Arabs and Byzantines. To build a cavalry army, he enfeoffed state land to subservient subordinates, meritorious soldiers, and nobles, and ordered that feoffees should perform cavalry service and fight for their kings in wartime, supplying horses and weapons. Other countries in Europe followed suit and the number of cavalry increased significantly. Some European cities began to recruit landless knights to make up for the lack of troops, and mercenaries became the main military force in the fifteenth century. The European cavalry, scattered among the fiefs and with little focused training, was mainly heavily armed: they wore chainmail that covered everything except their eyes and horses' hooves and tails. Light cavalry armor in contrast was made of leather, and did not cover the whole body. European countries held competitions presided over by kings and other feudal lords, in which knights competed in pairs. The winners were rewarded and encouraged to improve their fighting skills.

The basic tactical unit for some Western European countries, which implemented the cavalry system, was a small unit composed of knights, sword guards, archers, and spearmen. Twenty-five to eighty small units composed a brigade and a number of brigades composed a cavalry legion. Cavalry was the main force for medieval European armies. After the seventh century, the important role of cavalry in European war was well established and it became the force that determined the course of wars; serving in the infantry was despised as being the business of slaves and serfs. Though there were always more infantry than cavalry in European countries, they were mostly those who did not want to fight and rarely had even basic fighting skills. Some of the freemen infantry were too poor to provide their own weapons and had to fight with sticks. In the crusade age, European generals realized that multi-faceted armies were much more powerful than those that were composed of cavalry only. Many generals therefore replaced some of the knights and heavy cavalry with infantry, and after the use of firing weapons became established, infantry became the main force on the battlefield.

By modern times, with the wide application of gunpowder, the military field underwent significant transformation. Spears and swords were replaced by muskets, large numbers of mercenaries emerged, the heavy cavalry quickly retreated from the battlefield with the infantry becoming the main force, and artillery began to gain attention. Ancient phalanxes were replaced by a linear formation. New weapons such as tanks, rocket launchers, airplanes, submarines, aircraft carriers, and chemical weapons were used on battlefields. Air forces, navies, armored forces, engineering corps, and marines appeared subsequently.

4.1.2.2 Contemporary Western Military Revolution

This includes a number of military elements of which every Western country has a similar understanding. Research from America, namely the thesis proposed in the American Defense Report in 1997 that could be summarized into "three innovations and two transformations", has become the mainstream—new weapons, theories, and organizational structure, and transformations in how war and military action are undertaken.

Innovation in Military Technology

Military revolution often starts with military technological innovation. The major breakthrough in military technology, which promoted weapons and equipment systems and changed the means by which war could be waged, was the direct material basis for a military revolution. With the rapid development and wide application of information technology, the technology invested in weapons and equipment is more and more sophisticated. Taking the US Army as an example, more than half of its military equipment system has achieved informatization with the successful application of digital technology. The digital battlefield is characterized by high transparency, fast information transmission, low military density, and strong survivability. The US military has focused on the development of intelligent ammunition, combat platforms, robots, and command systems.

Innovation in Military Theory

Innovative military theory is the soul of military transformation. Its transformation plays a key role in military technological transformation and revolution. It sets the direction, scale, and structure of army building and determines the patterns both of wars and military educational training.

Innovation in Military Systems and Organization

Military systems and organization carry forward the use of advanced military technology, weapon systems, and innovative military theory, and combine military hardware and software. Transformation of military systems and organization does not only focus on the expansion or reduction in the size of armies, but also examines the optimized military structure. To deal with all kinds of fighting forces and military operations, modularization and integration have to be stressed. Modern combat formations have tighter internal bonds, more flexible grouping methods, and stronger combat capacity.

Changes of the Form of War

In the information era, because of the continuing improvements in maneuverability, reconnaissance, surveillance, and precise attack, a large number of precision-guided weapons have been developed. From intelligence and reconnaissance, object localization, command and control, to effect assessment, all can now be done very exactly. All-weather and all-spectrum high-tech surveillance systems allow commanders to reliably learn about battlefield situations. Advanced global navigation systems can automatically display three-dimensional coordinates, velocities, and precise times regarding a target and also provide high-precision positioning information. The fighting space is no longer limited to direct conflict areas, but expanded to multi-dimensional areas such as land, sea, air, and space.

4.2   MODERN WESTERN MILITARY TECHNOLOGY

The improvements in technology have caused changes in weapons and equipment, combat pattern, military theories, and culture. Intelligence systems include an early-warning plane that has a number of integrated technologies; new infantry fighting vehicles have combined functions, such as air and chemical defense, reconnaissance, and communication; hovercrafts perform well on water and on land; armed helicopters have created an airborne army. These changes have led to the development of different military concepts, thoughts, and culture.

According to its function, modern military technology can be divided into precision-guided technology, including missiles, guided bombs, and guided shells; automated command technology, such as control, communication, computers, and intelligence; reconnaissance and surveillance technology, including space (using satellites), aerial (early-warning planes), ground (radar), and underwater reconnaissance (sonar); camouflage and stealth technology; night-vision technology, which breaks the barrier of darkness; military laser technology, such as laser weapons and laser range finders; electronic warfare technology, mainly aiming to control the electromagnetic spectrum; military aerospace technology, which is applied to reconnaissance, surveillance, early warning, communications, navigation, and weather forecasts with the help of remote sensors, observation equipment, communications equipment, and weapon systems deployed in space; nuclear weapon technology; chemical weapon technology; and biological weapon technology. There are also new-concept weapons involving directed energy, kinetic energy, and anti-materiel (against military equipment instead of enemy combatants) features.

4.2.1   An Overview of Precision-Guided Weapons

Precision-guided weapons, whose direct hit probability is higher than 50%, include a variety of missiles, guided bombs, artillery shells, and torpedoes, and they have been used to attack tanks, aircrafts, ships, radars, command centers, and bridges. A direct hit means that the circular error probability is smaller than the lethal radius of the warhead.

During the Second World War, the Germans developed the V-1 missile and V-2 missile to bomb London. Research into and the manufacturing of precision-guided weapons leapt forward in the 1960s with the improvements in technology, especially the rapid development of micro-electronics and computer technology. The Vietnam War prompted the US military to develop guided weapons, and these were tested and improved in actual combat. To attack the important target of Thanh Hoa Bridge near Hanoi, the American Air Force dispatched fighter planes on more than 600 sorties and dropped more than 5000 tons of conventional bombs, but thanks to anti-aircraft defense from the ground, Thanh Hoa Bridge survived. Indeed, eighteen aircrafts were shot down and thirty-nine were damaged. Finally, the US military blew up the bridge by dispatching twelve fighter planes and using new laser-guided bombs; what is more, no fighter planes were damaged. Subsequently, the US military bombed twenty oil depots on the banks of the Haiphong River and destroyed nineteen of them. Precision-guided weapons shot to fame because of their success in the Vietnam War. In October 1973, during the fourth Middle East War, the Egyptian Army destroyed eighty-five Israeli tanks in five minutes and wiped out the Israeli 190th Armored Brigade by using Soviet-made wire-guided anti-tank missiles. The Israeli Army hit back with US-style anti-tank missiles. In the first three days, more than 300 tanks were damaged on both sides, 77% of which were destroyed by anti-tank missiles. Since then, the words "precision-guided weapons" have been indelibly recorded in the world's military history. In the 1980s, with the rapid development and wide application of information technology, micro-electronics, and photonics technology, more types of precision-guided weapons were developed.

4.2.2   Classification of Precision-Guided Weapons

Precision-guided weapons may be divided into precision-guided missiles and precision-guided munitions. A precision-guided missile is a weapon that relies on its own power to move forward, with a guidance system controlling its flight trajectory. Precision-guided munitions have locational devices but no internal power unit.

4.2.2.1 Guided Missiles

Missiles are generally composed of a warhead, propulsion system, control system, and a body. Lacking one of these elements, they cannot be called missiles. According to their operational tasks, they can be divided into strategic and tactical missiles. The strike range of strategic missiles is usually more than 1000 kilometers. According to range, they can be divided into international (>8000 kilometers), long-range (3000–8000 kilometers), and medium-range missiles (1000–3000 kilometers). They adopt stellar guidance (the use of angular measurements (sights) between celestial bodies and the visible horizon to locate one's position in the world, on land as well as at sea) and radar-related terminal guidance, and have high-performance independent warheads to raise hit accuracy and viability. Tactical missiles are those with a range of under 1000 kilometers that are used to attack targets deep inside enemy territory. They often adopt inertial or composite guidance with conventional, nuclear, or chemical warheads.

According to the relationship between launch point and target, missiles can be divided into:

- land-to-land missiles, launched from the ground to attack ground targets;

- land-to-air missiles, launched from the ground to attack air targets;
- shore-to-ship missiles, launched from the shore to attack ships;
- air-to-air missiles, launched from the air to attack air targets;
- air-to-land missiles, launched from the air to attack ground targets;
- air-to-ship missiles, launched from the air to attack on-water targets;
- air-to-submarine missiles, launched from the air to attack submarines;
- ship-to-ship missiles, launched from ships to attack on-water targets;
- ship-to-submarine missiles, launched from ships to attack submarines;
- ship-to-air missiles, launched from ships to attack air targets;
- submarine-to-submarine missiles, launched from submarines to attack submarines;
- submarine-to-ship missiles, launched from submarines to attack ships;
- submarine-to-land missiles, launched from submarines to attack ground targets.

With the development of space technology, the potential distance between launch point and target has expanded significantly. Missiles using space platforms as launching points to attack targets have appeared, examples being anti-satellite missiles and space-based intercepting weapons.

4.2.2.2 Guided Bombs

Guided bombs, launched from aircraft, include a guidance device that can control its trajectory and guide it to targets. Unlike a missile, a guided bomb has no power device in itself, and relies on the initial velocity given by the aircraft. With the help of guidance equipment, a guided bomb can correct flight deviation automatically until it hits its target. With a simple structure and low cost, a guided bomb can be used to destroy air defense systems, artillery, tanks, armored vehicles, bridges, rugged construction facilities, and airport runways. Currently there are TV-guided and laser-guided bombs.

A television-guided bomb is equipped with a television camera, by which the pilot can observe the position of a target. When the aircraft is a certain distance away from the target, the bomb is dropped. The tracker system tracks targets automatically and corrects any trajectory deviation to guide the bomb. It has high hit accuracy but is weather-sensitive. Equipped with a laser seeker, a laser-guided bomb adopts semi-automatic homing guidance, which fires a laser beam at targets. The seeker in the front of the warhead catches the reflected laser from the target surface, and then controls and guides the warhead toward the target. Owing to excellent directivity and tiny divergence of the laser beam, the accuracy of laser-guided bombs is quite high. They are costly, but their combat effectiveness is dozens or even hundreds of times higher than that of traditional bombs.

4.2.2.3 Guided Artillery Shells

Launched by ground artillery, a guided artillery shell is mainly used to attack armored targets. It is composed of a seeker, electronic components, control devices, and the warhead. While the shell flies to the target area, the seeker tracks the target automatically. By calculation and correction of the electronic control system, the warhead can attack small targets, such as armored targets, bunkers, and firing points.

There are three kinds of guided artillery shells. First is the semi-automatic laser-guided artillery shell, such as the "Copperhead," which was made by the USA in the 1980s. Its hitting accuracy is within 1 meter. Guided artillery shells can hit tanks, aircraft, and ships accurately at a distance of 40 to 90 kilometers. Second is the millimeter-wave guided artillery shell, such as the "Saddam" system developed by the USA and the "Merlina" system developed by the UK. The three warheads carried by this shell use a 35 GHz radiometer as passive homing guidance. After the artillery shell is fired, the fuse delay controls the warhead to the target. On the warhead there hangs a vortex-shaped parachute that can rotate automatically and scan targets. When it aims at the center of the target, the warhead detonates. Third is the infrared homing guided artillery shell, such as the "Manchester Lux" made by Sweden. The artillery shell is usually launched by mortars at a distance of 8 kilometers. When the artillery shell reaches its highest point of trajectory, the infrared seeker starts to search targets. Once it receives the infrared ray emitted by targets, the seeker will lock itself, and the artillery shell will then fly to the target under the control of the guidance system.

4.2.2.4 Guided Torpedoes

Guided torpedoes are offensive underwater weapons launched by submarines and ships to perform anti-submarine and anti-ship missions. Missiles are the main weapons in long-distance anti-ship combat, but in the field of underseas warfare torpedoes are of prime importance. Tracking targets by taking advantage of the sound of moving targets, guided torpedoes initially adopted passive voice and wired guidance and later active voice and active and passive combined guidance. The current (up to the year of 2017) operating distance of active voice is 1700 meters while the distance of passive voice is 2500 meters. To enhance their anti-jamming capability, modern guided torpedoes often adopt a multi-frequency system. Taking advantage of pulse code and spectral analysis, guided torpedoes can distinguish true from false target signals in the complex marine environment.

Wire-guided torpedoes appeared in the 1960s. They take advantage of a sonar system to make up for the shortcomings of shortening sound guidance distances at high speed. Initially there was one-way transmission but now it is mostly two-way. They operate by remote-control and use telemetry, while optical fiber is used instead of copper wire to reduce signal attenuation over long distances. Wake-guided torpedoes are powerful weapons in attacking ships. The changes in bubbles, water pressure, and temperature generated by the disturbance of propellers can guide torpedoes.

4.2.3   The Influence of Precision-Guided Weapons

Appearing during the Second World War, precision-guided weapons, known as "smart weapons" or "smart bombs," were very successful from the 1960s, although their development goes back to the 1940s.

4.2.3.1   Improved Operational Efficiency

According to statistics, during the Second World War the circular error probability of a B-17 bomber was 1000 meters, and it needed 9000 bombs on average to destroy one target. During the Vietnam War, the circular error probability of the F-105D fighter-bomber was 100 meters and it needed 200 bombs on average to hit one target. During the Gulf War, the circular error probability of the F-117 stealth aircraft was 1–2 meters and it needed only one or two bombs to blow up one target. The probability of destroying a tank with a "Copperhead" homing guided artillery shell is the same as that of 2500 general artillery shells.

In June 1982, Israel invaded Lebanon. Under the cover of electronic-interference equipment, the Israeli Army made an air attack on Beqaa Valley with a variety of air-to-ground precision-guided weapons. They destroyed nineteen "Sam-6" anti-aircraft missile bases in just six minutes. In the subsequent Beqaa air combat with Syrian Army, Israeli advanced air-to-air missiles helped them to obtain the impressive record of 50:0. In the Gulf War and Iraq War, precision-guided weapons became essential firepower. According to incomplete statistics, the precision-guided weapons' probability of hitting targets was 85% and the probability of destroying targets was 64.8%. Therefore, from the effect in actual combat, its value is far more evident than that of nuclear deterrence. Precision-guided weapons have played an important role in unbalanced military conflicts.

4.2.3.2 New Combat Theory

Precision-guided weapons brought changes to combat instruments, theories, and methods. Non-contact wars are the main combat form of contemporary wars. Precision-guided weapons make long-range precision strike a reality. In the Iraq War, air-launched cruise missiles were thousands of kilometers away and Tomahawk cruise missiles launched from the sea by the US Army hit the intended targets; the global positioning system (GPS) guidance system can work independently in harsh weather and the millimeter wave guidance system was hardly affected by clouds and dust; the Patriot air defense missile system can simultaneously track fifty to a hundred aerial targets and simultaneously control nine missiles to attack incoming targets from different directions and heights.

"Surgical strike" became a common military means that was adopted by powerful nations. In April 1986, in the air-strike action on the Libyan "Golden Valley," American F-111 fighters and carrier-based attackers conducted a surgical" strike to five targets on the ground. The military purpose was reached in twelve minutes. The size of battlefields was expanded and the boundary between front and rear was blurred. The striking range of precision-guided weapons was far beyond the definition of a traditional front. Hand-to-hand fighting on the front was reduced significantly and battlefields were no longer fixed. In the Gulf War, there were more than 1.2 million troops and 8000 tanks. However, ground fighting lasted for only 100 hours and no large-scale infantry fighting or tank warfare occurred, for the armored troops of the Iraqi Army had already been destroyed by the missiles of the multinational force. The Iraq War lasted for only three weeks. American and British forces occupied Baghdad and won the war with no serious resistance, and this was inseparable from the heavy use of precision-guided weapons.

4.2.3.3 Political Benefits

The relationship between contemporary war and domestic politics is intimate. A lot of national leaders have stepped down because of a poor record and heavy casualties in wartime. Precision-guided weapons have provided the technical conditions for quick victories and minimal casualties on the battlefield. Precision-guided weapons are aimed the enemy's war machine, and can force a surrender. Precision-guided weapons can significantly reduce civilian casualties and the destruction of infrastructure. This is effective in winning public support and trust in politics and diplomacy, and for the world economic order in general.

4.3   Western Military Thought

Military thought, an important part of military culture, is rational knowledge about wars and the army, representing the guiding theory and basic principles for national defense and army-building. Representatives of ancient Western military thoughts are those promulgated by the ancient Greek city-states and the Roman Empire. The military practice of the ancient Greek military commander Epaminondas, the Macedonian king Alexander III, the Carthaginian military commander Hannibal, and military masterpieces such as Herodotus' *History*, Thucydides' *History of the Peloponnesian War*, and Xenophon's *Expedition* reflect military thoughts in some ancient European countries. There is clear analysis of the relationship between war and politics and diplomacy, operational strategy, tactics, and military construction. In the seventeenth century, with the rapid development of capitalism in Europe and America, the industries that developed produced a large number of new weapons. The Renaissance and the bourgeois revolution quickened the formation of new classes and the development of ethnic relations. They also changed war and construction of armies from form to content. In the twentieth century, with the expansion in the scale of war, Western military thoughts became more sophisticated. For example, theories about the navy led to the rapid development of shipbuilding and marine technology. Later, theories about the air force and tank design produced important impacts on the development of military technology and weapons.

4.3.1   Modern Western Military Thought

Modern Western military thought originated in Europe. During the Renaissance, there was sign of its modernization. The main magnum opus is *The Art of War* by the Italian Niccolò Machiavelli in 1521. This book suggests that in order to consolidate their rule countries must focus on war, improve military strength, and implement compulsory military service. In the seventeenth century, some bourgeois military thinkers put forward revolutionary military thoughts. These were embodied in Clausewitz's *On War* and Jomini's *The Art of War*. The books summarized Napoleonic war experience and were the mark of the establishment of European modern bourgeois military thought. Compared with ancient Western military thought, modern military thought has different focuses.

4.3.1.1 Theorization

In ancient Western military thought, there were few specialized military theoretical writings. Rational knowledge about wars and armies was scattered, often mixed into historical works (such as *Histories* about the Greco-Persian Wars by Herodotus, *History of the Peloponnesian War* by Thucydides, *The Anabasis of Alexander* by Arrian of Nicomedia, and *Commentaries on the Gallic War* by Julius Caesar). Early in the first century, *Strategems* complied by the Roman Frontinus, tried to break the space–time structure of traditional history works, but it did not succeed. At the end of the fourth century, the publication of *Concerning Military Matters*, written by the Roman Vegetius, ended the sequence of conflicting military writings and historical works. A large number of military theoretical writings emerged in the modern West, such as Jomini's *The Art of War* and Clausewitz's *On War*. In the seventeenth century, owing to the rapid development of modern science, a research method relying mainly on "observation, experiment, collecting and accumulating material" gradually took form. What is more, the development of classical philosophy provided a basis and tools for the research of military thought. For example, by using the analysis method from Hegelian philosophy, Clausewitz reached new heights in explaining the reorganization of war. The comprehensive discussion of the relationship between war and politics, the profound understanding of the role of spirit, the analysis of offensive and defensive contradiction, and the elaborate study of winning factors were the outstanding achievements of modern Western military thought. In his introduction to *The Art of War*, Jomini demonstrated many basic military principles and rules and proposed a variety of factors determining the success or failure of wars.

4.3.1.2 Systematization and Diversification

In ancient times and the Middle Ages, although there were such military works as *Strategems* and *Concerning Military Matters*, the understanding of war was not systematic. What is more, cold weapon war and simple combat patterns revealed the lack of systematization and integrity. In the eighteenth century, the British-born soldier Major-General Henry Lloyd made a great contribution, writing the first analytical military history. While summing up the experience of war, Clausewitz and Jomini systematically analyzed and researched the basic issues in the military field.

4.3.2   Contemporary Western Military Thought

Military theory is closely related to the development of the practice of war. In the twentieth century, technology, complex international relations, and numerous wars developed. Historically, there are two ways to win wars: first, by reckless fighting; second, by non-violence or violence plus non-violence, especially by taking advantage of resources. Contemporary Western military thought is composed of a series of interconnected basic military strategic perspectives. "Direct military route" strategic thought can be divided into sea power, air power, nuclear weapon theories, mechanized war theory, and total war strategic theory. "Indirect military route" strategic thought can be divided into alliance and deterrence strategies. The ultimate goal of these strategies is to crush the enemy's will. The development of contemporary Western military thought has experienced three different historical periods.

4.3.2.1 The Hot War Period

The hot war period refers to the time from the early twentieth century to the end of the Second World War. In the first half of the twentieth century, humans experienced two world wars of unprecedented scale, which caused nearly 100 million casualties and huge property losses. To realize their strategic goals, countries in the West developed new military thought, weapons, and equipment to meet the needs of war. With heavy use of tanks, airplanes, and ships, the pace of war accelerated. On the basis of summarizing the experience of war, military theorists put forward new strategic theories and military thoughts.

As early as the end of the nineteenth century, the importance of the ocean aroused attention from Western militarists. The US naval officer Alfred Thayer Mahan was the most prominent US strategist, conducting strategic research into naval battles and proposing the theory of sea power. The core of this is that sea power, especially its major traffic related to national interests and trade, is the main factor for a powerful and prosperous nation. The theory attracted little attention from the Western military community when it was first put forward, but it caused a sensation in academia. After the First World War, the significant impact of naval operations led Western countries to recognize the theory's significance. It was followed by theories about the use of aircraft carriers and submarines. In 1903, the successful powered flight made by the American Wright brothers marked the coming of the aviation age. The invention aroused great attention among a number of Western militarists, including the Italian

Giulio Douhet, the American William "Billy" Mitchell and the British Sir Hugh Trenchard. Douhet foresaw that planes would dominate future war. With sharp military vision, he boldly proposed the air power theory: he believed that countries with air supremacy would win wars and that the losing sides would have to accept any conditions imposed by their conquerors. This new military thought was verified by the Second World War. In the early twentieth century, the advent of tanks and armored combat vehicles changed military theory and brought forth the mechanization theory, which was made full use of by the armies of Western countries during the Second World War.

During the interwar period, military thought changed a lot. One of the most representative theories was that of "total war," a strategy put forward by the German general and strategist Erich Ludendorff. In 1935, his book *The Total War* skillfully combined theories about land, marine and air fighting, and boldly proposed the new idea of-total war—the core of which was to mobilize all available strength, both the army and the general public, to participate in wars. This became the core military thought during the Second World War and was applied by Nazi generals. The Blitzkrieg theory, which included both tactics and strategy, was equally influential. This theory was first proposed by the German Marshal Alfred von Schlieffen during the war against France during the late nineteenth century and was used by Germany in the First World War. Learning from military theories that concerned air power, mechanization, and total war, Heinz Guderian and other generals came up with a new strategy concept early in the Second World War: that with the co-operation of aircraft and airborne troops, troops in armed vehicles could raid the enemy's rear lines in high-speed attacks. This theory initially brought tremendous success to German troops.

During the hot war period, especially after the First World War, wars were becoming increasingly complex, involving politics, economy, the military, technology, and diplomacy. It was difficult to solve conflicts between nations simply by military force. Under this context, the British strategic theorist Liddell Hart proposed the indirect route strategy theory, which was a big step forward for Western military strategic thought. He also proposed the "grand strategy," expanding military strategy to a discipline that encompassed many fields.

In addition, every Western country had to strengthen its military superiority over neighboring countries to safeguard its own interests. The alliances strategy was gradually formed, the core of which was a focus on collective security. However, owing to the constraints of science and technology, military exchanges and alliances between countries were restricted.

The First World War was the first world-scale war between the Central Powers, formed by Germany, Austria, and Italy, and the Entente countries, formed by Britain, France, and Russia, redividing colonies and spheres of influence to assure world hegemony.

4.3.2.2 The Cold War Period

The Cold War period started at the end of the Second World War and ended with the collapse of the Soviet Union. After the Second World War, and considering the effect of two world wars, the Western countries concluded that it was necessary to organize certain military alliances to ensure national security. Therefore, early in the post-war period, Western countries continued to pursue this strategy and established two military alliance systems, the North Atlantic Treaty Organization (NATO) and the Warsaw Pact, formally the Treaty of Friendship, Cooperation and Mutual Assistance. The purpose of these two organizations was to carry out "collective defense," which meant that when any contracting state went to war with other countries, other member states must offer assistance, including the use of military force. In fact, the field of co-operation between the two unions was not limited to military alliance, but also included economy and politics. Later these two unions became tools of the USA and the Soviet Union, both of which were aiming at world hegemony.

During the Cold War, the most representative military thought in Western countries was the nuclear deterrence theory. The huge military effect produced by the nuclear strikes on Hiroshima and Nagasaki prompted Western strategists to recognize the enormous power of nuclear weapons; and then countries competed in developing nuclear weapons and pursuing nuclear deterrence. During the Cold War, the US (or NATO) nuclear strategy had five stages: containment, massive retaliation, flexible response, actual deterrence, and new flexible response. Through implementing this strategy, Western countries had a lengthy nuclear arm race with the Warsaw Pact, led by the Soviet Union. The race weakened the Soviet Union's economic strength, eventually dragging it down.

In the late 1970s, with the rapid development of micro-electronics, new materials, new energy sources, and space technology, Western countries started to research and develop space weapons. A space race with the Soviet Union was launched, proposing the "high frontier" military strategy, stressing strategic defense as being "the perfect way to protect American deterrence." The direct result of this strategy was the Reagan administration's "strategic defense initiative," which was known as the

"Star Wars" program. On June 10, 1984, the USA launched a missile from a South Pacific island that successfully hit the warhead of a multiple warhead international missile that had been fired from Vandenberg Air Force Base in California to an altitude of 160 kilometers. This was the beginning of "Star Wars". To implement the program, the United States invested $35 billion. The Soviet Union invested tens of billions of dollars to fight the program, severely weakening its national strength.

4.3.2.3 Post-Cold War Period

East European upheaval and Soviet disorganization marked the end of the Cold War, which lasted for more than forty years. After a careful analysis of the new strategic environment, Western military strategists realized that in this period the most critical issue was to identify an imaginary enemy that threatened Western countries' national interests. They started to develop new strategic approaches, for example, the USA adjusting its national security strategy while continuing to pursue the nuclear deterrence strategy. A regional defense strategy was proposed in 1992, based on the idea that there was no strong opponent to compete with the United States, yet non-military threats were increasing. After Bill Clinton took power in 1993, the USA proposed flexibility and an optional participating strategy. Then in 1997 a new military theory with trans-century significance, "Shape, Respond, Prepare Now" was proposed by the USA.

In addition, Western countries further developed the alliance strategy theory after the Cold War. The disintegration of the Soviet Union and the Warsaw Pact plunged Central and Eastern Europe into a power vacuum, so to protect their national interests some European countries that had previously been members of the Warsaw Pact moved closer to NATO and proposed the idea of joining. Western strategists in NATO put forward NATO's eastward expansion as a strategy, but NATO was reluctant to discard the old mentality and enlarge upon the fruits of its victory in the Cold War. With a new military revolution and changes in the world strategic situation during the twenty-first century, Western countries actively explored new military strategies that were in their own interests.

National Security as the Basic Starting Point

National interests, especially national security, are the starting point and destination of military strategy. After the Cold War, the international strategic situation changed dramatically. The security threat to NATO was no longer in existence, so the USA and other Western countries adjusted their national security strategies. Western countries have successively proposed new-century national security strategic thoughts. For example, the USA believed that, before 2015, no single country or group could rival itself, so there emerged a so-called "period of strategic opportunities." According to this judgment, the USA realized that the focus of the new-century strategy was to protect American global economic interests. This was the "Shape, Respond, Prepare Now" strategy in action. "Shape" means to participate in international affairs and closely combine military action with diplomacy to create an advantageous environment for the USA; "Respond" is to improve military capabilities by preventing and coping with a variety of local conflicts; "Prepare Now" is to prepare for unpredictable major challenges. Other Western countries also made timely strategic adjustments.

Strategic Alliance Thought Playing a Greater Role
During the Cold War, most of the unions established among Western countries were military–political alliances whose major mission was to guarantee security through military deterrence. But with the end of the Cold War, these unions turned to political-military alliance. Western military thought emphasizes alliance and regional co-operation, joint security responsibilities, rational power use, and group security. NATO proposed the "NATO new strategy" concept, which is a US-led, globally oriented military strategy. In the new century, Western countries' alliance strategy is more aggressive, and NATO will become the master of Europe. The current military forces including Russia cannot compete with it as they did in the Cold War period. In the Kosovo crisis of 1998–1999, NATO took a tough attitude and upgraded its military presence to the extent of invading a sovereign state, which was unprecedented before the end of the Cold War. This all shows that in the new century the strategy of the Western alliance is more aggressive than before.

Strategic Information Becoming the Focus
In 1995, the US Department of Defense commissioned the famous strategic research think-tank the Rand Corporation to conduct research into "information war." The Rand Corporation proposed a "strategic information war" in 1996. It affirmed the important role of information dominance in future high-tech wars and new-century military conflicts. This involves the manipulation of the information flow in networks, destroying the enemy's telephone network, oil and gas pipelines and other power networks, air traffic control system, national fund transfer, bank transfer system, and so on. Because the targets could hold information about a

country's basic structure, military, politics, economy, and society, the information war is strategic and powerful. Taking advantage of superiority in information, American military force can ensure its leading role in the twenty-first century. The strategic information war challenges traditional military strategic thought, and it is foreseeable that theories about the information war could change military strategy in the twenty-first century.

BIBLIOGRAPHY

Buzan, Barry. 2001. *The Arms Dynamic in World Politics.* Changchun: Jilin People's Publishing House.

Chang Qiaozhang. 2004. *New Concepts in the Military Revolution.* Beijing: Chinese People's Liberation Army Publishing House.

Gu Wei. 2004. *Military Technology and Revolution in Military Affairs.* Shanghai: Fudan University Press.

Li Shenming, and Wang Yizhou. 2001. *Yellow Book of International Politics: Annual Report on International Politics and Security.* Beijing: Social Sciences Academic Press.

Nie Yunlai, and Li Xiaodong. 2004. *Annual Report on World Military Development.* Beijing: Military Science Publishing House.

Niu Xianzhong. 2003. *Three Expositions of Military Science of Sun Zi: From the Ancient Art of War to New Strategies.* Nanning: Guangxi Normal University Press.

O'Hanlon, Michael. 2001. *Technological Change and the Future of Warfare.* Beijing: Xinhua Publishing House.

Shen Weiguang. 2003. *The Lead in the Future Warfare: Information-Based Army.* Beijing: Xinhua Publishing House.

Slipchenko, Vladimir. 2004. *The Sixth Generation War.* Beijing: Xinhua Publishing House.

Wang Baocun. 1999. *The World Military Affairs Revolution.* Beijing: Chinese People's Liberation Army Publishing House.

Wang Yue. 2004. *A Course in National Defense Technology and Military Affairs.* Harbin: Harbin Engineering University Press.

Xu Guobin. 2007. *Military Theory Course.* Guangzhou: Guangdong People's Publishing House.

Xue Guoan, and Wang Hai. 2004. *Answers to the Hot Issues on the World Military Affairs Revolution.* Beijing: Chinese People's Liberation Army Publishing House.

Zhang Zhixue. 1994. *The Chinese Micropedia (Military Science).* Chengdu: Sichuan Education Press.

Zhang Xiaoxiang, and Zhang Yiren. 2005. *Modern Technology and Warfare.* Beijing: Tsinghua University Press.

CHAPTER 5

Education System

5.1 History

5.1.1 Primary and Secondary Education

5.1.1.1 Emergence of School System

School systems in Western culture emerged as early as the Archaic Period (800–500 BC), when private schools for grammar, music, and physical culture (gymnasiums) arose in Athens, in ancient Greece. During the Classical Period (500–330 BC), what are recognized today as institutions of secondary or higher education were created by famous scholars such as Socrates, Plato, and Aristotle.

Hellenistic Greece (330–30 BC) witnessed the establishment of secondary grammar schools that studied classical plays and poems as well as grammar and natural sciences. In the same period, a more formal and coherent system was shaped in Athens, which, much like the one predominating in modern society, included three tiers of education—primary, secondary, and higher.

In the Roman Republic (509–27 BC), a dual-track system came into being, under which the plebs and the patricians attended school in two different systems: children of the rank and file went to extremely shabby primary schools, while those from noble and rich families progressed from primary tutorials at home to secondary grammar schools, and then to higher rhetorical schools.

© The Author(s) 2018
G. Xu et al. (eds.), K. Chen et al. (trans.), *Understanding Western Culture*, https://doi.org/10.1007/978-981-10-8150-7_5

5.1.1.2 Rise of Modern Primary and Secondary Schools

In the Middle Ages (*c.* 500–1500), formal schooling mostly fell under the control of the Church and was largely the purview of monasteries, cathedrals, and parishes, primarily aiming to train clergymen for holy orders. In the sixteenth century, when the Protestant Reformation (1517–1648) against the Roman Catholic Church dismantled the unity of medieval European Christendom, the divided ecclesiastical denominations and entities that broke from the stranglehold of Catholicism began to set up larger numbers of primary schools to teach the common people to read, using this as a tool to preach their particular doctrines. Primary education was therefore expanded to wider classes of people and much larger populations. At the same time, in the wake of the Renaissance (fourteenth century to seventeenth century), which brought about widespread and far-reaching educational reforms, capitalist industry and commerce rose in importance. In response to the changing society and the capitalists' demand for a better education for their children, there appeared in Europe new types of secondary schools, which, standing outside the traditional monastery and cathedral system, may be recognized as the precursors of modern secondary schools.

5.1.1.3 Establishment of National Education Systems

Germany

Germany was the first country in the world to establish a national education system. In 1619, regulations were issued in Weimar stipulating that all school-age children should attend school all year round and that local government should take responsibility for urging parents to send their children to school. This is recognized as initiating German compulsory education. In 1872, the German government promulgated its first general school law providing compulsory education for all children from the age of six to fourteen, which increased primary school enrollment in Germany to 100% by the end of the nineteenth century and made it the world's pioneer in promoting and practicing universal compulsory education.

France

On the eve of the French Revolution of 1789, many French people were influenced by Enlightenment thought. They criticized feudal monarchy and supported secularization and democratization in education. Secularization of education involved the ending of the Church's monopoly on education and the establishment of a national education system; changing the social function of education from serving the Church to serving the state; and ensuring that religious preaching in schools was replaced by secular moral education. The democratization of education urged the implementation of universal education, extending educational rights to every citizen and at the same time guaranteeing that men and women should enjoy equal opportunities in education.

After the Revolution, Napoleon issued a decree that set up the Imperial University, which, from January 1, 1809, was in charge of public instruction throughout the France. The Imperial University was the highest administrative authority, supervising and organizing every aspect of French national education, with authority over the twenty-seven previously independent universities (*"académies"*). A highly centralized educational administration system is still in use today, remaining a unique feature of French education.

In 1881 and 1882, the Jules Ferry Laws established mandatory education for six to thirteen year olds as well as free public primary schooling. In 1889, the School Act defined primary school teachers as being as important as government functionaries. Under these laws and acts, in France there was founded a system of free, mandatory, secular, public education. By the end of the nineteenth century, French compulsory primary education had benefited 100% of school-age children.

The USA

Since the late eighteenth century, the USA has been making continuous attempts to tailor education to the needs of the nation. It first established a non-sectarian, single-track, free, public, primary education system in the nineteenth century. For example, in 1834 the Pennsylvania State Congress, prior to other states, passed a non-compulsory free school act. In 1852, Massachusetts enacted the first mandatory attendance law, the first in the USA. Another historical event which was a turning point in American education history was the famous Kalamazoo School Case, which occurred in 1873–1874, in which a lawsuit was filed by three Kalamazoo citizens who intended to prevent the local school board from taxing the citizens in order to fund a high school; they failed. When the ruling in favor of the school board was made by the Michigan Supreme Court, a tax-supported high school was explicitly signed into law. This decision was soon cited by many other states, and there was a surge in the number of publicly funded high schools throughout the country. Thus was a universal public school system shaped in the USA.

5.1.1.4 Foundation and Institutionalization of Vocational Education

Germany
Germany also led the way in vocational education. In the early eighteenth century, the growing industry, commerce, and urbanized lifestyle that all demanded practical knowledge gave rise to a new type of school, the *Realschule*, which focused on practical sciences and expertise. They reached their most rapid growth in the mid-eighteenth century.

In the years between 1760 and 1840, the Western world witnessed the Industrial Revolution, which, dominated by mechanized production and changing employment relationships, promoted technical and vocational education and training, but failed to make them an officially indispensable part of the national school education system.

It was in the twentieth century that vocational education was institutionalized in most Western countries. For example, in 1919 the French parliament ratified the Vocational Technical Education Bill, historically referred to as the Charter of Technical Education. Since then, the French government has repeatedly promulgated supplementary statutes to perfect a system of technical and vocational education. Similar to France, Britain issued the Butler Education Act in 1944. Consequently, technical secondary schools began to share an equal position with other schools, and they were included in the main body of the British education system.

At the end of the nineteenth century, a variety of high schools were established in the USA for different purposes: industrial, agricultural, commercial, polytechnic, and so on. At first, these schools were unequal in status, regarded as less worthwhile than general public schools. To eliminate this imbalance, in 1918 the Commission on the Reorganization of Secondary Education issued the "Cardinal Principles of Secondary Education," which required both general and vocational aspects in secondary education and the establishment of comprehensive schools for instruction in a range of subjects across the academic, liberal, and vocational spectrum. Following these principles, in the 1920s various specialized middle schools were converted into comprehensive high schools that embraced all curricula in a single unified organization.

In the first half of the twentieth century, most Western countries enacted legislation to define and regulate vocational education, making it an indispensable part of national education systems and one of the major impetuses for social production and economy growth.

5.1.1.5   Formation and Development of Modern Primary and Secondary School Systems

Western modern primary and secondary school systems were shaped in the mid-nineteenth century and were basically institutionalized in the mid-twentieth century, with dual-track and single-track systems developing.

The dual-track system comprised two educational systems which were separated from and unrelated to each other, serving children of the ruling classes and of the lower classes respectively. Some European countries such as the UK, France and Germany were historically typical in their implementation of such a system. For this reason, it was also referred to as the European or Western European system. In the above-mentioned three countries, the system serving the ruling classes was developed first, made up of secondary and higher schools. Grammar schools in the UK, French national schools, and German liberal arts schools all fell into this category.

The system for the masses, on the other hand, was mainly made up of primary schools for elementary instruction and secondary schools for vocational education. Primary schools could trace their origin to the medieval schools founded in Western Europe by the burghers who were becoming more prominent in the increasingly important cities and newly founded population centers. Secondary schools, such as the *Realschule* of Germany and the modern schools of England and France, however, were built up by the emerging bourgeoisie during the first Industrial Revolution, which taught the mother tongue, basic knowledge of modern sciences, and modern foreign languages. Unfortunately, until the beginning of the twentieth century governments in most cases neither recognized the secondary schools as formal educational institutions nor admitted their pupils as qualified candidates for higher education.

To improve the situation, in the first half of the twentieth century the UK, France, Germany, and some other Western countries set a goal to establish a single-track school system, which was basically achieved around the Second World War.

The single-track school system covered several stages of national education. Citizens in principle had equal opportunities to receive education at every stage, and had equal access to schools with the same quality of services. Such a system played an important role in guaranteeing equal education opportunities. The USA was one of the countries that employed such a system, so the single-track system is also referred to as the American-style system.

5.1.1.6 Diversification of Secondary Education
After the mid-twentieth century, in response to the diversification in industrial structures, the branch-type school system was created to cultivate varied types and levels of talents.

A branch-type system is one that introduces a single and uniform elementary and partial secondary system for all children, after which the system is diversified into a variety of grade-level configurations or streams. The system formed in this way is like a fork, so it is also called the fork-system. One example is US grade-level schools. After the Second World War, several reforms were made in the USA and, succeeding the 8–4 plan that dominated the country from the 1920s to the 1950s and the 6–6 plan that followed, the 6–3–3 pattern was formed, covering six years of elementary school, three years of middle school, and another three years of high school. This plan began to bloom in many other countries after the Second World War and was developed into different variations or schemes in the USA, such as 5–3–4, 4–4–4, and 6–2–4 patterns. Meanwhile, in Britain, on the other hand, four major types of public secondary schools were established: grammar schools, technical schools, secondary modern schools, and comprehensive schools; in France general high schools, technical high schools, and vocational high schools developed; and in Germany there were four distinct tracks: the *Hauptschule*, *Realschule*, *Gesamtschule*, and *Gymnasium*.

5.1.2   Higher Education

5.1.2.1 Enriched Discipline
Western higher education may date back to ancient Greece, when poets and natural philosophers began to impart their doctrines and theories to their students. Akademia, founded by Plato in 387 BC, for example, was a place for himself and his students to study and research philosophy and to

carry out group activities; this is believed to be the origin of ancient Western higher education.

In the first century BC, institutions focusing on rhetoric began to take form. Their curricula were partially adopted by some of the universities that were organized in the medieval period.

After the Roman Empire split, the Eastern Roman Empire became the center of higher education. In 425 AD the University of Constantinople was founded, offering a variety of higher learning.

5.1.2.2   Establishment of the Basic University Structure

It is generally believed that the establishment we call a university today was first founded in medieval Italy and France, and gradually spread to other regions, such as Britain, in the Late Middle Ages.

In the late eleventh century, crowds of eager students from many parts of Europe headed for Bologna in northern Italy to study law. They banded themselves into various unions and associations divided by language and ethnicity, then recruited masters and scholars; and eventually in 1088 the University of Bologna was created, autonomously administrated by students. It is recognized as the first independent legal higher education entity.

However, the University of Paris, which took shape between 1150 and 1170 and was characterized both by discipline-based organizational and administrative units (faculties) and by a wider variety of courses such as liberal arts, law, medicine, and theology, among which theology was the highest and liberal arts was preparatory for the others, is more widely regarded as the mother of European universities and the archetype of all other medieval universities throughout Northern Europe.

Different from those on the European continent, the medieval universities in the UK, typically the University of Oxford founded in 1185 and the University of Cambridge established in the early thirteenth century, took colleges as their essential teaching and administrative units. At first these were boarding and lodging houses arranged for poor students, then they gradually developed into places where teachers and students of the same discipline lived, taught, and studied, and later they became autonomous or semi-autonomous academic bodies, equipped with libraries, accommodation, and dining halls, as well as teaching facilities. In the sixteenth century, colleges became autonomous institutions specializing in teaching. Except for the privilege of awarding degrees, the universities at this time had no right to interfere in the administrative affairs of their colleges.

In conclusion, by the end of the fifteenth century European universities embodied four chief features. First, they enjoyed autonomy. Second, permitting students and scholars to flow freely at least within Europe, they were really international academic institutions. Third, with their strong religious overtones, a large number of medieval universities were dominated by the Christian Church. Fourth, the syllabus was typically limited to four disciplines: liberal arts, law, theology, and medicine. The so-called "liberal arts" covered both arts and sciences: grammar, rhetoric, logic, arithmetic, geometry, astronomy, and music. Completion of liberal arts was a prerequisite for students who wanted to study the other three disciplines.

5.1.2.3 Rise of Universities for Applied Sciences

In the first half of the eighteenth century, in response to the demands made by the growth in national economies, institutions that aimed to foster practical talents began to emerge in Western countries. France and Germany were among the earliest countries in the world to open such institutions.

France enjoyed a boom in economy and industry in the eighteenth century. To drive the wheels of expanded production, a variety of professionals and specialists were in great demand. In the meantime, ambitions for colonies throughout the world put the nation in urgent need of qualified servicemen. The government therefore decided to open up small professional schools (*écoles spéciales*) to cultivate applied talents that would provide professional knowledge and production skills. These schools were higher institutions established under the principle of imparting a science, a skill, or a profession. Among the earliest were the Artillery School (1720), the Road & Bridge School of Paris (1747), and the School of Mines in Paris (1783). These schools, covering engineering, business, administration, agriculture, and higher education in general, initiated a new level of specialist training in France, and later they were collectively referred to as the *grandes écoles*. Of these *grandes écoles*, engineering institutions accounted for a large proportion, and as they stood out for being prestigious and for training high-qualified engineers, they were also called engineering schools. With the rise of education for practical professionals, the domination of four disciplines (arts, law, theology, and medicine) in higher learning, which had been the case in the Western world since the Middle Ages, was broken.

Late in this period, a large variety of specialized schools and technical colleges, such as the Mine College, Berlin Technical Institute, the Veterinary School, and Berlin Architecture School, were opened in Germany, laying much weight on practical applications and concentrating on training students to be capable technicians and administrators. By the mid-nineteenth century, some of these schools had developed into poly-technical schools or technological universities.

In the nineteenth century, cultivating qualified professionals became a prestigious task for higher education in many Western countries. In 1826, for example, London University was established in the UK. Theology was dropped from the syllabus but a wide range of natural sciences and engineer-ing subjects were introduced, with a focus beginning on training applied professionals. This ushered higher education in the UK into the modern era.

Under the influence of London University, in the latter half of the nine-teenth century the UK witnessed the rise of city colleges to train qualified commercial and industrial personnel, such as factory managers, designers, industrial researchers, and sales forces.

Similar changes were made in the USA. After the American Revolutionary War (1775–1783), voices that suggested building practical studies became louder. The Military Academy at West Point and Rensselaer Polytechnic were set up in 1802 and 1824 respectively, thus triggering the reform of disciplines and specialties in traditional arts and science insti-tutes. Thereafter, professional and technical training was made part of American higher education. A few decades later, responding to the indus-trial revolution, the Morrill Act of 1862 was enacted, and accordingly federally controlled land was granted to every state: this could be sold for funds to establish and endow "land-grant" colleges, most of which ulti-mately became large public universities.

5.1.2.4 Creation of the Research University

Under the leadership of Wilhelm von Humboldt, a liberal Prussian educa-tional reformer, the first Western research-oriented university was founded in Germany in 1810, and given the name Humboldt University of Berlin. With ideas centered around the new humanism, such as independence of academia, autonomous administration, academic freedom, the unity of research and teaching, and the integration of the natural sciences, social sciences, and humanities, the Humboldt University emphasized both teaching and research and established an academic degree system that granted PhD degrees, thus setting an example for other Western universities.

Under the impact of this, the renowned yet traditional Cambridge and Oxford decided to introduce natural sciences and scientific research into their curricula, beginning the move to intensive academic specialization. The German model also attracted students from all over the world, especially from the USA, most of whom on returning to their own countries became the main force behind the spread of modern German higher education ideals—and the backbone of prestigious US universities such as Harvard, Yale, Johns Hopkins, and Princeton.

5.1.2.5 Diversification in the Level and Structure of Higher Education

After the Second World War, the recovery and prosperity of social production and economic construction promoted an unprecedented development in higher education: the educational structure became more diversified and more rational. A large number of non-traditional higher institutions emerged: the French STS and IUT, the British polytechnic, the German *fachhochschule*, the US community college, among others. Meanwhile, all the higher institutions, traditional or non-traditional, were included in the same system, with credits equally granted and interchanged.

Besides the STS and the IUT, which were short-run higher technical programs, France established the master's degree in 1966 for the *universités* and the doctorate in the 1970s for the *grandes écoles*, the two long-term institutions that made up the French dual system of higher education.

Like France, the UK also diversified its higher education structure. After the Second World War, the British tradition which gave too much emphasis to elite education changed with the increased demands of society for practical talents. In 1963, the government issued the Robbins Report, recommending the immediate expansion of universities and stating that all post-secondary education should be regarded as higher education. In 1965, the UK further stated that the relatively autonomous traditional university sector should co-exist with the predominantly public institutional establishments (mostly technical colleges and colleges of education). Thereafter thirty-one polytechnics were set up, mainly responsible for training technical engineers. These offered more professionally oriented and locally relevant courses, which created more chances for the students to apply their knowledge in practice. At the start of the 1990s, all the polytechnics were promoted to universities.

In the post-war years Germany, responding to economic and social development, also put more weight on the cultivation of practical talents.

With the Humboldt tradition broken, new types of universities such as Ruhr-University Bochum and the University of Konstanz were established in the 1960s and onwards. Meanwhile, vocational higher education was enhanced and the "3+1" curriculum structure was defined: three years learning theory at school and a one year internship in firms and factories.

Improvements were also made in the USA. At the turn of the twentieth century, two-year junior colleges were established. The University of Chicago took the lead in 1896 by defining the first two years of university studies as "junior college," and associate degrees were awarded from 1900. Following this, in 1907 the California State Legislature authorized high schools to found local junior colleges. This triggered a nationwide surge in the number of junior colleges, which stood apart secondary schools and universities. In 1947, the President Commission Report titled "Higher Education for Democracy" renamed junior colleges as community colleges. In 1960, California initiated a tripartite system in its Master Plan, which once again blazed a new trail ahead of other states.

5.1.2.6 Transdisciplinary Reforms

A further transition began in the 1980s, with transdisciplinary and multidisciplinary studies highlighted in higher education. In the UK, for example, integrated curricula were set up: physics plus mathematics, biology plus economics, and mechanical engineering plus French, for example.

5.2   Unique Features

The history of social development and educational traditions being different from country to country, there are various education systems in Western cultures. The unique features of five typical systems are sketched in this section.

5.2.1   The UK: Diversified Secondary and Further Education

The UK system is quite complex, with lots of variants in different areas. Mainly it covers early years, primary, secondary, further, and higher education. Primary and secondary education is compulsory for all children aged five (four in Northern Ireland) to sixteen years old, upon the completion of which children (except those in Scotland) take GCSE examinations, and then move on to diversified options.

5.2.1.1 Secondary Education

A wide variety of secondary schools co-exist in the UK. Because of their sources of funds, these schools can be broadly classified into two groups: state-maintained schools and independent schools. State schools include grammar schools, modern schools, technical schools, and comprehensive schools, the last being the most common. The different types are distinguished from each other in their tasks and purposes.

Almost all secondary schools in the UK provide both junior and senior levels of secondary education, which, often covering three and two years respectively, have no clear cut-off point in between. In general, what is taught at school in the first three years is a broad base of mandatory subjects, while in the fourth and fifth years most are selective courses for GCSEs, which normally mark the end of compulsory education. However, after taking GCSEs at sixteen, some pupils stay at school and choose to study GCE A-level courses or more vocational qualifications. To meet the needs of these pupils, many secondary (mostly grammar or comprehensive) schools extend their service to seven years, spanning three consecutive stages, the last of which, covering the final two years (Year 12 and Year 13), is for post-secondary further studies. In England and Wales, this stage is commonly termed the sixth form.

5.2.1.2 Further Education

By law, children who have completed their GCSEs at the age of sixteen can either leave school for work or continue into further education. Further education in the UK is a general heading for a long list of post-compulsory learning and training, ranging from very basic to university entrance level, covering the required preparatory courses offered to sixteen- to eighteen-year-old school children who plan to move on to college or university and part-time or full-time career-based training for adults who are at work.

There are a wide variety of further education institutions in the UK. They include sixth forms within secondary schools, independent sixth-form colleges, and further education colleges.

Originally designed to prepare academically elite students who stayed on in grammar schools to transit from secondary to higher education, sixth forms are characterized mainly by specialized academic subjects that most typically lead to A-level (or equivalent) qualifications, a prerequisite for admission to colleges and universities.

Further education colleges, on the other hand, offer a wider range of subjects to a greater diversity of population. Apart from full- or part-time academic programs, there are a long list of work-based training courses, such as technology, craftsmanship, art and design, catering, engineering, and finance, from which the students can choose more flexibly. Alongside secondary school leavers, a further education college also serves community members, on-the-job employees who hope to receive further training, adults who want to enter a new career or return to school to study, and those who want to develop new skills or specialties.

In institutions for further education, students are free to choose courses or create their own selections. The most popular programs include A-levels, GNVQs, BTECs, NVQs, and international baccalaureate diploma programs. Some of these programs can be taken in a wide range of subjects and at different levels.

5.2.2   France: Coherent School System

The school system in France is well planned, with all its parts interlinked. It covers three major consecutive stages: primary, secondary, and higher education, each of which includes several substages or cycles. All the substages, cycles, and stages are streamlined and tightly interlinked. The overall framework contains nursery school (*école maternelle*) for ages two to five, primary school (*école primaire*) for ages six to eleven, lower secondary school (*collège*) for ages twelve to fifteen/sixteen, upper secondary school (*lycée*) for ages sixteen to eighteen, followed by university (*université*).

5.2.2.1 Nursery, Primary, and Secondary Education

Nursery schooling in France is not mandatory or compulsory, but it is given exactly the same importance as primary education. Although affiliated to primary schools, French nursery schools have their own specific teaching programs, which take games as the major teaching method.

In primary schools, pupils sharing similar intelligence, learning ability, and interests join in homogeneous groups, where the members, at their own physical and life pace, work on the subjects that particularly cater to their groups.

Primary school students are given time to rest and relax. Normally, a year's schooling time involves only thirty-five academic weeks and five equal terms. Besides the two-month summer vacation, students enjoy two weeks of rest after each term, which lasts only seven weeks.

French secondary education contains two substages: the lower and the higher. The lower is fulfilled by *collèges* and often lasts four years, while the upper is carried on by *lycées* in three or four years.

The classes at *collège* level are structured into four grades, the sixth, fifth, fourth, and third (from lower to upper). In the sixth grade, students consolidate the knowledge they acquired in primary schools, begin to study new subjects, and explore new learning methods, and as a result they transition from primary to secondary education. The fifth and fourth are grades in which students learn in depth and in breadth. In the third grade, guidelines for entrance to three different types of upper secondary education and information about jobs are given, so that the students can decide which type of lycée they would like to go to and which major they should choose.

Similar to primary schools, the collèges also adopt homogeneous groupings. These groups are not fixed in the *collèges*. To ensure educational equality, they manage to keep pace with the changes in the students' learning levels in a reflection of French educational ideals: no student is to be given up on or underestimated.

Lycées, on the other hand, are divided into three streams: the *lycée général*, the *lycée technologique*, and the *lycée professionnel*. At the end of the final year of schooling in each type, the vast majority of students are awarded a *baccalauréat* diploma (colloquially *le bac*). To obtain it they must pass the multi-subject national *baccalauréat* examinations, different types of which vary with the series and streams the students have chosen at their *lycée*.

The *lycée général* and the *lycée technologique* are the mainstream part of French upper secondary education. Both of them cover three years of study and two learning cycles, namely *cycle de détermination* (the first year) and *cycle terminal* (the second and third years). The first year involves as many as nine major subjects covering a wide range and two specialist subjects selected from a prescribed list, which ensures a broad general education. In the second year the pupils are divided into general and technological streams, where they stay until the end of the third year. Under these streams, there are several series of courses to choose (four series for the general stream and eight series for the technological stream). Students from different series take different *baccalauréat* examinations at the end of their secondary education, after which those from the general stream often step on to two or more years of post-*baccalauréat* university studies, while those from the technological stream mostly go on with short-term studies.

Unlike general and technological education, good-quality vocational training and vocational courses are provided in separate professional *lycées*, where career-based curricula are offered to students who prefer a hands-on educational approach and would like to go straight to work rather than continue into higher education. To satisfy the specific needs of various industries that the students may work for after graduation, a total of more than 100 types of vocational diplomas are arranged for the students. French professional high school programs may last two or four years, leading to the Certificate d'Aptitude Professionelle (CAP), the Brevet d'Etudes Professionelles (BEP), or the Diplôme du Baccalauréat Professionnel (DBP).

5.2.2.2 *Higher Education System*

The French higher education system provides three levels of programs, with short or long cycles. Short-cycle programs are offered by university Institutes of Technology (IUT) and Sections of Technicians Superiors (STS) in *lycées*. Long-cycle programs are provided mainly by publicly funded universities (universités) and the elite higher education establishments known as *grandes écoles*.

To gain entry to public universities, students must possess a *baccalauréat*. For this reason, the academic levels in university are identified in four grades, with *Bac*+1 +4 respectively recognized for grades 1–4.

Public university comprises three successive cycles, each corresponding to a nationally recognized diploma. The first cycle, which is multidisciplinary, covers two years of learning and leads to the Diplôme d'Etudes Universitaires Générales (DEUG). The second cycle lasts one to two years, and is open to students with a DEUG. Qualified graduates who complete the first year of learning get a *license*. If they stay on for a second year and fulfill all the learning tasks, they are awarded a *maîtrise*. The third cycle (two phases of another one to four years) opens up three tracks after the *maîtrise*. The first lasts one year and leads to a Diplome d'Etudes Approfondies (DEA), the prerequisite diploma preparing students for PhD studies, or the parallel Diplome d'Etudes Supérieures Spécialisées (DESS), an advanced professional qualification for access to professional life. In most cases, if you hold a DESS you cannot apply for a doctorate degree. Following the DEA is the second phase of doctoral study, lasting two to three years. In this phase, students further study a specific field or subject and learn to undertake research by working in a research team, based on which they prepare their dissertations, this being overseen by their doctoral supervisors. After successfully completing their studies and passing their dissertation examination, the candidates are awarded a doctoral degree.

In 2002, the French government issued a significant decree, demanding the implementation of the tripartite LMD system which is widely adopted in Europe: License (Bachelor, *bac* + three years), Master (*bac* + five years), and Doctorate (*bac* + eight years).

Different from the public universities, the *grandes écoles*, often presti-gious institutions focusing on a single subject area, such as engineering or business, offer three-year programs to elite students who have stood out in national written and oral exams. Before being enrolled in a *grande écoles*, students must attend two or more years of initial higher education after receiving a baccalauréat from high school. For the most part, this preparatory education is given in special classes known as *prépas*. *Prépas* are located in a number of selected high schools throughout the country and are often quite selective in their admission of students. After two years of *prépas*, students take the most selective examinations. Only those who achieve excellence are granted admission to a *grande école*. These are widely regarded as prestigious, and traditionally have produced the most competitive graduates for the government and prestige enterprises.

5.2.3   Germany: Unique Secondary and Vocational Education

Germany was one of the first countries in the world to have enforced national compulsory education. The twelve years of compulsory education begin for all children at the age of six and end at the age of eighteen. Students must attend at least nine years of full-time general education (although the school day ends fairly early). Afterwards, they must receive three more years of compulsory education at upper secondary level in either a full-time school (general or vocational) or a part-time vocational school, such as a *Berufsschule*, which teaches part-time vocational courses in conjunction with on-the-job training, such as apprenticeship by industry.

In general, children attend primary school (*Grundschule*) for four years (six years in Berlin and Brandenburg). Having completed their primary education, those in most states often attend one of the three traditional types of secondary schools: the *Hauptschule* (typically five to six years), the *Realschule* (typically six years), and the *Gymnasium* (typically eight to nine years). So beginning with primary schooling, the longest basic education in Germany lasts thirteen years.

Traditionally, the German education system is dominated by public schools, and almost all of these are tuition fee free (international students may have to pay fees for some programs); textbooks and other school sup-plies are partly free.

Despite the general situation described above, it should be noted that since each of the federal states (*Länder*) is responsible for its own educa-tional policies, the German education system has a decentralized struc-ture, with quite a few variants from state to state.

5.2.3.1 Secondary Education

Secondary education in Germany is unique, with the traditional tripartite system as its distinguished feature; this includes the above-mentioned three types of traditional schools.

Pupils complete their primary education at such a young age that it tends to be their parents as well as teachers who help them to make the choice about which type of school to attend for their secondary education; this in some ways determines their prospects for self-development and potential job orientation after leaving school.

If children get into the *Hauptschule*, they will learn both fundamental academic courses and a wide variety of specific courses that are closely related to their real-world life and future career. As a general intermediate school for mandatory education in Germany, the *Hauptschule* places a major emphasis on preparing students for vocational education or training. Graduates with a leaving certificate from a *Hauptschule* typically go into vocational schools for a wide range of job training. Upon completion of the training, they often start their work as technicians.

The *Realschule*, a popular type of secondary school in Germany, is an intermediate school that underlines both general academic learning and various specialized capability training, so as to cultivate all-round talent. Applied natural and social sciences closely related to students' lives are highlighted. The *Realschule* entitles its graduates to transfer to a regular *Gymnasium* or to enter a full-time vocational school, such as a dual vocational school or a *Fachoberschule* (higher technical school).

As opposed to the *Hauptschule* and the *Realschule*, the more distinguished *Gymnasium*, historically the top selective school for a small number of royal or gifted children, provides the most stringent and top-ranking academic education in the liberal arts to the academic elite. A *Gymnasium* contains two phases: orientation (under Grade 7) and post-orientation (Grades 7–13), the latter covering two levels. Level I (Grades 7–10) is compulsory, focusing on the foundation courses; while Level II (the last two to three years) offers selective courses according to individual preference (with certain prerequisite conditions and restrictions).

An eligible *Gymnasium* leaver can go straight to university, which produces senior professionals, high-level executives, and competent vocational trainees. In comparison with those from the *Hauptschule* and the *Realschule*, graduates from a *Gymnasium* often have more promising futures and broader choices of career.

Beyond the tripartite system, in some German states there is a new type of secondary school—the *Gesamtschule*, a combination and substitute for the three traditional types, similar to the US comprehensive high school in some ways. It was first introduced in Germany in the spring of 1969 on the initiative of the German Education Council and was established during the 1970s and 1980s as an experimental alternative to the tripartite system for three reasons: to accommodate the growing democratic trend and to release the competition for entry to the *Gymnasiums* or the *Realschule*; to provide equal education opportunities for all young people and thus eliminate the barriers that exist between different social classes; and to integrate all types of programs into a single school, thus facilitating the students' switching between different tracks in accordance with their aptitude and special requirements. In 1982, secretaries for cultural and educational affairs from each state attended a joint conference at which they arrived at an agreement that recognized the equivalent validity of *Gesamtschule* diplomas awarded across the country, making the *Gesamtschule* an integral part of the recognized school system. But eventually factors such as politics, economy, and historical culture stopped the *Gesamtschule* system from taking the place of the tripartite system; it developed into a supplementary track.

The *Gesamtschule* may be co-operative or integrated. A co-operative *Gesamtschule* retains the traditional hierarchical structure by incorporating the three traditional tracks (*Hauptschule, Realschule*, and *Gymnasium*), but allowing convenient transfer across the three tracks. An integrated *Gesamtschule*, on the other hand, does not use the three-track organizational structure but combines them into one, in which students are divided into different classes based on their subject competence or their preferences. The *Gesamtschule* leavers stream into different paths, similar to the corresponding traditional school leavers.

5.2.3.2   Vocational Education and Training

The German government has always put vocational education and training (VET) at the core of its ambition, and has set the world a good example in pushing forward the nation and its economy through the development of a successful and sophisticated VET. German citizens do not run the rat race in pursuit of higher education diplomas; instead, youngsters are offered opportunities to receive various types of VET. The Vocational Education and Training Act is a solid basis for vocational training, under which the completion of three years' compulsory vocational training is required of every citizen who has failed to continue their secondary education in a *Gymnasium* after completing nine years of compulsory general education.

German vocational education enjoys a high reputation because of its capacity for cultivating high-quality talents in a broad spectrum of professions. For example, in 2006, the country recognized 342 training occupations (legally regulated and given national validity), covering almost all aspects of life, society, and economy, and establishing a complete, interactive, and integrated system of job training. The VET services in Germany are mainly offered in the following types of school.

Dual Vocational School

The dual vocational school is a major type of German compulsory vocational school, serving those who have passed through a *Hauptschule* or a *Realschule*. It is noted for its dual-track training system, which combines part-time theoretical grounding in the school and practical training in an enterprise.

Based on the framework of a dual training contract, every week the trainees take one to two days of part-time courses at school and three to four days of practical job training at a host company. There is also a choice of block release programs, in which both theoretical learning and practical training are offered.

This schooling and apprenticeship normally lasts three years in total. Successful completion leads to a graduation diploma offered by the school and a certificate of training by the company, with which the school leaver can enter a particular field of work as an apprentice, an assistant, or a skilled worker. But in fact most graduates choose to move to a specialized vocational school and study there for one to three years, and then sit the examinations for various vocational qualification certificates; for master craftsman, technician, decorator, sculptor, accountant, and so on.

Specialized Vocational School

Of the other important establishment for vocational education in Germany is the specialized vocational school. This is responsible for both practical training and theoretical instruction. Unlike the dual-track school, it prepares and trains students for a specific vocational area within the school independently, instead of in co-operation with an enterprise. It offers a wide range of training, including those normally not undertaken by enterprises or workshops, such as childcare, geriatric nursing, business assistant, music, and foreign languages. The duration of schooling and admission requirements vary from school to school. Normally, one to three school years are required. Graduates from the *Hauptschule*, the *Realschule*, and the dual-track vocational school are enrolled in different schools based on the schools' entry requirements. Those who successfully complete their schooling in a three-year full-time specialized vocational school graduate with a vocational qualification certificate, which is nationally recognized for the relevant jobs.

Specialized School
In Germany, people who need to run businesses individually or do any administrative job at middle level need more than a junior-level vocational qualification certificate. They are required to sit further examinations to obtain an advanced qualification certificate in their particular area of business or industry. For this purpose they go to a specialized school, which is designed to offer further education to those who enjoy both practical experience and a junior certificate. The educational tasks mainly cover more specialized vocational education, special training for changing jobs, and further general education. Successful completion of this is a prerequisite for starting a business in one's own name and for careers in the middle levels of business, administration, and so on. A specialized school is available to students who have some work experience or a junior-level qualification certificate in their field.

Specialized school courses may be taken part time, full time, or in the evening, for six months to two years. Upon completion, students are granted both recognized professional and technical certificates and qualifications for a specialized college.

Specialized Upper Secondary School
Combining general education with vocational training, this type of school mainly aims to prepare students for a specialized college, and thus focuses on both general knowledge and professional theory and practice.

A specialized upper secondary school lasts two years (Grades 11–12), with graduates from the *Realschule* or the equivalents as its major enrolment.

5.2.4   *Sweden: Unique Upper Secondary Curriculum and Extensive Adult Education*

Sweden attaches special importance to education. Education from primary school to university is free, and the cost of adult education is shared between the government and employers.

The nine-year compulsory education is mostly completed in the same school, without primary or secondary division. There are also some schools that divide the nine years into sections that are six and three years in duration.

5.2.4.1 Upper Secondary Education

Upper secondary education is not mandatory, but about 98% of students enter a senior high school after the nine-year compulsory schooling is complete. Senior high school lasts for three years, with a uniquely designed curriculum structure.

In 1971, upper secondary education in Sweden was reorganized into an integrated system that encompassed both general and vocational high schools. In 1993, the content and organization underwent substantial changes. The curricula were further divided into sixteen national programs, including natural and social sciences, arts, business administration, and childcare. In the school year 2000–2001, a technology program was added. Which programs a student takes depends on his specific interests and skills. For example, a student who aims to go to college may take the natural or social science program, while another may choose the arts program. Whichever programs the students choose, they must study eight common core subjects, which cover a third of total class periods.

The programs are endowed with the following characteristics:

1) The sizes of programs vary greatly. Of the seventeen national programs, the most common two are social science (*samhällskunskap*) and natural sciences (*naturvetenskap*), which give priority to general education and enjoy about 45% of the total enrolment. Each of the other fifteen programs, primarily oriented toward vocational education, cover less than 5% of the total enrolment.
2) There is only one type of comprehensive upper secondary school in Sweden, but no single school covers all seventeen programs. About half of the schools teach natural sciences and social science; the less common programs, such as those focusing on energy, food, and natural resource utilization, are taught by only less than a tenth of the schools.
3) It is the types and the timing of the programs, rather than the ages of the students, that determine which classes they will attend. Grades do not exist. The students do not stay down but re-take if they fail a program.
4) Whichever program is taken, it leads to students' qualifications for higher education.

5.2.4.2 Adult Education

Adult education in Sweden is basically free of charge. Laws and regulations stipulate that the government has an obligation to offer job training to those aged sixteen to eighteen who failed to enter high school and failed to get a regular job. Employees have the right to ask for leave with pay for further studies, and are able to obtain special financial aids. People can receive free labor market (re-employment) training and at the same time get a living allowance. Since the 1990s, vocational and adult education have been the focus of Swedish education reform, which mainly aims to build a more flexible education system to better adapt to the demands of the market and society.

Adult education takes many different forms. The following are the major types.

Folk High School: The Boarding Adult College

The folk high school is one of the oldest adult education institutions in Sweden. In 2008, there were about 150 folk high schools throughout the country, with an enrolment of about 250,000 students each year. They have the freedom to decide on syllabuses under the relevant laws and regulations and offer various courses to students. These last two or three years and some entitle students to attend college.

Study Circles

A study circle is a group of friends who collectively decide on a subject or topic of study and then embark on a journey of discovery in an organized and collaborative way, often through conversations and discussions.

The most distinctive features of study circles include: they are made up of friends and have overall criteria and specific terms that all the members must abide by; members must work together in advance to make their choice on the fields or subjects to be studied; and they must create a systematic scheme to fulfill their pre-planned learning tasks.

A study circle does not need teachers. To facilitate study, one of the members acts as the leader. Content and learning methods are determined by the participants themselves, based on their common interests and needs. Reading material is often used. Arts and citizenship lessons take up about two-thirds of the total learning time. Study circles can enjoy government subsidies.

The study circle began in 1902 in Lund in northern Sweden, and is now is the most common Swedish adult education method.

Comprehensive Universities

Comprehensive adult universities in Sweden offer extensive educational services at both upper and post-upper secondary levels, ranging from popular education (such as culture, language, and arts) to vocational training (such as continuing education and labor market training). The courses, either formal or informal, can be provided during the day or in the evening. The teaching is organized in accordance to adults' characteristics, highlighting the development of their abilities and skills, stressing the link between theory and practice.

The Swedish adult education system also covers other kinds of schools and programs, such as adult schools run by the municipalities, training programs supported by the Swedish National Labor Market Board, free programs for short-term training, on-the-job training offered by enterprises, broadcast education programs, correspondence courses offered by post-secondary institutions, and those by many upper secondary schools and universities. All such organizations and programs help to make up an extensive educational network for adults.

5.2.5   The United States of America: Community College and Education

There were two great educational inventions in the USA in the twentieth century. First was the foundation of the "6–3–3" system in middle and primary schools, which deeply influenced countries all over the world; second was the establishment of a higher education system that has special characteristics and also community colleges.

5.2.5.1 Community College

American community colleges grew rapidly in the years between 1955 and 1965, when a new one emerged every week on average. The colleges adhere to the principle that they should serve the local community all the time, claiming not to set restrictions based on students' backgrounds, such as skin color, race, religious beliefs, and age. Their multiple educational functions, flexible teaching management system, diversified methods of learning, cheap tuition, and high graduate employment rates mean they are well received by the US public and are widely recognized as institutes of the people. At present, 44% of US college students and 50% of freshmen are studying in community colleges. They have taken a very important place in the education system.

Community colleges are different from the general institutions of higher education in the following ways.

First, they belong to and are an important part of the community. With their supreme aim to serve the needs of the community, they often update their departments, subjects, and teaching content. They also open their stadiums, theatre auditoriums, libraries, and other educational resources to community residents. Taken as cultural and educational centers and a powerful force in the construction of community, they receive community funds and resources that improve convenience in research, teaching, and other aspects.

Second, they perform multiple functions:

1) Transfer. Having completed the first two years of courses for an associate degree in a community college, students can transfer to Grade 3 of a four-year institution of higher education and begin to study the last two years of courses to obtain a bachelor's degree.

2) Vocational preparation. Roughly half of the community college students are majoring in vocational or technical courses, and this number continues to increase.

3) Remedial education. This is for high school graduates who are not academically ready to enroll in college-level courses.

4) Community courses. These are, for example, housekeeping, employment counseling, leisure entertainment, gardening, and crafts, which in most cases do not lead to a degree, diploma, or credit.

5) General education. The colleges provide a comprehensive education with a variety of disciplines and fundamental studies from multiple perspectives, teaching students to practice rights and obligations, to develop ideas about ethics and values, and to improve their abilities, such as those related to effective communication and reading, substantive independent thinking, problem-solving, and value identification, as well as imparting knowledge about culture and environment, health and disease, conflict and insecurity, family life arrangement, and activity creation.

6) International education. Educating and training globally competitive and multi-cultural citizens by offering international study plans, short term study and travel plans, special lectures or courses, international exhibitions, and learning resources exchange.

Third, they enjoy remarkable adaptability:

1) They have multi-disciplinary and comprehensive faculties and curricula which cover almost everything: mechanics, chemical industry, vehicle repairing, medical care, automation, accountancy, law, cosmetology, sculpture, tailoring, photography, and so on.
2) They meet the various needs of the students. There are courses for two-year associate or four-year bachelor's degrees, or a one-year life education certificate as well as those without credits or certification. The teaching differs from one person to another to provide the most convenience for the students. Special conditions of learning are created for the disabled and there are nurseries for the children of young parent students.
3) They keep pace with the development of the community, making timely extensions and adjustments in their goals and continuous renewal of the courses, departments, and teaching content. For example, originally they focused on transfer education, but today vocational technical education accounts for half of the total courses. On the other hand, some departments have been eliminated.
4) The cheap tuition favors students. Apart from the public and various foundations, funding for community colleges in large measure comes from local tax revenue. With favorable tuition fees (generally only 50–60% of those of a public university) the colleges have promoted the popularization of higher education in the USA.
5) Part-time teachers, who account for more than half of the faculty, outnumber full-time teachers, although the courses they are responsible for are in smaller demand. As entrepreneurs who are familiar with the status quo of their industries, experts in their fields, or experienced front-line engineers and technicians, they are in a good position to teach short-term professional courses. Full-time teachers, in comparison, tend to teach long-term basic courses that are in greater demand.
6) Several community colleges in a big city can be combined into a city university. The city university headquarters is based at one of the community colleges, mainly playing a role in coordinating the needs of city education, so as to avoid the waste of resources and allowing direct intervention regarding the administration of the staff and college property.

5.2.5.2 Community Education

A community college functions as just one of the major bases for community education. As an indispensable part of life for the public, community education must be adjusted to different residents who have different needs, and therefore should be organized and implemented through a diversity of channels.

Together with community colleges, general schools at all levels and newly built community schools can provide education for communities.

The general-school-based programs cover more than 200 topics in forty-seven categories and are usually timetabled in the evenings or at weekends to accommodate full-time working people. Besides courses, the programs include seminars, lectures, cultural and sports activities, exhibitions, consultations, and other kinds of services. Some of the courses are related to credits and the granting of certificates and diplomas. Others aim to help people gain occupational skills that will better prepare them for the workplace and potential job openings, or raise the quality of their participation in household management, recreation, and leisure.

With the common goal of recognizing and serving the needs of the local community, education offered by the newly built community schools or colleges is diverse in objective, form, and content. The schools of the community mainly provide secondary-level education. Such schools include common community schools, community central schools, community comprehensive secondary schools, and community primary professional schools. The community colleges are mostly engaged in higher education.

In community activity centers and other public places, there are programs provided by community organizations related to health, welfare, youth, and so on, focusing on physical and psychological health, ethnic relations, employment, environmental protection, pollution control, citizenship, and combating crime. Community education also comes from some business people and enterprises, mainly involving business management, vocational and technical skills, interpersonal relationships, and leisure activities. This kind of education is often provided to members of the community and employees. To ensure the implementation of public policies, the government at all levels also carries on educational activities for the community.

5.3   POPULAR TRENDS

5.3.1   *Learning Society and Life-Long Learning System*

American educator Robert M. Hutchins, in a book first published in 1968, argued that a "learning society" not only offers part-time adult education to every man and woman at every stage of life, but succeeds in transforming society's values in such a way that learning, fulfillment, becoming human is its aim, and that all its institutions are directed to this end.

In its report "Learn to be: the World of Education Today and Tomorrow," issued in 1972, the United Nations Educational, Scientific and Cultural Organization (UNESCO) states that the advent of a learning society "can only be conceived as a process of close interweaving between education and the social, political and economic fabric, which covers the family unit and civic life. It implies that every citizen should have the means of learning, training and cultivating himself freely available to him, under all circumstances."

In 1990s, many countries aimed to build a learning society. For instance, in 1995 more than a dozen member countries of the European Union co-signed the white paper "Teaching and Learning: Toward the Learning Society." This sets out the actions to be taken in member states and the support measures to be introduced at community level. The main courses of action envisaged at the European level for 1996 include the following objectives:

- to encourage the acquisition of new knowledge;
- to bring schools and the business sector closer together;
- to promote social harmony;
- to develop proficiency in three European languages;
- to treat capital investment and investment in training on an equal basis.

The idea to build a learning society was also put forward by the British government in the green paper "The Learning Age: a Renaissance for a New Britain," which was issued in 1998. A scheme to build universities for industry in a learning society began in 1999: this attempts to provide high-quality products and services for British society through modern web and communication technology, developing relationships and links between the resources of the learning providers and the needs of the learners. In this scheme people can learn flexibly and conveniently at home, at work, and in community learning centers. The study circles in Sweden and the community colleges of the USA, mentioned above, are both typical organizations in a learning society.

On the way to building a learning society, all Western countries emphasize that learning and education are a life-long process, which is ongoing and is interwoven through society.

The idea of life-long learning dates back to the 1960s and the term came into use more generally in the 1970s to replace "life-long education," indicating that learning should be a personal, self-motivated, and voluntary pursuit. In 1996, the International Commission on Education for the Twenty-First Century delivered a report which pointed out that, in order to progress to a learning society, long-life learning must be the citizens' first choice.

In life-long learning, all the stages, levels, and types of learning are component parts of a single process. The development of the theory and practice of life-long learning is closely related to and largely affects adult education, including its overall concepts, development strategy, systems, structures, and personnel training. The emphasis is on a combination of various forms and content of learning.

5.3.2   Links Between Vocational Education and General Education

The idea of life-long learning has enlarged the connotation and denotation of education, and led to changes and adjustments in the global education structure.

To cope with this trend, many Western countries have managed to bridge the gaps between general education and vocational education at the secondary level.

5.3.2.1 Equivalent Value at Secondary Education Level

In the USA, for example, the two tracks are integrated. This can be seen from how comprehensive high schools, first established in the 1920s, organize the curricula. Typically, the courses are organized into three tracks, namely vocational, academic, and general, from which the students may freely choose according to their specific needs and interests. Under this curriculum system, general education and vocational education are considered equally important. Students may make plans of studies to suit their individual needs, and may shift from one plan to another in order to experience a broad variety of courses.

Another example is Sweden, which in 1993 integrated more than 500 previously specialized courses into sixteen national study plans, all leading to higher education qualifications.

Similarly, in Germany higher education is equally available to vocational secondary school graduates and their equivalents from complete secondary schools.

5.3.2.2 Interplay Between Higher Vocational and Higher General Education

While vigorously developing short-term technical institutions and junior colleges, Western countries are showing a growing concern for links between different types and stages of higher education. For example, in France those who have received a certificate from a short-term higher education program are allowed, if qualified enough, to move on either into a job, a higher school, or even a *grande école*.

5.3.3   Informatization

In the 1990s, information technology was rapidly developed, exerting a great influence on global education. In many countries, it became an indispensable part of national curricula and an important aid to teaching. To a large extent, it facilitates not only classroom learning, but also long-distance teaching and learning. As a key strategy of adjusting to the knowledge-based economy, online education became popular. It breaks up the limitation of traditional campuses and is a convenient channel that allows people to learn what they want, without worrying about conditions such as time, age, and occupation. Online education has also helped to guarantee people's equal chance of learning. In June 2006, the Annual Conference of European Distance and E-learning Network Association held at Vienna University of Technology pointed out that information and communication technology would help to promote the linking of education training with enterprises; an integrated lifetime learning model was taking shape, connecting education, training, workplace, and home.

To respond to the requirements of learning under these new high technology conditions, Finland, France, and Scotland designed a new type of experimental schools, which had fewer classrooms and more flexible teaching space than traditional schools. Based on existing libraries, the new schools expanded their electronic resource centers and added videotapes, DVDs, and interactive learning software. The multimedia system began to be widely applied to teaching. As this function was expanded, these schools become full-time community learning centers, and they are open to the public all the year round.

In France, the government encourages everyone to make full use of Internet resources to develop their education. To achieve this goal, the French Ministry of Education has taken a series of measures that include setting up a digitized university, increasing the Internet surfing rate on campuses and among families, and offering information technology training to teachers.

By the autumn of 2004, when the new term began, more than half of the public universities in France were able to access wireless Internet surfing. The French Ministry of Education is taking efforts to co-ordinate universities and colleges, so that resources can be shared among people who work in the same field. As a result, the French government has successfully established several digitized universities, which predominantly serve medical science, engineering, law, economy, and management.

5.3.4   *Internationalization*

The integration of the global economy, the rise of the knowledge economy, and the rapid development of information technology have largely extended education service trades and increasingly strengthened international co-operation in education. To make up for possible educational deficiencies, most countries have opened the door and continue to try to learn how to make use of the resources that can be provided by other countries. A typical example is the efforts made by European countries at the turn of the twenty-first century toward the integration of higher education.

In 1998, the Ministers of Education from France, Germany, Britain, and Italy signed the Sorbonne Declaration at the University of Paris to promote the integration of European higher education. In 1999, the twenty-nine European Ministers in charge of higher education convened in the famous Italian city of Bologna and signed the Bologna Declaration regarding the harmonization of the European higher education system's architecture. The objectives and action plan proposed in this declaration inherited and developed the theme laid down in the Sorbonne Declaration, and hence started the Bologna Process: this aimed at creating a European

Higher Education Area by 2010. The declaration was followed up by a series of meetings between European ministers, in which relevant schemes were outlined, including the following:

- the adoption of a system of easily readable and comparable degrees;
- the establishment of a system of credits, the European Credit Transfer and Accumulation System (ECTS);
- the promotion of mobility of students and teachers between institutions;
- the promotion of international competition, attractiveness, and prestige;
- the provision of life-long education;
- the involvement of higher education institutions and students in the Bologna Process.

With more and more transnational franchises, course cohesion, overseas branch campuses, and distance education, Europe has accumulated much experience in such aspects as development speed, scale, and school pattern.

Franchising is a common operation in transnational higher education. A franchiser (an institution) will grant a foreign institution (a franchisee) the privilege to import services such as course-teaching and degree-awarding to its country. Through the mandate and agreement of both sides, the franchiser can enhance its reputation and benefits, while the franchisee can fulfill its obligations and offer a diversity of choices of education to meet the needs of different students.

Another operation is course cohesion. To allow credits to be interchangeable, and thus to facilitate further education and employment, two or more universities or colleges will co-operate to define the curriculum according to the credit transfer principles. At present, the ECTS is the most influential. This is a standard for comparing study attainment and higher education student performance across the European Union and other collaborating European countries. The ECTS provides a common measure which facilitates the transfer of students and their grades between European higher education institutions, and tackles the problem of different grading approaches in distinct educational systems across Europe.

The internationalization of education can also be achieved through degrees awarded by an overseas campus, which are the same as those awarded by the main campuses in the host country.

A new development is online education, which is rising as the development of network technologies increases in speed. It is offered by cyber universities and numerous media corporations in collaboration with traditional universities and other traditional educational institutions.

To promote the integration of European education, the Bologna Process has constantly been accelerated. More than forty European countries have participated in it. Obviously, the internationalization of education has become an irreversible and indispensable trend.

BIBLIOGRAPHY

Chen Yuan. 2004. *Basic Education in France*. Guangzhou: Guangdong Education Publishing House.

Fang Tong. 2004. *Basic Education in the Kingdom of Sweden*. Guangzhou: Guangdong Education Publishing House.

Faure, E., et al. 1972. *Learning to Be: The World of Education: Today and Tomorrow*. Paris: UNESCO.

Hutchins, R.M. 1969. *The Learning Society*. Harmondsworth: Penguin.

Lü Da, and Zhou Mansheng. 2004. *Important Literature on Contemporary Educational Reforms in Foreign Countries*, The Book of the United Kingdom. Vol. 1 & 2. Beijing: People's Education Press.

Shan Zhonghui. 2006. *A History of the Problems of University Education in Foreign Countries*. Ji'nan: Shandong Education Press.

Yang Huimin. 2004. *Basic Education in the United States*. Guangzhou: Guangdong Education Publishing House.

Yang Yingsong. 2000. *Introduction to Community Education in Different Countries*. Shanghai: Shanghai University Press.

Zhang Kechuang, and Li Qilong. 2005. *Basic Education in the Germany*. Guangzhou: Guangdong Education Publishing House.

Zhang Dewei, and Liang Zhongyi. 2006. *A Comparative Study of International Upper Secondary Education*. Beijing: People's Education Press.

Zhong Wenfang. 2006. *A History of Modern Western Elementary Education*. Shanghai: Shanghai Scientific & Technological Education Publishing House.

Zhu Huaixin. 2003. *Basic Education in the United Kingdom*. Guangzhou: Guangdong Education Publishing House.

CHAPTER 6

European and American Literature

6.1 ANCIENT GREEK LITERATURE

6.1.1 Epic

The Ancient Greek epics, the *Iliad* and the *Odyssey*, represent the culminating accomplishment of ancient Greek literature, and some even regard these two works as the fountainheads of European and American literature. They are believed to have been written by the blind poet Homer (about 580 BC), and thus are called the Homeric epics for short. However, some people believe that epics should not be ascribed to one author, and indeed these are made up of oral lore that was collected and then rewritten by Homer or a group of poets. This is a common feature of early literature. In China, *The Book of Odes* comprises ballads compiled by Confucius. The Homeric epics draw on material from the Trojan War, the difference between them being that the *Iliad* describes the war and its heroes, while the *Odyssey* concentrates on one Greek hero Odysseus and depicts his arduous ten-year journey returning from the war. The two epics are written with grand structures, plain language, and abundant metaphors. They contain a huge number of myths and heroes and are the main sources for Greek mythology.

© The Author(s) 2018
G. Xu et al. (eds.), K. Chen et al. (trans.), *Understanding Western Culture*, https://doi.org/10.1007/978-981-10-8150-7_6

6.1.2   Ancient Greek Tragedy

Ancient Greek tragedy marks the high point of all tragedies. From Aristotle's time to the eighteenth century, ancient Greek tragedies were a yardstick for critics to measure the value of a play. The three most famous ancient Greek tragedians are Aeschylus (*c.* 546–525 BC), Sophocles (*c.* 496–406 BC) and Euripides (*c.* 480–406 BC). Aeschylus is described as the father of tragedy, and his plays include *The Persians, Seven against Thebes,* and *Orestes.* Sophocles' masterpieces are *Oedipus the King* and *Oedipus in Colonus,* and *Antigone,* while Euripides' masterpieces are *Medea* and *The Trojan Women.*

6.1.3   Ancient Greek Comedy

Both ancient Greek comedy and tragedy developed from parades celebrating the wine god Dionysus. Tragedy indicates the irresistibility of destiny, while comedy derides life and expresses irony about the weakness of human nature, embodying the conviviality and absurdity of life. The greatest Greek comedian is Aristophanes (*c.* 456–386 BC). Eleven of his comedies survive, including *The Wasps, The Frogs,* and *Lysistrata.* Aristophanes' comedies cover a wide range of topics: some concern war and peace, some attack authority, some ridicule sages, and others retell myths. His language is either buffoonish or elegant and exerted a profound influence upon later playwrights, such as Shakespeare.

6.1.4   Ancient Greek Lyric

Another important constituent of ancient Greek literature is lyric poetry. Unfortunately, only a small amount of this is preserved. The beloved and widely-read Greek lyrical poets are Pindar (*c.* 522–443 BC), Theocritus (third century BC) and particularly the poetess Sappho (*c.* 630–570 BC). Her poetry depicts the tender inner world of love, and several ancient sources refer to her as the "tenth Muse." Sappho was adept at writing odes, and was believed to be the founder of this form. Theocritus was the father of pastorals and his writing style was copied by the Roman poet Virgil (70–19 BC).

6.1.5   Ancient Greek Mythology

Greek mythology is not an independent literary genre. Most of it is preserved through the Homeric epics, Greek plays, and historical and philosophical works, yet its significant influence cannot be neglected. Because

Greek mythology was well preserved during Roman times, it is also called Greek and Roman mythology. It describes the origin and pedigree of gods, the duties of and stories about gods, the origin of human beings, and the disputes between humans and gods. One feature that distinguishes Greek and Roman mythology from Chinese mythology is the endowment of gods with human characters. Gods in Greek and Roman mythology are just as aggressive, jealous, and revengeful as human beings. In spite of the differences between gods and human beings, their intimacy is beyond the imagination of Chinese mythology. The humanism derived from Greek and Roman mythology became one of the backbones of Western culture and was the impetus for Renaissance literature and romantic literature in the nineteenth century. The abundant myths and characters in this mythology become an eternal fountainhead for Western literature and an indispensable part of Western language.

6.2   Ancient Roman Literature

6.2.1   Virgil and the Epic

Similar to the *Iliad* and the *Odyssey*, the *Aeneid* also draws on the Trojan War. The *Iliad* and *Odyssey* focus on Greece, while the *Aeneid* mainly deals with the Trojan War hero Aeneas, and describes how he leaves Troy and builds the city of Rome. Virgil's language was exquisite and he was adept at rhetoric, even exceeding Homer in his descriptions of the inner world and sensations.

6.2.2   Drama

With regard to plays, there were no major achievements in ancient Roman literature. Roman plays were basically an imitation of Greek works. Some people believe that the Roman preference for wrestling and other physical activities were responsible for their mundane plays. Large-scale state patronage of sports meant the theatre was neglected.

6.2.3   Poetry

Ancient Roman poetry, by contrast, displayed significant achievement. Besides the great poet Virgil, other renowned Roman poets are Catullus (*c.* 84–54 BC), Ovid (*c.* 43–17 BC), and Horace (*c.* 65–27 BC). Catullus expressed romantic emotions with enthusiasm and passion and his style was inherited by later poets, including Sidney, Shakespeare, Burns, and Shelley. Ovid's *Metamorphoses* assembles all myths involving metamorphoses in Greek and Roman mythology and seems more influential than Virgil's *Aeneid*, in spite of its inferior literary achievements. The myths in *Metamorphoses* also become inspirational sources for later writers and artists. The poetry written by Horace is elegant and Nietzsche spoke highly of him: "To this day no other poet has given me the same artistic delight that a Horatian ode gave me from the first." The famous painting *Primavera* by Italian Renaissance artist Sandro Botticelli was inspired by Horace's poem "Spring": "Now Cytherean Venus leads her dancing bands with the moon hanging overhead, and the seemly Graces linked with Nymphs shake the earth with alternating feet, while burning Vulcan visits the great forges of the Cyclopes."

6.2.4   Prose

Ancient Romans excelled in meditation and debate. Their representative here is Cicero (*c.* 106–43 BC). He was a statesman, a philosopher, a historian, and an orator. His prose is masculine and eloquent, and he has received the epithet "the father of Western prose."

6.3   MEDIEVAL LITERATURE

6.3.1   Church Literature

The Middle Ages were ruled by Christianity, and church literature played a significant role. Church literature includes biblical stories, hagiography, prayers, miracle plays, and religious plays.

6.3.2   Knightly Literature

Chivalry prevailed in the Middle Ages. Knights were loyal to their lords and valued reputation over everything; and of course they were devout Christians. Every knight had a beloved lady and dared to attempt any adventure for her: knightly literature was a vivid portrayal of this phenomenon. France was at the heart of the chivalric spirit and was the place where knightly literature was the most prevalent. Its predominant forms are lyrical and narrative poems. Lyrical poems describe knights' admiration for noblewomen and originate from southern France, specifically Provence. On the contrary, narrative poems originate in northern France. They describe the adventures that knights go through in order to win honor and the admiration of noble ladies, and the expeditions they undertake to denounce heretics and to protect Catholicism. A constant topic in narrative poems is King Arthur and his knights of the Round Table, a theme that appears in literary works from France, Germany, and England. The twelfth-century legend of Tristan and Iseult is one of the most widely retold narratives.

6.3.3   Epic

Just like the epics of Homer and Virgil, epics in the Middle Ages portrayed important historical events of a specific nation and eulogized national heroes. The most well-known in this age are the Teutonic *Song of Hildebrand*, the Anglo-Saxon *Beowulf*, the French *The Song of Roland*, the Spanish *The Poem of the Cid*, and the German *The Song of the Nibelungs*.

6.3.4   Ballad

Apart from these epics, a number of ballads were also handed down from medieval times. A well-known example is the English *A Geste of Robyn Hode*, which exerted a huge influence upon later literature.

6.3.5   Civic Literature

Another part of medieval literature was generated from daily life; it was thus called civic literature. It satirizes and mocks monks and feudal lords. One masterpiece is the *Roman de Renart*, which tells the story of Reynard the Fox. Many stories originating in France in the ninth and tenth centuries were based on the same character, and circulated around other countries in Western Europe. Another representative work is the thirteenth-century *The Romance of the Rose*, which also originated in France. Although it was written in two stages by two poets, about forty-five years apart, stylistically and structurally it was consistent. The stated purpose of this long poem is both to entertain and to teach readers about the Art of Love. It illustrates secular life under the religious culture and chivalric fashion of medieval times. The fourteenth-century English poet Chaucer was influenced by the poem.

6.3.6   *Dante and* The Divine Comedy

Dante's long poem *The Divine Comedy* is widely considered to be the greatest work in Italian literature, and indeed one of the greatest in Western literature since the Homeric epics and Virgil's *Aeneid*. *The Divine Comedy* offers a vivid description of the hero's experience in Inferno, Purgatorio, and Paradiso, using dreams and imagination. This magnum opus embraces all the knowledge in the world and builds a wide range of characters successfully, including historical characters, contemporary characters, and gods in Greek and Roman mythology. It follows medieval Christian theology, particularly the redemption of humanity, and affirms secular emotions as well, combining deity, rationality, and human nature. *The Divine Comedy* is divided into three *canticas*, with each part comprising thirty-three *cantos*. An initial *canto* serves as an introduction to the poem, and this is generally considered to be part of the first *cantica*, bringing the total number of *cantos* to 100. The verse scheme used is *terza rima*, which hendecasyllabic (with lines of eleven syllables), the lines having the rhyme scheme aba, bcb, cdc, ded, and so on. Such a form implies veneration of a trinitarian God (one God with three aspects) and achieves a uniformity of form and content.

6.3.7   *Chaucer*

The appearance of Geoffrey Chaucer (*c.* 1343–1400) on the literature stage marked an end of English literature's reticence and the beginning of the English Renaissance. Chaucer's perennial masterpiece is *The Canterbury Tales*, which adopts a frame-narrative structure (another example being *The Arabian Nights*), in which stories with assorted themes are arranged in a coherent order. The storytellers in *The Canterbury Tales* are a group of pilgrims heading for Canterbury Cathedral. They are representatives from different social classes: knight, miller, reeve, cook, "man of law," friar, merchant, and so on. Everyone's story is different: some are serious and tragic while others are joyous and comic. The characters are so vivid and lifelike that readers are offered a panorama of the social life in fourteenth-century England. Chaucer wrote in medieval English, laying the foundations of English as a literary language and confirming the London dialect as standard English, although the influence of the court and bureaucracy is a more likely influence on the development of modern English. Chaucer's other long poems such as *Troilus and Criseyde* were also written with wit and humor. There is no doubt that he deserves the title of "the father of English literature."

6.4   RENAISSANCE LITERATURE

6.4.1   Petrarch and Boccaccio

The representative writers of Italian Renaissance we will discuss are the poet Petrarch (1304–1374) and the novelist Boccaccio (1313–1375). Petrarch was the most famous early master of the sonnet form, opening up a new era for verse. With a higher reputation even than Dante, he was regarded as the second "poet laureate" since the classical age. The "Petrarchan sonnet" was a model for English Renaissance poets. Petrarch's masterpiece is Song Book, a collection of 366 love poems for Laura.

Boccaccio is deemed as one of the founders of Western literature thanks to his work *The Decameron*, which includes 100 stories narrated by ten men and women gathering at a villa just outside Florence to escape the Black Death. Some stories are drawn from the author's imagination, while some are adaptations of folktales and others draw on ancient French ballads. Boccaccio portrayed every aspect of fourteenth-century Italian society in humorous and witty language. *The Decameron* is a masterpiece of Italian prose and an important work of European literature. English poets from Chaucer to Keats were all inspired by it (with Chaucer's *The Canterbury Tales* being an obvious imitation in both structure and content).

6.4.2   English Literature during the Renaissance

England was the center of the European Renaissance, and English literature was at the peak of Renaissance literature. The main accomplishments of the English Renaissance were poetry and plays. The most famous poets are Sir Philip Sidney (1554–1586), Edmund Spenser (1552/1553–1599), Ben Jonson (1572–1637) and William Shakespeare (1564–1616), Jonson and Shakespeare being more famous for their plays. Sidney excelled in short poems; while Spenser's short poems are as beautiful as his longer works, laying a foundation for his notable status: the late eighteenth/early nineteenth-century essayist and poet Charles Lamb praised him as the "poet's poet." His long poems are *The Shepherd's Calendar* and *The Faerie Queene*. Shakespeare's sonnets descended from and further developed the Italian Petrarchan sonnet, and were an incomparable accomplishment.

The most stupendous achievement of the English Renaissance was its drama. A group of playwrights named the "University Wits," represented by Christopher Marlowe (1564–1593), emerged before Shakespeare, and Shakespeare's contemporary playwright Ben Jonson was also a gifted writer, but unfortunately, being born in Shakespeare's era, their artistry is overshadowed.

Shakespeare composed thirty-seven plays in his lifetime, and they are generally separated into histories, comedies, and tragedies. They have been constantly put on stage and adapted to films for almost 400 years, and no other works from other writers can compete with their popularity. Shakespeare's plays are perhaps the most widely studied texts except for the Bible. Most of his plays are based on history, Greek and Roman mythology, or previous writers' stories; nevertheless, his genius infused an immortal vitality into these characters and materials. When reading Shakespeare's plays, even today readers cannot sense the chronological barrier between history and the present, because his language is fresh and interesting and feels contemporaneous. It is reasonable to call Shakespeare our contemporary. The overarching motif in Shakespeare's plays, whether history, comedy, or tragedy, is always humanity, though the histories may carry another intention, that of admonition. The theme of Shakespeare's comedies is generally love, the plot is charming yet convoluted, and the language is quick-witted and humorous. *A Midsummer Night's Dream, As You Like It, The Taming of the Shrew, Much Ado About Nothing*, and *The Merchant of Venice* are names familiar to everybody. Shakespeare's tragedies are usually believed to be his most accomplished work; the four most renowned are *Hamlet, King Lear, Macbeth*, and *Othello*. These expose the weaknesses of human nature. The heroes are either of noble birth or of celebrated status, and their dignified qualities match their notable position. However, flaws in their character result in their tragic ends, examples being Hamlet's irresolution and vacillation, King Lear's prejudice and credulity, Macbeth's avarice and ambition, and Othello's undue suspicion. The tragedy caused by the weakness of human nature forms a sharp contrast with the heroes' noble quality, which arouses strong compassion among readers and audiences. Another reason for the eternal vitality of Shakespeare's plays is his deep understanding of human nature.

Brilliant as Shakespeare is, the light that he shines does not show us all the wonders of English Renaissance literature. In the same way the splendor of Dante is not able to lighten the gloomy skies of the Middle Ages. Another eminent playwright is Ben Jonson. In the seventeenth century, his fame exceeded even Shakespeare's. He was of great erudition and versatility, and this is expressed in his plays. Jonson's Roman play *Poetaster* is composed of dialogues between Virgil, Horace, Ovid, and Timbales, and the language that each speaker utters resembles the ideas in his own writings. Some believe that even Shakespeare could not have written such a talented work. The eighteenth-century English critic John Dryden said: "I admire him, but I love Shakespeare." As with Shakespeare, Ben Jonson was an excellent poet and a greatly talented playwright.

Apart from Shakespeare and Jonson, other notable playwrights during the English Renaissance were John Webster (*c*. 1580–*c*. 1634), Francis Beaumont (1584–1616), and his collaborator John Fletcher (1579–1625). Together with other great writers, they bedeck the starry night of the Renaissance.

Francis Bacon (1561–1626) was a great Renaissance scholar, philosopher, and essayist. His most prestigious work, *Essays*, was written in precise and accurate language, and is imbued with wisdom. Many famous sayings in it have been passed down through history, examples being. "Knowledge is power" and "Histories make men wise; poets, witty; the mathematics, subtle; natural philosophy, deep; moral, grave; logic and rhetoric, able to contend." Francis Bacon is the founder of British philosophy and the father of English prose.

6.4.3   Renaissance Literature of France and Spain

The Renaissance literature of France and Spain is no less remarkable than that of Italy and England. French literature had already achieved a few notable accomplishments in medieval times, but in the sixteenth century two literary masters emerged in France: one was the author of *Gargantua and Pantagruel*, François Rabelais (between 1483 and 1494–1553), and the other was the essayist Michel de Montaigne (1533–1592). *Gargantua and Pantagruel* is a novel in five volumes that describes the adventures of the giant Gargantua, his son Pantagruel, and the useless jokester Panurge; it faithfully reflects every aspect of contemporary society through their adventures. The novel ridicules all kinds of malpractices through the use of amusing stories and language. On one hand, it criticizes society's hypocrisy and cruelty and the harm caused to children by scholasticism; on the other hand, it confirms the humanity and creativity of men. The giants in the novel are powerful, knowledgeable, broad-minded, and peace-loving, incarnating the spirit of the Renaissance.

Very different to Rabelais, Montaigne was tranquil and calm. His essays feature wisdom, humor, and skepticism. He has been called "the king of the essay" and was the first great French essayist, exerting much influence on other writers. It is said that Shakespeare's *The Tempest* was based on one of Montaigne's essays.

Spanish literature started to gain attention because of a great novelist who lived during the sixteenth century, Miguel de Cervantes (1547–1616). His original intention in writing *Don Quixote* was to satirize the romantic knightly literature that had been popular since the Middle Ages. Surprisingly, the novel gradually developed its own life and developed into a work of unique style and thought. The hero Don Quixote is enchanted by knightly novels, and his behavior is ridiculous because of his frenzied addiction. However, he later becomes a hero because of his perseverance, his lack of vice, his integrity, and his kindness. He is a funny yet pitiful hero. As it goes on, the novel changes from satire to an attack on society, also being a eulogy to humanists who are courageous enough to make changes. Don Quixote and his servant Sancho Panza are a pair of classical literary characters, but to the average person one of them appears to be a lunatic with an unrealistic imagination, while the other is a fool who appears to only accidentally speak words of wisdom.

6.5   European Literature in the Seventeenth Century

6.5.1   French Literature

The most accomplished form in seventeenth-century French literature is drama. Great playwrights who abided by classicism were Pierre Corneille (1606–1684), Jean Racine (1639–1699), and Molière (1622–1673). Corneille composed more than thirty tragedies and comedies, and many of them are still in theaters' repertoires, an example being *Le Cid*. Racine was also a great playwright, his masterpieces including *Andromaque*. The most remarkable playwright in French history is Molière. His works include *The Misanthrope*, *The School for Wives*, and *Tartuffe*. Moliere's comedies contain far-reaching ideas that appear amid laughs and mockery, and readers may feel a sense of misery behind the humor. He infused the majesty of tragedy into comedy.

Another influential writer in seventeenth-century France was the allegorist Jean de La Fontaine (1621–1695). Fontaine ridiculed human life through fable. Children lose themselves in the fairy tales while adults savor the gorgeous writing and its implied meanings.

Seventeenth-century French poetry dedicated itself to the imitation of ancient Greek poetry. The seven poets who venerated Greek poets called themselves "The Pléiade." Members of the group attached great importance to form and shared the defining characteristics of Baroque style. Although their poetry was not popular for long, their impact on the forms of French poetry was decisive and crucial. Three representatives of the Pléiade are Pierre de Ronsard (1524–1585), Joachim du Bellay (*c.* 1522–1560), and Jean-Antoine de Baïf (1532–1589).

Nicholas Boileau-Despreaux (1636–1711) was a seventeenth-century French poet and critic. It was he who discovered the aesthetic interest of Racine and the talent of Molière. His work *The Art of Poetry* was modeled on T*he Art of Poetry* (*Ars Poetica*) by the Roman poet Horace and presents detailed guidance for the composition of poems, laying a foundation for French poetry. He is regarded as the most talented critic after Aristotle and before the English Matthew Arnold (1822–1888).

René Descartes (1596–1650) was a seventeenth-century philosopher. "I think, therefore I am" is one of his renowned philosophical propositions. His admiration for reason corresponded with the literary classicism of the time. Descartes' rational philosophy influenced following generations to a great extent.

6.5.2   English Literature

The representative poet of the metaphysical school is John Donne (1572–1631). He was adept at using elusive and inventive metaphors in his poetry and was referred to as a metaphysical poet by the poet and critic John Dryden in the eighteenth century. The metaphysical poets were undervalued for a long time, with the artistic value of their work not being valued until their re-evaluation by the great twentieth-century poet and critic T.S. Eliot. Donne is now deemed to be one of the best British poets ever.

John Milton (1608–1674), born thirty years after Donne, was stylistically different from him. His metaphysical poems are short and contain magical images; they resemble Homeric epics in form and draw on material from biblical stories. Composed of grand structures and magnificent language, they are imbued with courage and heroism. His masterpieces are *Paradise Lost* and *Samson Agonistes*. Milton is another great master, second only to Shakespeare.

Another writer worth-mentioning from seventeenth-century England is John Bunyan (1628–1688). His allegorical novel *The Pilgrim's Progress* describes how the hero Christian experiences arduous hardships before finally arriving in Paradise. His language is clear, plain, and simple, but is occasionally decorated with sentences that have a biblical style. The work is intended to enlighten people through the use of uncomplicated stories, and is a paradigm of Protestant literature.

6.6   EUROPEAN LITERATURE IN THE EIGHTEENTH CENTURY

6.6.1   French Literature

Charles-Louis de Secondat, Baron de La Brède et de Montesquieu (1689–1755), generally referred to more simply as Montesquieu, was a writer as well as a historian. He is well known for his early work *Persian Letters*, which satirizes the malpractices of Church, government, and literature. His historical work *Considerations on the Causes of the Greatness of the Romans and their Decline* (1734) influenced Edward Gibbon's *The History of the Decline and Fall of the Roman Empire* (1776–1789). Montesquieu's work *On the Spirit of the Laws* is a documentation of law, society, and government, as well as a study of the customs of various countries from ancient times until his times.

Voltaire (1694–1778) was the nom-de-plume of François-Marie Arouet. He was a leader of the French Enlightenment, his works covering almost all genres of literature, including plays, poems, novels, histories, literary criticism, and letters. In essence, they all serve the same end, that of campaigning for Enlightenment ideas. For instance, the tragedy *Brutus* advocates the idea of a republic, another tragedy *Mahomet* is a study of religious fanaticism, and the romantic tragedy *Zaïre* reveals sin caused by religious prejudice.

Jean-Jacques Rousseau (1712–1778) was also an important leader of the Enlightenment movement. His works *Emile, or On Education, Julie, or the New Heloise, The Social Contract*, and *Confessions of Jean-Jacques Rousseau* exert a far-reaching influence upon philosophy, history, literature, politics, and society in general.

Denis Diderot (1713–1784) compiled *Encyclopedia, or a Systematic Dictionary of the Sciences, Arts, and Crafts*, which is a collection of science, literature, philosophy, and other disciplines, and contains the wisdom of many influential philosophers.

Three major playwrights emerged in eighteenth-century France: Alain-René Lesage (1668–1747), who was also a novelist, Pierre de Marivaux (1688–1763), and Pierre Beaumarchais (1732–1799). Lesage's novel *Le Diable Boiteux* is witty and humorous. Marivaux experimented with different genres using unique language. Just as the word "Kafkaesque" (grotesque) was coined to describe the work of Czech writer Franz Kafka (1883–1924), the new French word *Marivaudage* refers to Marivaux's elusive literary style. His masterpieces are *A Matter of Dispute* and *The Game of Love and Chance*. Beaumarchais' comedies, *The Barber of Seville* and *The Marriage of Figaro*, accompanied by Mozart and Rossini's music, are well known to virtually everyone.

6.6.2 English Literature

Representative writers of English prose in the eighteenth century are journalists who wrote for The Spectator, Joseph Addison (1672–1719) and Richard Steele (1672–1729). Their articles are enjoyable, educational, witty, and funny. The writing is clear, and a model of English prose. However, the greatest master of prose from the era is Jonathan Swift (1667–1745), whose *Gulliver's Travels* uses human beings and other creatures, for instance Lilliputians (tiny people), Brobdingnagians (giants), and Houyhnhnms (intelligent talking horses), to satirize the ridiculousness of human society. The novel has been popular among children and adults ever since it was published. The word "Yahoo" (describing the deformed creatures that resemble human beings whom Gulliver meets) has entered the English language. *Robinson Crusoe* by Daniel Defoe (1660–1731) exerts the same wide influence as *Gulliver's Travels*. The story of Robinson surviving alone on an island (later with his companion "Friday") provides readers with endless space to imagine and courage to adventure. Perhaps this is one of the key elements to inspire early American immigrants.

The stories of Gulliver and Robinson Crusoe are similar to contemporary travelogues in some respects, but the epistolary (letter form) *Pamela, or Virtue Rewarded* by Samuel Richardson (1689–1761) can be considered to be the first English novel. Published in 1740, it is equipped with all the elements a novel requires. Based on the thread of the heroine's emotions, it describes a poor maidservant whose master makes unwanted and inappropriate advances toward her. The novel was a huge success when it first appeared, and its fame spread to France and Italy. It had a profound effect on contemporary novels. Because of this,

Richardson has been called "Father of the English Novel." However, the first great novelist was Henry Fielding (1707–1754). Carrying on the tradition of Spanish and French picaresque novels, *The History of Tom Jones, a Foundling* portrays the emotional life and ups and downs of Tom, a foundling who became a gentleman. Although this is not a unique subject, Fielding's humor and his reflections on human nature together create a classic among English novels. "Since the author of Tom Jones was buried," said the novelist William Makepeace Thackeray (1811–1863), "no writer of fiction among us has been permitted to depict to his utmost power a Man." Another novelist, Laurence Sterne (1713–1768), left his name in the literary arena thanks to *The Life and Opinions of Tristram Shandy, Gentleman*, which can be considered as the first stream of consciousness fiction thanks to its loose structure, jumping from one subject to another. Some critics regard Sterne as the founder of contemporary narrative styles.

The central figure of literature and culture in the eighteenth century is Samuel Johnson (1709–1784). He integrated knowledge, wit, and humor, and attracted myriad admirers. He established the highest standard of literary criticism in the era. His most influential work was *A Dictionary of the English Language* (1755), the preeminent English dictionary until the publication of the *Oxford English Dictionary* 173 years later. Because of his larger-than-life personality, Johnson made a huge impact on the first great biography writer James Boswell (1740–1795). Through their close contact and communication, Boswell's *Life of Samuel Johnson* (1791) achieved the most vivid and personal biography published up to that point, and often described as the greatest biography ever written.

While prose enjoys full blossom, play remains silent. Richard Brinsley Sheridan (1751–1816) was the only master playwright at this time. *The Rivals* and *The School for Scandal* are rich in wit and humor, and the latter is considered to be the best English comedy since Shakespeare. Another interesting writer is Oliver Goldsmith (1728–1774). He wrote novels, plays, and poems, creating unforgettable masterpieces in all these genres. His novel *The Vicar of Wakefield* is only next to *Robinson Crusoe* in terms of popularity. His play *She Stoops to Conquer*, along with Sheridan's *The Rivals* and *The School for Scandal*, were staged regularly for half a century. His poem *The Deserted Village* remains melodious and touching for readers today.

Edward Gibbon (1737–1794) was perhaps the greatest English historian. His *The History of the Decline and Fall of the Roman Empire* is the most spectacular historical document among English works.

Four very influential English poets appeared at this time. They are John Dryden (1631–1700) and Alexander Pope (1688–1744), representatives of classicism, and William Blake (1757–1827) and Robert Burns (1759–1796) of romanticism. Dryden was an excellent poet, a literary critic, and a playwright. His poetry is neo-classical: he used heroic couplets, which established their status as one of the fundamental rhyme schemes in English poetry. Dryden was appointed Poet Laureate in 1668. In literary criticism, he was the first great critic, whose reflections on metaphysical poetry led to its neglect for centuries. It was not until the twentieth century, when T.S. Eliot reassessed its value, that people rekindled their interest in metaphysical poetry. Dryden's best-known drama is *All for Love*. Pope was the most outstanding neo-classical poet. His poetry is smooth, symmetrical, refined, and delicate, and he skillfully used heroic couplets. *The Rape of the Lock* is his most famous work. Pope was also a great critic. Many of his sayings have become epigrams, for instance, "To err is human, to forgive, divine," "Fools rush in where angels fear to tread," and "A little knowledge is a dangerous thing." He was also a brilliant translator, translating the *Iliad* and *Odyssey* into English.

In the late eighteenth century, William Blake and Robert Burns were considered as the pioneers of romanticism. They both loved nature, human beings, and animals. Their poems are a natural flow of emotions. Blake believed in God, and his poems are suffused with mysticism. Burns is unique because of his preservation and application of Scottish ballads. His sincere and melodious poems, such as "A Red, Red Rose" and "Auld Lang Syne" enjoy fame not only in English-speaking countries, but also around the world.

6.6.3   German Literature

After the civil war of 1648, German literature started to attract the world's attention. Two consummate masters entered the arena: one was Johann Wolfgang von Goethe (1749–1832) and the other was Friedrich von Schiller (1759–1805). As epoch-making as Dante and Shakespeare, Goethe won German literature an important place in European literature. Just like *The Divine Comedy*, his monumental play *Faust* is also a personal epic that searches for the meaning of life. The hero Faust is a scholar who is avid for life. Under the allurement of the devil Mephistopheles, he dedicates himself to the empirical world, indulging in erotic enjoyment and the acquisition of power. He is a hero who pursues dreams as well as a playboy who is addicted to enjoyment. Goethe indicated the abundance, complexity, and the meaning of life. The fame of his earlier novel *The Sorrows of Young Werther* is treated as marking the beginning of German romanticism.

Schiller was a great playwright, poet, and literary theorist. He followed the freedom of spirit. His play *The Robbers* expresses his liberal thought and is a milestone of German drama. His other works include *Intrigue and Love* and *Don Carlos*. Schiller's literary theory influenced later philosophers and theorists, such as Hegel.

Another person that is worth mentioning here is the playwright, ideologist, and critic Gotthold Ephraim Lessing (1729–1781). His aesthetic work *Laocoön: An Essay on the Limits of Painting and Poetry* is a classic text about painting and poetry criticism.

6.7   European and American Literature in the Nineteenth Century

6.7.1   French Literature

Honoré de Balzac (1799–1850) is renowned for *The Human Comedy*, a book consisting of ninety-one realist novels with more than two thousand varied characters, thereby providing what can be regarded as an encyclopedia of human society, and because of this Balzac, transcending boundaries of geography and time, gains eternal vitality through his works.

Victor Hugo (1802–1885) was Balzac's friend. It is difficult to compare their literary talent and status, so few objections can be made if Hugo is considered to be the greatest French writer. His representative writings are *The Hunchback of Notre-Dame* and *Les Misérables*. While we may find it hard to judge whether Balzac's *The Human Comedy* belongs to romanticism or to realism, Hugo's writings are very evidently romantic. Besides his talent for fiction, Hugo was also a great playwright, poet, and political commentator.

Alexandre Dumas, père (1802–1870), one of the most popular authors of the nineteenth century, succeeded in gaining a great reputation as a historical novelist, especially for such works as *The Three Musketeers* and *The Count of Monte Cristo*.

The most outstanding work of Alexandre Dumas, fils (1824–1895) is *The Lady of the Camellias*. With beautiful sentences and sincere emotion, the novel indicts the destruction of truth by hypocritical capitalism; moreover, the novel has been adapted as a drama and is one of the early works that expresses French realism.

George Sand (1804–1876) was the greatest French female writer, and she is often compared with Englishwoman George Eliot partly because of their literary status and partly because they take country life as their theme. The common themes explored by George Sand are the rights and obligations of life and free love. She may be regarded as one of the earliest feminists.

If the aforementioned writers and their works are more or less romantic, Gustave Flaubert (1821–1880) and Guy de Maupassant (1850–1893) were undoubtedly masters of realism. Flaubert's representative work is Madame Bovary, while Maupassant is famous for his short stories, such as "Ball of Fat" and "The Necklace."

Concerning other writers such as Émile Zola (1840–1902), Marie-Henri Beyle (1783–1842), better known as Stendhal, Prosper Mérimée (1803–1870), Alphonse Daudet (1840–1897), Pierre Loti (1850–1923), and Marcel Proust (1871–1922), they may all be classified as naturalist writers except Loti, who is regarded as an impressionist. Naturalism is extreme realism or naked realism in which writers use almost cruel methods to uncover the reality, the animality of humans, the cruelty of nature, and so on. Zola's works include *Nana* and *The Downfall.* A couple of Stendhal's works are *The Red and the Black* and *The Charterhouse of Parma*, while the novella *Carmen* by Mérimée became a household name after it formed the basis of Bizet's opera.

The nineteenth century also witnessed the development of French poetry. Briefly speaking, they can be classified into three groups: romantic, Gothic and symbolic.

Representative romantic poets are Alphonse de Lamartine (1790–1869), Victor Hugo, and Alfred de Musset (1810–1857). A representative Gothic poet is Théophile Gautier (1811–1872). Poets such as Charles Pierre Baudelaire (1821–1867), Stéphane Mallarmé (1842–1898), and Arthur Rimbaud (1854–1891) represent the school of symbolism. However, this classification is not absolute, because the Gothic poets also used elements of reminiscence and nostalgia from romanticism, while both the Gothic and symbolist poets valued form above all.

It is worth mentioning is that the French symbolist poets were influenced by the American poet Edgar Allan Poe (1809–1849), and in turn transmitted that influence into English poetry.

6.7.2   German Literature

Although the nineteenth century witnessed a multitude of poets, playwrights, and novelists, the overall achievements were not as great as they had been in the previous century. Poetry stood out among all the genres, and the Romantic lyric poets are represented by Heinrich Heine (1797–1856), Georg von Hardenberg (1772–1801), who wrote under the name of Novalis, Friedrich Hölderlin (1770–1843), and Ludwig Uhland (1787–1862). Their poetry was set to music by Franz Schubert, Robert Schumann, and Johannes Brahms, so they are well known.

The North Sea, a cycle of poems, is Heine's best work. Another romantic writer worth mentioning is E.T.A. Hoffmann (1776–1822), who was a composer as well. His works are weird and absurd, and his usage of techniques such as alienation, free association, inner monologue, and a multi-level structure has influenced many modernist or postmodernist writers. His works have inspired lots of musicians; for example, Pyotr Ilyich Tchaikovsky got his inspiration for *The Nutcracker* from Hoffmann's "The Nutcracker and the Mouse King".

6.7.3   Russian Literature

The nineteenth century was the golden age for Russian literature, which started with romanticism and then turned into realism and critical realism. Poets such as Alexander Pushkin (1799–1837) and Mikhail Lermontov (1814–1841) were representative romantic poets, while romantic novelists included the renowned writers Leo Tolstoy (1828–1910), Fyodor Dostoyevsky (1821–1881), and Ivan Turgenev (1818–1883).

Alexander Pushkin symbolized the beginning of Russian literature, being described by Maxim Gorky as "the father of Russian literature." In early times, his poems were romantic, but his style later changed to realism. A representative work is *Eugene Onegin*, a novel written in poetic form, which describes faithfully the aristocratic life of Russia in the 1820s, presents the customs of Russia, and successfully shapes an image of the noble youth.

Leo Tolstoy was one of the greatest writers of the twentieth century, with the two books *War and Peace* and *Anna Karenina* being his masterpieces. *War and Peace* is set during the Napoleonic wars, and the grand set-pieces contain vivid descriptions of people from different social classes. *Anna Karenina* becomes more and more exquisite and touching as the characters develop. In the two books, the description of reality both in its breadth and depth reaches new heights. In his later years, Tolstoy wrote another great work, the novel *Resurrection*.

Fyodor Dostoevsky, virtually as famous as Tolstoy, was good at revealing people's inner hearts against the social and historical backdrop of the nineteenth century. His works include *Crime and Punishment* and *The Brothers Karamazov*, among many others. Dostoevsky is regarded by many as "the father of realism," using objective descriptions without commenting on characters' divergent views on a certain event, and using the stream of consciousness technique to reveal people's inner worlds. All these techniques are well presented in the novel *Crime and Punishment*. Another novel, *Notes from Hell*, expresses the absurdity and agony that is later shown in works by existential writers.

Ivan Turgenev was another great Russian novelist of the nineteenth century. He is always mentioned together with Dostoevsky and Tolstoy, yet while the latter two often explored religion and morals, Turgenev was dedicated to art itself. He was particularly adept at describing inner emotions, especially those of women. As Turgenev himself said about the way in which he portrayed nature, "I am hard to be surpassed." His works include the short story collection *A Sportsman's Sketches* and the novels *Fathers and Sons*, *On the Eve*, and *Torrents of Spring*.

6.7.4   English Literature

The nineteenth century was another glorious time for English literature. The first half of the century was occupied by romanticism, while realism began to prevail in the second half. Romantic poetry was the greatest flowering of romantic literature, which started with the publication of *Lyrical Ballads* by William Wordsworth (1770–1850) and Samuel Taylor Coleridge (1772–1834). Wordsworth and Coleridge were both pioneers of romanticism and practiced their theories in their poetry. Wordsworth used plain words to praise nature, the natural spirit, and the common people. In 1843, he became Britain's Poet Laureate. His argument that "poetry is the spontaneous overflow of powerful feelings" has become a poetic definition that is agreed upon by most people. Coleridge's poems, full of exoticism and mystery, represented another tendency of romanticism. His poem "Kubla Khan" stemmed from his dream of China and was involved with mysterious oriental beauty. Other famous romantic poets include Lord Byron (1788–1824), Percy Bysshe Shelley (1792–1822), and John Keats (1795–1821). Byron and Shelley had a great influence on poets in France and other European countries. They created both short and exquisite lyrical poems such as "Ode to the West Wind" by Shelley and epic poems such as Byron's *Don Juan*, Shelley's *The Revolt of Islam* and *Prometheus Unbound*. Although Keats wrote no epic poems, his lyrical poems are exquisitely formed and are infused with fierce emotion, so that readers cannot put them down. His most famous poems include "Ode to Autumn" and "Ode to a Nightingale."

With the reciprocal radiance that romanticism and realism shone upon each other and the talent of both male and female writers, the nineteenth century became a fabulous era for English novels. An exemplar of romantic novelists was Walter Scott (1771–1832), who drew material from Scottish historical legends and myths to create romantic stories that enchanted readers in Britain and indeed throughout Europe. Writers after Scott included Charles Dickens (1812–1870) and William Makepeace Thackeray (1811–1863), with Dickens being the most popular novelist after Scott. His novels reveal the craftiness and cruelty of real society as well as exposing the innocence and naivety of children. Children are the heroes of many of his novels, which seek to make observations about this sophisticated world by contrasting it with the innocence of children. His fifteen novels (he also wrote hundreds of short stories and non-fiction articles) include *David Copperfield*, *The Pickwick Papers*, *Nicholas Nickleby*, and *Oliver Twist*. In his masterpiece *Vanity Fair*, Thackeray portrayed characters and society with depth and craftsmanship: he was one of the greatest realist writers of the nineteenth century and one of the greatest novelists in English history.

The nineteenth is the epoch when English female writers gained more prominence. They include Jane Austen (1775–1817), Charlotte Brontë (1816–1855), Emily Brontë (1818–1848), Anne Brontë (1820–1849), and George Eliot (1819–1880). Austen's novels are based on family life and mainly concern romantic love and marriage. They exhibit the marital problems of women and English families with humor, wisdom, and delicacy. Her novels have won everlasting popularity, so that even today readers and movie directors alike admire them greatly. Representative works of the Brontë sisters are *Jane Eyre* (Charlotte), *Wuthering Heights* (Emily), and *The Tenant of Wildfell Hall* (Anne). *Jane Eyre* is the novel that first depicts the love story of a girl who is marked by an independent personality rather than an attractive appearance, and the eponymous character has become a paradigm for female literature. The violent passion, unsociable hero, and solitary environment of *Wuthering Heights* brought a new perspective to the English novel. Some people regard George Eliot as the most remarkable female writer in nineteenth-century England, for her books are full of in-depth psychological insights. Her masterpieces are *Adam Bede*, *The Mill on the Floss*, and *Middlemarch*.

There are other great writers in nineteenth-century England: they include the great essayists Charles Lamb (1775–1834) and Thomas Carlyle (1795–1881), the great critic Matthew Arnold, and the scientist and writer Thomas Huxley (1825–1895). Lamb's prose is of great wit and humor as well as extraordinary talent. His masterpiece is *Essays of Elia*. Arnold's essays are classics of criticism. Huxley's essays "Man's Place in Nature" and "Debate with Wilberforce," combining science and literature, are examples of clearly expressed scientific thinking.

6.7.5   American Literature

With the gradual independence and increasing prosperity of America, American literature started to attract attention. In succession to the romanticism seen in Europe, American literature in the nineteenth century was also colored by romantic characteristics. Two leading figures were the philosopher and writer Ralph Waldo Emerson (1803–1882) and Henry Thoreau (1817–1862). They denounced traditional Christian doctrines and espoused nature and natural being, and exerted a seminal effect on later poets, such as Walt Whitman (1819–1892) and Emily Dickinson (1830–1886). Washington Irving (1783–1859) was the first internationally best-selling American writer, and his masterpiece was *The Sketch Book*, a collection of short stories that included "The Legend of Sleepy Hollow." A contemporary of Emerson's was Nathaniel Hawthorne (1804–1864), who was famous for his novel *The Scarlet Letter*. This revolves around a love affair between a married woman and a priest, and reveals the struggle between religion and human nature. Hawthorne also wrote a Gothic novel *The House of the Seven Gables*.

A great master of the Gothic novel in the nineteenth century was Edgar Allan Poe (1809–1849). His novels share the features of Gothic, detective, and psychological novels, and develop each of these genres. The greatest American novelist is perhaps Mark Twain (1835–1910). When reading his masterpieces *The Adventures of Tom Sawyer* and *Adventures of Huckleberry Finn*, readers find themselves living the curious and adventurous childhoods he describes. Though there is shadow among the childlike world in these novels, it is cast by the sun, which is the opposite of the evil world seen by children in Charles Dickens' novels. Mark Twain also unfolded an idyllic picture of the American landscape in these two novels. Another great novelist after Mark Twain was Henry James (1843–1916), who was a master of psychological description. His works center on genteel society, and his masterpieces include *The American, The Portrait of a Lady*, and *The Golden Bowl*.

The best poets in nineteenth-century America are Edgar Allan Poe, Walt Whitman, and Emily Dickinson. Poe's poetry is characterized by aestheticism and concentrates on rhyme and meter as well as diction. He preferred the theme of death, and his representative works are "The Raven" and "Annabel Lee." If Poe's poetry represents the decadent beauty of gloom and death, Whitman's poetry is a powerful song of self, song of nature, and song of liberty, and represents the bright and optimistic American spirit. His poetry is an embodiment of the doctrine of self-reliance expressed by Emerson and Rousseau and marks the beginning of free verse. Whitman is deemed to be the representative poet of American spirit and was an exemplar for later poets. Opposed to Whitman's bold and unrestrained passion, Emily Dickinson lived in her own private world, although she agreed with Whitman in terms of her fervent love for nature and acquiescence regarding religion. She paid close attention to tiny creatures as well as her own internal world. Another contemporary poet was Henry Wadsworth Longfellow (1807–1882). His poetic accomplishments were less conspicuous than those of the poets mentioned above.

6.8   European and American Literature in the Twentieth Century

6.8.1   English Literature

Thomas Hardy (1840–1928) was a good poet and an excellent novelist. His novels are filled with pessimism and helplessness against irresistible fate. His masterpieces include *Jude the Obscure* and *Far from the Madding Crowd*.

George Bernard Shaw (1856–1950) was a critical realist playwright who was influenced by socialism. His plays humorously mocked and criticized social evils in education, marriage, government, and social welfare. For his outstanding achievements, he was awarded the Nobel Prize for Literature in 1925. Shaw's works include *Man and Superman, Pygmalion, Saint Joan*, and *Major Barbara*.

Though H.G. Wells (1866–1946), John Galsworthy (1867–1933), and William Somerset Maugham (1874–1965) wrote in the twentieth century, their works continued Hardy's realist tradition. H.G. Wells is famous for his science fiction, represented by *The War of the Worlds*. The Nobel Prize winner John Galsworthy's achievement in literature is manifested in his trilogy *The Forsyte Saga*, *Modern Comedy*, and *End of the Chapter*, which recounted the history of the fictional Forsyte family. Through their story, John Galsworthy portrayed a realistic picture of British society from the late nineteenth century to the early twentieth century. This series also described the vicissitudes of the British bourgeoisie.

Somerset Maugham was famous for his novels *Liza of Lambeth* and *Of Human Bondage*, and he also wrote a large number of short stories. Many of his works are full of exotic flavor owing to rich experiences during his extensive travels.

James Joyce (1882–1941) was one of the pioneers of Modernism. His masterpiece *Ulysses*, which is based on one day's experience of an ordinary man, imitates Homer's *Odyssey*. While the *Odyssey* describes the experience of Greek hero Ulysses, who surmounted all sorts of obstacles before finally returning home, Joyce's *Ulysses* reflects the spiritual journey of a modern person through the device of a single day in the life of an ordinary man. In this book, despite the seemingly common materials, the past and the present permeate each other and daily trivia becomes profound, while extreme erudition is mixed with crude humor, fully reflecting the primary characteristics of modern literature. Another of Joyce's masterpiece is *Finnegans Wake*, which general readers can barely understand because of all the allusions and innuendos that are included.

Virginia Woolf (1882–1941) was a distinguished writer in the twentieth century, and is famous for her skillful use of the stream of consciousness. Representative novels are *To the Lighthouse*, *The Waves*, and *Mrs Dalloway*.

The novels of D.H. Lawrence (1885–1930) novels reflect the repressed humanity in industrial society. The bold depiction of sex in his novels meant that some of them were banned, but he is now recognized as one of the pioneers of modern fiction. His works include *Sons and Lovers* and *Lady Chatterley's Lover*.

Joseph Conrad (1857–1924) was dedicated to revealing the dark side of imperialism. His novels, such as *Heart of Darkness* and *Lord Jim*, established his position as a great novelist.

W.B. Yeats (1865–1939) was one of the greatest British poets and play-wrights of the twentieth century. His early works were influenced by romanticism and symbolism, whereas his later works could be defined as including aspects of postmodernism. He was awarded the Nobel Prize for Literature in 1923 and his poems include "Sailing to Byzantium" and "The Tower."

T.S. Eliot (1888–1965) was a British poet who was born in the United States. He was a leading modernistic writer and is particularly famous for his poem *The Waste Land*. The historical allusions and references in the book are as elusive as in Joyce's *Ulysses*. Eliot expounded upon the spiritual steril-ity of modern people and modern society. He was also the best critic since Arnold, and his criticism has contributed to the re-reading and re-assessment of many literary works. For instance, the metaphysical poetry of the seven-teenth century was given attention again thanks to his evaluation of it. Eliot won the Nobel Prize for Literature in 1948.

W.H. Auden (1907–1973) was also an important poet in the early twentieth century, and his political poetry and poetry of war affected Chinese poets of the 1930s.

In the mid-twentieth century, British literature was represented by the so-called "Angry Young Men," who expressed their dissatisfaction with war and social injustice. Among their number were the novelist Kingsley Amis (1922–1995) and the playwright John Osborne (1929–1994).

William Golding (1911–1993) was a famous writer in the 1950s and later. He is represented here by *Lord of the Flies*, and he won the Nobel Prize for Literature in 1983. *Lord of the Flies* is an allegorical novel that reveals the evil of human nature in its description of the process whereby a group of children on an deserted island change from kind to vicious, civilized to savage: it aroused strong responses on publication.

In the late twentieth century, there were two prominent female writers. They were Doris Lessing (1919–2013) and Iris Murdoch (1919–1999). Doris Lessing, who was often viewed as the spokesperson for the feminist movement, wrote many works with communist, psy-chological, and sci-fi themes during different phases of her life. Concern about women's fate in modern society is the theme of a large number of her books. Lessing's masterpieces are *The Grass is Singing*, *The Golden Notebook*, and *Memoirs of a Survivor*. For her outstanding contribution to literature, she was awarded the Nobel Prize for Literature in 2007, the oldest winner ever of this award.

Iris Murdoch was another prominent writer of the twentieth century. Influenced by Freud and Sartre, most of her novels were about ethics and sex. They often center on middle- and upper-class intellectuals, and are usually humorous, dark, and mysterious. Her novels include *Under the Net*, *The Bell*, and *The Black Prince*, with *Under the Net* being selected by the American Modern Library as one of the best 100 English novels of the twentieth century.

In the twentieth century, the greatest playwrights in Britain were Samuel Beckett (1906–1989) and Harold Pinter (1930–2008). Samuel Beckett was one of the founders of the Theater of the Absurd. In his masterpiece *Waiting for Godot*, two tramps endlessly "wait for Godot" in the wilderness. The waiting is boring. What are they waiting for? Why are they waiting? How long will they wait? And what is Godot? Neither the characters nor the audience know the answers. By distinctively displaying an ordinary situation, Beckett revealed the awkward position of humans in an absurd world, and this won him the Nobel Prize for Literature in 1969.

Harold Pinter was also a representative of the Theater of the Absurd and the greatest playwright in Britain after Beckett. His masterpieces are *The Room*, *The Birthday Party*, and *The Caretaker*. He won the Nobel Prize for Literature in 2005.

6.8.2   American Literature

With America's rising economic status in the twentieth century, its literature began to flourish and many writers became celebrities during this period. In addition to white male writers, black female writers and Jewish writers won international recognition, accomplished great achievements, and became eminent representatives of literature in the second half of the twentieth century.

In the first half of the twentieth century, the most outstanding writers, who mainly focused on realist writing, included Theodore Dreiser (1871–1945), Jack London (1876–1916), John Steinbeck (1902–1968), Ernest Hemingway (1899–1961), and F. Scott Fitzgerald (1896–1940).

The works of Theodore Dreiser mainly exposes American society's pursuit of money and status and the resultant disasters that ensue. His works include *Sister Carrie* and *An American Tragedy*.

Jack London's masterpieces are *The Call of the Wild* and *White Fang*. The former exposes the law of the jungle, while the latter is written from the viewpoint of the titular canine character and depicts the violent worlds of wild animals and men, also exploring themes of morality and redemption.

John Steinbeck was a typical writer of the American Great Depression of the 1930s. His novels depict how poverty-stricken ordinary people create beautiful lives by fighting and working hard. *The Grapes of Wrath* is his most outstanding work. In 1962 he was awarded the Nobel Prize for Literature.

Ernest Hemingway wrote about wars in the twentieth century; other themes include love and loss. His works are characterized by their narrative conciseness. The heroes of his stories are often very brave, striving to keep their dignity even in a harsh environment. His works include *For Whom the Bell Tolls, The Sun Also Rises,* and *The Old Man and the Sea*. He won the Nobel Prize for Literature in 1954.

F. Scott Fitzgerald represents the writers of the 1920s Jazz Age. His novels reflect the uproar and the pursuit of pleasure of that era. *The Great Gatsby* is his most renowned work.

In the first half of the twentieth century, representatives of modernism among American writers included the poet Ezra Pound (1885–1972), the playwright Eugene O'Neill (1888–1953), and the novelists William Faulkner (1897–1962) and J.D. Salinger (1919–2010).

The poetry of Pound shares many similarities with that of T.S. Eliot, such as the frequent employment of cultural metaphors and the outstanding mastery of crafted images rather than logic on which traditional poems are based. Pound sought the redemption of Western society through the employment of metaphors and observations about history and culture. He is a representative poet of imagism, and his master work is *The Cantos*.

Eugene O'Neill was a pre-eminent and prolific American playwright of the twentieth century. His works include *The Emperor Jones, Desire under the Elms, The Hairy Ape, The Iceman Cometh*, and *Long Day's Journey into Night*. His plays reflect the stress experienced by and the historical destiny of modern people, and their dilemma concerning an eagerness to communicate that contrasts with a fear of communication.

William Faulkner took Yoknapatawpha County, a fictional Southern town, as the background for his novels and short stories, vividly elaborating the historical and cultural psychology of Southern society. With the application of the stream of consciousness style as well as multi-angle, multi-level viewpoints, his works reveal the complexity and mystique of modern life. His novels include *The Sound and the Fury* and *Absalom, Absalom*.

J.D. Salinger was a writer who gained worldwide literary fame for just one novel, *The Catcher in the Rye*, and a number of short stories. Through the narration of the young protagonist Holden Caulfield, the novel deals with the complex psychological nuances and problems that young people experience as they grow up. It has been a bestseller ever since it was published in 1951.

To simply divide writers of this period into realists and modernists would lead to the exclusion of many writers, because many realistic writers employed modernistic writing traits in order to depict reality. Looking at authors from another perspective, it is noteworthy that in addition to mainstream writers a lot of non-mainstream authors, such as Toni Morrison (1931–) and Alice Walker (1944–), rose to fame in the twentieth century. With talent and intelligence, they composed a series of classics that have brought them international fame. Their works not only attach great significance to racial and feminist issues but also incisively touch upon the universal problems in American society. In 1993, Toni Morrison was awarded the Nobel Prize for Literature; her most famous work is *Beloved*. Alice Walker's most important works include *Meridian* and *The Color Purple*, which won her the Pulitzer Prize for Fiction and the National Book Award for Fiction. Both authors are innovative in their approach to writing and language.

Jewish authors have also achieved much in the twentieth-century American literary world, with the most renowned including Saul Bellow (1915–2005), Isaac Bashevis Singer (1902–1991), and Arthur Miller (1915–2005).

Saul Bellow won the Nobel Prize for Literature in 1976, and his works include *Herzog*, *Henderson the Rain King*, and *Humboldt's Gift*. His works often have a Jewish hero, pay special attention to how modern people live, and insightfully uncover their various material and spiritual problems.

Another Nobel Prize-winning writer is Isaac Bashevis Singer. Jewish elements and culture abound in his works, the most famous being *The Magician of Lublin*.

Arthur Miller, among much else, wrote the play *Death of a Salesman*, which is one of the classics of modern tragedy.

6.8.3   French Literature

Romain Roland (1866–1944) succeeded Honoré de Balzac as the master of the realist tradition. His most renowned work is the ten-volume novel *Jean-Christophe*. With epic grandeur and profundity, his works are broad-minded, insightful, and vivid, combining poetic passion, philosophical exploration, and realist depiction. With symphonic structure and splendor, *Jean-Christophe* develops a new artistic style of its own, in which the presentation of nature is saturated with musical beauty. As the author remarked, this book is "a musical novel."

Roger Martin du Gard (1881–1958) was the author of the eight-volume novel *The Thibaults*, which shows the social contractions and the mindset of intellectuals during the First World War in France. With the approach of the stream of consciousness, the work reflects social reality in a modernistic way and shows an anti-war attitude on humanitarian grounds. The author won the Nobel Prize for Literature in 1937.

André Gide (1869–1951) was another French writer who won the Nobel Prize for Literature. His early works usually have some symbolic elements, but he opposed excessive attention to form and a detachment from reality. His most outstanding work is *The Counterfeiters*, in which the counterfeiters are not only the outlaws who make counterfeit money, but also symbolize those writers who only have names as authors but no really good works. The novel has many modernistic characteristics, such as a complex plot, numerous characters, and a structure in which stories develop simultaneously but with no connections between them.

Louis Aragon (1897–1982) was a poet, novelist, and journalist, and a master of French surrealism, whose long book *Le Paysan de Paris* describes a bizarre and colorful France from the perspective of a peasant in an imaginative manner. It became one of the most successful surrealist works in French literary history. The author later joined the Communist Party and adopted some principles of socialist realism, but finally gave up on this and returned to his surrealist roots. His works cover novels, prose, poetry, and literary criticism, in which not only the history of the political struggle is recorded, but also the trends in French literature are foreseen.

Paul Verlaine (1844–1896) was a renowned scholarly poet. His representative poem is "A Seaside Cemetery," in which he shows his philosophical thinking about statics and dynamics, life and death. With abundant images, profound thought, and strict poetical meter, the poem is a masterpiece, in which modern ideology is expressed in a classical way.

The French novelist Marcel Proust was the writer of the seven-volume novel *Remembrance of Things Past*, which won him fame as master of modern fiction. The interwoven remembrances in the novel make the work a symphony of time from which reality emerges. It is a classic work that describes modern people's understanding of life and time.

Representatives of French existentialism are Jean-Paul Sartre (1905–1980) and Albert Camus (1913–1960).

Jean-Paul Sartre was both a philosopher and a writer. His main philosophical works include *Being and Nothingness* and *Existentialism is a Humanism*. His existential philosophy reflects Western people's increasing awareness of crisis, sense of alienation, and consciousness of insecurity after the Second World War. Beginning with the premise that "existence precedes essence," his philosophical works come to the conclusion that "freedom of choice" provides a way to get out of the survival predicament. As a writer of fiction, his most famous works are the novel *Nausea* and the play *Hell is Other People*, which expose the absurdity of modern society and the indifference, entanglement, and frustration of interpersonal relationships.

Albert Camus was another representative of French existentialism. He also revealed the absurdity of modern society and the impossibility of totally changing it. However, unlike Sartre, he advocated that people should confront and resist this absurdity with the hero spirit, and in the course of this show the beauty of human nature. His work *The Plague* perfectly shows beautiful human nature fighting absurdity; while another work, *The Stranger*, expounds the real passion behind the superficial "flatness" that people experience when confronted with absurdity in a plain style. He was awarded the Nobel Prize for Literature in 1957, "for his important literary production, which with clear-sighted earnestness illuminates the problems of the human conscience in our times."

Eugene Ionesco (1909–1994) was a distinguished Romanian French writer, who was also one of the founders and representatives of the Theatre of the Absurd. His works include *The Chairs*, *Rhinoceros*, *Exit the King*, and *The Bald Soprano*.

6.8.4   German Literature

Gerhart Hauptmann (1862–1946) was a great playwright. He showed great compassion toward human beings and viewed the tragic sins as something inside the universe or the human race instead of in individual lives. The characters are lifelike and his works render readers a general picture of the life in an era or a country. Gerhart Hauptmann was awarded the Nobel Prize for Literature in 1912. His works include *The Sunken Bell*, *Henry the Leper*, *Lonely People*, and *The Weavers*.

Thomas Mann's (1875–1955) masterpiece is *Buddenbrooks*. The writer explored the aristocracy in nineteenth-century Germany by describing the vicissitudes of the Buddenbrooks family using sarcastic and exquisite language. This, together with *The Magic Mountain*, won him the Nobel Prize for Literature in 1926.

Bertolt Brecht (1898–1956) was an eminent poet, playwright, and drama theorist. He proposed the theory of defamiliarization, which exhibits to the audience the taken-for-granted incidents in life in a non-traditional manner, in order to surprise people and make them think. In terms of acting and stage design, Brecht tried to deliberately break the illusion created while watching a traditional play, intending audiences to be ready to judge and criticize everything they saw on stage. His works include *Drums in the Night*, *Man Equals Man*, *Life of Galileo*, and *Mother Courage and her Children*.

Heinrich Theodor Böll (1917–1985) was a writer who focused on the catastrophe and trauma that war brought to human beings and society in general. His masterpiece is *Group Portrait with Lady*, and in this novel he exploits pastiche, reflecting on the historical appearance of German society over half a century through the description of the relationship between a woman and people of various sorts. He won the Nobel Prize for Literature in 1972.

Günter Grass (1927–2015) is famous for *The Tin Drum*, a novel with an all-pervading sense of absurdity. The story is told from the bizarre perspective of a dwarf, Oscar, with the physical height of a three-year-old child and a superior intelligence, and it reveals the deformed history of German society between the two world wars. The author won the Nobel Prize for Literature in 1999.

6.8.5   Russian Literature

Leonid Andreyev (1871–1919) was an early realist writer, yet his works exploit contemporary writing techniques, such as expressionism and symbolism. With exaggerated features and intense colors, *The Red Laugh* combines a series of absurd scenes, like nightmares, to express the horror of war. In the play *The Life of Man*, a candle is lit, burning and extinguishing to symbolize a man's life. *The Seven That Were Hanged* even blends different writing skills. With the help of writing techniques other than realism to explore reality, his works are extraordinary.

Vladimir Mayakovsky (1893–1930) was the most prominent Russian poet of the twentieth century. He wrote on different themes with intense emotion and created the ladder poem, which strengthened rhythm and enriched expressive power. His works include *Vladimir Ilyich Lenin* and *All Right!*.

Maxim Gorky (1868–1936) was called an outstanding representative of proletariat literature by Lenin. His most famous works include *The Mother* and an autobiographical trilogy, *My Childhood, In the World*, and *My Universities*. By portraying a series of proletariat revolutionists, especially the working class, *The Mother* represents the awakening of Russian revolutionists, the combining process of Marxism, the labor movement, and the prospect of the doom of capitalism and the success of socialism. Gorky's autobiography describes the living conditions in Russia during the 1870s and 1880s, exposes the cruelty of the exploiting class, the mean habits of the petite bourgeoisie, the misery of the working class, and a real image of Alexei, who is diligent, never surrenders to dark powers, pursues the brightness, and explores the revolutionary truth.

Mikhail Aleksandrovich Sholokhov (1905–1984) was also a remarkable Russian writer, his most famous works being *And Quiet Flows the Don* and *Virgin Soil Upturned*. *And Quiet Flows the Don* is an epic novel. Based on the two revolutions (February Revolution and October Revolution) in 1912 and 1922, the First World War, and the Russian Civil War, the novel describes the huge changes that 5 million Cossacks went through during the war. The novel has a complicated yet well-knit structure with threads of social life and personal life intertwined. Well-rounded portrayal of characters, vivid language, the use of unique and funny Cossack dialects, many folksongs, a depiction of the magnificent scenery of the grasslands of the Don River, all create a romantic atmosphere. Sholokhov was awarded the Nobel Prize for Literature in 1965.

Boris Pasternak (1890–1960) was a prominent Russian poet and novelist. The first half of *Doctor Zhivago* is a novel, and this is followed by over twenty poems. Centering on Zhivago and his lover Lara, and many other characters, the novel presents the themes of life in both society and family. By describing the experience of the decade of the October Revolution and Russian Civil War, the novel shows the old intellectuals' ambivalence and confusion about the revolution. With minute expression of family and emotion issues, the novel is a tragicomedy of love. It brought Pasternak tremendous fame, and he was awarded the Nobel Prize for Literature in 1958. However, the work was claimed to be "resenting Socialist revolution," and the Communist Party of the Soviet Union was enraged, and this brought suffering to the author.

Ivan Alekseyevich Bunin (1870–1953) inherited the Russian Realist tradition. He mainly portrayed life in aristocratic manors and in his early works criticized the spiritual sterility and degeneration of the aristocrats. Later he moved on to rustic subjects, depicting the darkness and backwardness in rural areas and the peasants' ignorance. Bunin emphasized the depiction of characters and environment, and his language is vivid. Gorky praised him as "one of the finest Russian stylists." Ivan Bunin's famous works include *To the Edge of the World and Other Stories, The Village*, and *Antonov Apples*. He won the Nobel Prize for Literature in 1933.

Aleksandr Isayevich Solzhenitsyn (1918–2008) was conferred the Nobel Prize for Literature in 1970 for revealing the conditions in forced labor camps in his novel *The Gulag Archipelago*, and was consequently expelled from the Soviet Union.

BIBLIOGRAPHY

Chen Jia. 2002. *A History of English Literature*. Beijing: The Commercial Press.
Fang Hanwen. 2005. *A History of Comparative Literature of the East and the West*. Beijing: Peking University Press.
Grant, Neil. 1998. *History of Literature*. Trans. Qiao Heming, et al. Taiyuan: Hope Publishing House.
Macy, John. 2004. *The Story of the World's Literature*. Trans. Yu Huiping. Guiyang: Guizhou People's Publishing House.
Sporre, Dennis J. 1990. *A History of the Arts*. London: Bloomsbury Books.
Wikipedia, the free encyclopedia. http://en.wilcipedia.org/wiki
Xu Baogeng. 2003. *The Pilgrimage of Western Literature*. Shijiazhuang: Hebei Education Press.
Zhu Weizhi, Zhao Li, and Huang Jinkai. 2004. *A Concise History of European and American Literature*. Beijing: China Renmin University Press.

WEBSITE

http:dxnc.gs.edu.cn/jiaoan/auweiwangye/jal-l.htm

CHAPTER 7

Western Organizational Culture: EU Organizational Culture

Organizational culture usually refers to a shared value system that may be distinguished from other value systems. The organizational culture of the European Union (EU) can be regarded as the best example of Western organizational culture. Formed on March 25, 1957, the EU has become a twenty-eight-member regional organization, with a population of about 500 million and a GNP amounting to $12 trillion (2007), the biggest in the world. With this overall strength, its willingness to participate in international affairs is increasing, and so is its influence on the international stage.

Cultural factors have played a crucial role in the European integration process, leaving an influence not only on the mode of development, basic tenets, legal system, institutional setting, and voting mechanism, but also on the scope and standards of the EU's eastward expansion. Meanwhile, European culture itself has become more embracing and colorful.

7.1   THE ORIGIN AND DEVELOPMENT OF EU CULTURE

7.1.1   Definition of EU Culture

In the *Modern Chinese Dictionary*, culture is defined as "the total of material and spiritual wealth created in the development process of human history, especially spiritual wealth, such as literature, art, science, etc."

© The Author(s) 2018   181
G. Xu et al. (eds.), K. Chen et al. (trans.), *Understanding Western Culture*, https://doi.org/10.1007/978-981-10-8150-7_7

Culture is the accumulation of national intelligence, the prerequisite for national development, the reflection of economic and political status, and the foundation of national integrity. Since the 1980s, because of globalization and the quick development of information technology, the importance of culture in shaping social and economic activities has been more evident than ever. It has become a sign of self-identification in many areas, since the first criterion in telling the difference between two societies is the value system and creativity of their people rather than monetary or natural resources.

Initially, EU integration was focused on the economy. As the economic integration level rose, culture was found to be extremely important in cultivating a sense of belonging in Europe. The renowned American scholar Samuel P. Huntington pointed out that "the EU is the result of European shared culture" since "the basis of economic cooperation lies in similarities of culture," and held that "Countries with cultural kinships could cooperate economically and politically. International organizations that are built with cultural similarities are more likely to be successful than those that are not." All EU member countries should respect each other's unique national characteristics. This consensus should be extended to a higher level to enrich European cultural heritages and to encourage international cultural exchange.

7.1.2   The Formation of EU Culture

7.1.2.1 Homogeneous Culture
European integration was based on a shared culture. Commercial interaction and wars among European countries had led them to know each other better. Though there were differences, they shared the same basic historical tradition and cultural origin.

Ancient Greek and Roman Civilizations
Greece is the fountainhead of European civilization, and the word "Europe" originates from Greek myth. The Greeks made important achievements in philosophy, mathematics, science, and city-building, and the Greek civilization became the cultural origin of Europe. Later, Ancient Rome inherited and developed Greek civilization; more importantly, as its territory expanded it combined several European countries, which had a significant cultural impact on them. Ancient Roman civilization became the origin of the Renaissance and Enlightenment. These two civilizations together provided a framework for European civilization, which has been deemed "one of the top events in human history."

Christian Culture

Religious factors were important in laying the foundation for European integration. All European countries have a Christian cultural background, which was significant in inheriting European civilization. Christian culture, including ancient ethics and dogmas, evolved into a spiritual bond that broke individual, familial, or even national boundaries, and was expected to, through the work of missionaries, combine the individualistic Greek culture, the Roman culture that stressed the importance of nation, legion, and law, and the familial Germanic culture. Europe is a Christian continent, where people share the same "heaven" and god, the same spiritual world that brought forth "European awareness". There are Christian characteristics in social structure, painting, music, and architecture, as well as in other areas. Democratic peace reduces the conflicts between European countries, and since they share the same cultures and values, their ideologies have common features. This is exactly why the EU can be such a powerful unity. Some have argued that "Christianity could bond the disintegrating western Europe through religion and religious organizations. It facilitated the cultural and social exchange between western European countries, accelerated the recognition process, and laid a base for the development of Christian culture in the Middle Ages."

Shared Cultural Values

J. Aldebert et al., the authors of *History of Europe*, commented, "Though European history witnessed hatred and plundering, or even betrayal, blood-shedding, there was mutual beneficial interaction." Having experienced the "Renaissance" and "Enlightenment," the Europeans pursue freedom and democracy, believe in Kant's philosophy, and stress justice and reason. European countries have built the democratic legal system that takes constitutionalism, the separation of powers, universal suffrage, representative system, judicial independence, and the supremacy of law as the basic principles and core contents. Democratic and legal awareness, rooted in public attitudes, became a principle of daily life. Cultural values, such as democratic politics, scientific thinking, a humanistic spirit, rationalism, and romanticism, were accepted by the Europeans.

7.1.2.2 The "European Union Dream"

After the seventeenth century, as wars plagued European countries, men of insight came up with the idea of building a European union that would ensure peace and development. In 1713, the French Abbé de Saint-Pierre proposed the establishment of a "European Confederation" in the "Plan for Perpetual Peace". Napoleon once said, "We should have a

European Code, a Supreme Court of Europe, unified European currency, measurement, and law. I should see the people of Europe as a unified people ... this is the only ideal outcome." In 1925, the Prime Minister of France, Édouard Herriot, said that his ultimate hope was that one day he would be able to witness the emergence of the United States of Europe. In 1929, the French Minister of Foreign Affairs, Aristide Briand, proposed the idea of a United States of Europe to the German government, and in 1930 submitted a memorandum to the governments of European countries that proposed a union for sovereign states. The two world wars destroyed not only the sense of pride cultivated by the European industrial revolution, but the overall strength of the whole of Europe. Post-war division and the Cold War were frustrating, forcing Europeans to reflect on the past. They realized that their suffering was caused by the splits in Europe, and the only way to recover was to build a European unity. Therefore, the voice calling for the establishment of a unified Europe was louder.

In September 1946, British Prime Minister Winston Churchill proposed the establishment of a United States of Europe. "We must create united states of Europe, which is the only way that the hundreds of millions of the hardworking people can regain the joy of making life valuable and hopeful ... Why cannot there be a European organization, in which people on this turbulent and powerful continent could be more patriotic and have a common citizenship? Why should not it have its rightful place and, together with other large groups, decide its people's destiny? There must be a faith that hundreds of millions of families voluntarily believe in."

On May 9, 1950, the French Minister of Foreign Affairs Robert Schuman proposed the establishment of the European Coal and Steel Community. "The first step of the European Confederation is to stimulate the economy. Association of coal and steel industries immediately provides the basis for it, and changes the fate of those areas engaged in the manufacturing of weapons of war ... for peacekeeping, the establishment of European Confederation is essential. We have to work together to start basic production and set a senior authority to constrain the power of France, Germany and other member states." On April 18, 1951, France, Germany, Italy, the Netherlands, Belgium, and Luxembourg signed the Treaty on Establishing the European Coal and Steel Community in Paris. On July 25, 1952, it was established. On March 25, 1957, in Rome, six countries signed two treaties regarding the establishment of the European Economic Community and the European Atomic Energy Community, which together were called the Treaty of Rome. On April 8, 1965, the same six countries signed the Treaty of

Brussels, which was aimed at merging the three organizations and renaming it the European Community (EC).

In 1973, the United Kingdom, Denmark, Ireland, Greece, Spain, and Portugal joined the EC, whose number of member states therefore expanded to twelve. Within the EC there was established a Customs Union, which unified foreign trade policy and agricultural policy, and created the European monetary system, a unified budget, and a political co-operation system. The EC gradually became an agent for European economic and political interests. In this way, the dream of European integration gradually came into reality.

7.1.2.3 From the European Cultural Agreement to the Maastricht Treaty

In 1954, fourteen member states of the EC (Belgium, Denmark, France, Germany, Greece, Iceland, Ireland, Italy, Luxembourg, the Netherlands, Norway, Sweden, Turkey, and the United Kingdom) signed the European Cultural Agreement. In this agreement, the signatory states expressed their desire to promote European culture and committed themselves to taking joint actions and adopting similar policies. In 1985, the Berlin Declaration was passed at the Meeting of Ministers of Culture of the European Commission, and this further clarified the goals. It was held that cultural, social, economic, and technological factors together constituted the realization of social harmony and development.

On December 11, 1991, the Maastricht summit passed the Treaty of European Union, known as the Maastricht Treaty, to form the EU and establish European economic, monetary, and political union. Culture was under consideration in it. Section 128 in Chapter 9 of the Maastricht Treaty reads: "the Community is committed to promoting the common cultural heritage and cultural development of all member states, to respecting the cultural diversity of the other countries." In Section 151, it is proposed that the EU should strive to improve cultural development through education and training in member states. According to the Maastricht Treaty, the EU can take action when member states cannot fully achieve these objectives. Such action by the EU was not to replace the function of member states, but was used as reinforcement, aimed at encouraging cultural co-operation. Cultural terms stipulated that in the implementation of the Maastricht Treaty cultural factors should be considered for the purpose of promoting cultural diversity.

7.1.3   The Goals of the Establishment of European Culture

7.1.3.1   Consolidating the Political and Economic Achievements of European Integration

After continuous efforts over half a century, the EU has become a successful union of sovereign states. The EU has become one of the major economic entities in the world with its GDP being equivalent to a quarter of the world, exceeding that of the USA. However, in the integration process, with the increasing number of member states, cultural differences between member states brought considerable distress to the EU. Various arguments, doubts, or even conflicts appeared between different cultures. Jean Monnet, "Father of the EU," after experiencing several setbacks in applying common foreign and defense policies, said, "if we can restart the process, I will start from culture." In order to strengthen the sense of belonging so that "European consciousness" could be rooted in people's minds, and then to consolidate the political and economic results of European integration, the EU found that the only way was to use various cultural carriers and cultural activities to popularize the idea of European integration. Europeans should know how to understand and respect each other. They need to be aware that their own national culture is an integral part of the common culture of Europe. EU member states will not lose their own culture because of integration, but will share the common cultural development and the civilization of Europe as a whole. On January 1, 1999, the Euro was issued and on March 1, 2002 this single European currency went into circulation. The EU entered a new developmental stage. The Euro presented a unified image of Europe, enhancing the identification of European citizenship.

7.1.3.2   Contending with American Cultural Hegemony, and Strengthening European Cultural Independence

After the Cold War, American culture, in the form of digital content, controlled the production of 75% of television shows and 60% of radio shows throughout the world thanks to a combination of advanced commercial mechanisms and high-tech industries. No European country can avoid the influence of American films. According to European film critics, they accounted for 70–80% of the European film market. The percentage in France was slightly lower, yet American films also accounted for 50% of the film market there. Through the export of cultural products, the USA not only obtained huge economic profits, but also spread its social and political philosophy, values, ideology, and culture, which was a kind of cultural colonization. In fighting against this American cultural hegemony and monopoly, European countries were consistent in believing that they should stop American cultural products from jeopardizing European culture. At the final phase of the 1993 Uruguay Round, the EU was in intense confrontation with the USA in terms of market access for cultural products, and was resolutely against the idea of opening up the market. The EU refused to give specific commitments and a schedule, and the USA had no choice but to compromise. Facing the massive invasion of American culture, the EU on the one hand struggled with the USA and on the other hand adopted a policy of cultural diversity to support the development of European culture, so as to compete with American culture. In order to reduce American cultural influence, the EU adopted a series of measures. First, some EU member states introduced restrictions on films, and a ceiling on the number of non-European films in cinemas; for example, the French ceiling was set at 40%. Second, a control for film imports was introduced: only a small number of American films were imported to meet the needs of the EU film market. In France, from each ticket sold by the French cinemas, a small part of the revenue would be used to fund French film production. Third, the EU member countries further opened their markets to each other, and at the same time introduced a number of non-European and non-American films.

7.1.3.3 Participating in International Affairs, Spreading European Culture, and Enhancing the Status of the EU in the World

The EU believed that culture was not only one of the most important elements in economic and social development, but also played an important role in democracy and social stability. If there was no cross-cultural communication, it was impossible to have peaceful co-existence. Therefore, the EU member states not only advocated the protection and promotion of European culture, but also incorporated culture into the management of such major issues as peace, aid, and development. The EU participated in international affairs to spread its culture. It signed cultural co-operation agreements with many non-member states. Cultural affairs were jointly dealt with by international organizations such as the Council of Europe and the United Nations. The EU's Culture 2000 subsidized cultural co-operation projects, such as exhibitions and carnivals, with non-member countries. The Media Plan subsidized the spread of European cultural products in the international market.

Plans for visual arts supported, in addition to projects in European countries, a number of major projects in Africa, Asia, and the Caribbean areas. Examples include an exhibition of paintings in Dominica and Haiti, and a cultural co-operation agreement between Angola, South Africa, Cuba, and other non-member states. Early cultural co-operation between the EU and non-member states appeared in Africa, the Caribbean region, the Mediterranean region, Latin America, Eastern Europe, and Central Asia. Based on the European Development and Cooperation Policy, the EU and seventy-seven Pacific countries strengthened co-operation to spread national cultural elements, stimulate cultural creativity, and build necessary cultural infrastructure.

In Asia, the 1996 Bangkok Summit was aimed at strengthening Asia–Europe relations. The President of the EC and the heads of states in Asia (China, Brunei, Indonesia, Japan, South Korea, Malaysia, the Philippines, Singapore, Thailand and Vietnam) laid out a co-operative scheme. This was later called the Asia–Europe Meeting, focusing on political, economic, and cultural affairs. Under the scheme, exchanges were encouraged to promote Asian and European culture, protect intellectual property, and deal with specific events (mainly for young artists). The Eurasia Foundation supported meetings, seminars, and carnivals relating to cultural industry, protection of cultural heritages, heritage tourism, and cultural works (dance, painting, and music). The Asia Urbs Program supported joint programs in the cities of Europe and Asia. The successful integration of the EU made a set of systems, rules, standards, values, and cultures influential in other countries and regions, including those surrounding the EU, such as Russia, Ukraine, Belarus, and the Mediterranean countries. Many of these countries had expressed a willingness to participate in the European integration process, and meet European standards in practice. This was significant in further expanding the influence of EU culture on the international stage.

7.2   CULTURAL FEATURES OF THE EU

Although there is a homogeneous history, EU culture has been diverse. Every country has its proud culture, such as Austrian music, Dutch windmills, Italian fashion, French wine, and German industrial design. On December 7, 2000, The EU published the Charter of Fundamental Rights of the European Union. Section Twenty-Two specifies that the EU respects the diversification of culture, religion, and language. In Portugal,

France, Italy, Spain, Luxembourg, Monaco, Ireland, and Poland, more than 90% of the residents are Catholic; but other religions, such as Judaism, Buddhism, Islam, and Hinduism, also have their space.

The multi-lingualism of the EU reflects the diversity of European culture. In accordance with the principle that "all languages are equal regardless of their usage," the EU must ensure that, in addition to the official languages, all other languages are respected. On the electronic screen at the daily press conference, several languages are used in displaying questions and answers. With the arrival of the Bulgarian people, Cyrillic characters will become the third alphabet, after the Latin and Greek, to be adopted by the EU. With Ireland using Gaelic as its second official language, and Spain adopting the Basque language, Catalan, and Galician as "semi-official languages," the number of EU official languages has increased to twenty-three, and official documents, including the 90,000 pages of treaties and agreements, must be written in all of them. The EU has a special Commissioner responsible for language services, which reflects the degree of attention paid to the subject.

The Council of the EU, the main decision-making and constitutional body, used a unanimous voting system from the very beginning. But this mechanism was not practical, especially when the number of member states increased. When the efficiency of decision-making decreased and the process of European integration was hindered, the "simple majority" and "effective majority" voting systems came into being, the latter becoming the Council's main voting mechanism. From the cultural aspect, different voting systems reflected different meanings. "Unanimous agreement" expressed national characteristics by expressing a consciousness of nationalism, as each member state had a veto. With a strong nationalist mindset, the French Charles de Gaulle implemented the "empty chair" policy for up to six months in order to amend the voting mechanism. But "simple majority" and "effective majority" had supranational attributes and a strong "European" consciousness, giving voice to the unity of Europe. This was the developmental trend in the EU's political culture.

The Euro designs represent the cultural unity and diversity of the EU. Designs for Euro notes and coins are different. Euro banknotes show some common characteristics with other currencies. The European Parliament, in the design of banknote patterns, denied the use of buildings that were nationally recognizable such as the Eiffel Tower, Arc de Triomphe, or the Colosseum. Therefore, there were no evident national characteristics expressed on the Euro notes. Seven kinds of Euro notes illustrated the European Classical, Roman, Gothic, Renaissance, Baroque, Rococo, and steel and glass styles, as well as doors and windows of the 20th century. On the other side were bridges in various styles, symbolizing the exchange among countries in Europe and the results of integration. In 1996, the EU gave each member state the right to design a pattern on the back of coins of its own, on the condition that there should be twelve stars, the symbol of the EU. Therefore, one side of all the coins was the same: 1 and 2 Euro coins included a map of EU member states, symbolizing a no-border Europe; the 50 cents, 20 cents, and 10 Euro coins used a map of Europe, showing the EU was a combination of different nations; the remaining three coins illustrated Europe on a globe. The symbol of the Euro is the third English letter "C" (the fifth Greek letter) with two horizontal lines in the middle. The EU states that this symbol originated from the Greek letter ε, which symbolizes the cradle of European culture and the first set of European letters. Parallel lines represent the stability of the Euro. Whichever country it is issued in, a Euro coin is usable in all Eurozone member states. The unified yet distinctive characteristic of the Euro patterns embodies the basic principles of the EU cultural integration policy: emphasizing the European shared culture and at the same time striving to protect its diversity.

7.3   EU CULTURAL POLICY

European integration started with economic integration. Against the background of a higher level of economic integration, the EU started to take culture into consideration, and formed an EU cultural policy. In 1992, the Maastricht Treaty officially gave the EU the right to manage cultural affairs. Section 128 of Chapter 9 of the Maastricht Treaty specifies that the EU is committed to protecting common cultural heritage, facilitating the development of each member country's culture and respecting cultural diversity. The EU, according to specific circumstances, has coordinated the uneven cultural regulations of each member state into a series of cultural policies that can be directly or indirectly applied to all EU members. It has advocated the development of national cultures and encouraged the free flow of personnel and products. The EU has stressed the national macro-management of culture, and provided support to the protection of intellectual property rights and local culture. These measures have played a positive role in prospering European culture, and have quickened the European integration process.

7.3.1   Protecting Historical and Cultural Heritage

The EU attached great importance to the protection of cultural and natural heritage. In 1974, the European Parliament adopted a resolution that pointed out the necessity of common actions in order to protect cultural heritage. In 1993, the Maastricht Treaty provided a legal basis for the protection of cultural heritage. Section 151 stipulates that member states must take action to protect their heritages. In 1997, the EC, in order to conduct a comprehensive assessment of city development, held a city forum and gathered a group of experts. This led to a resolution passed by the European Council and the European Parliament in 2001. This was about the establishment of a co-operation framework that was aimed at the sustainable development of cities, covering tourism and leisure activities related to cultural heritages. A key objective of the Culture 2000 plan was to promote the value of cultural heritage and to provide funds for important heritage projects, and about 34% of the total budget for this plan was devoted to the realization of this objective. Culture 2000 also supported co-operation projects in the field of cultural heritage, such as training and experience-sharing. In 1999, the EU put forward three guidelines in the European Spatial Development Perspective, one of which was the "special management and protection of cultural and natural heritage." The goal demanded effective protection and reasonable development of cultural and natural heritage.

To deal with the illegal transaction of cultural products, the EU has taken measures. In 1992, the EU accepted the French concept of "cultural exception" and introduced six standards related to this. It held that cultural products were different from other commodities. In the trade among member states, the EU banned import, export, or transshipment of artistic, historical, or archaeological treasures. The EU monitored exports of cultural products and facilitated the return of illegally exported national treasures. In June 2001, the European Parliament passed a resolution that required co-operation between member states in prohibiting the illegal trading of cultural products, especially in the expanded EU. The project City and Cultural Heritage of Tomorrow, carried out by the EU, funded the repair, preservation, and promotion of cultural heritage. From the fourth French five-year (1961–1965) plan onwards, culture was included. The protection of cultural heritage was always listed at the top of the list. The EU tried to promote the understanding of cultural heritage through education and training programs. The Socrates Plan funded education programs in schools and museums involved in cultural heritage. The Da Vinci Plan financed other projects, such as training in traditional arts and crafts and the restoration of cultural heritage. In addition, the EU took special action to protect local and minority languages. In 1999, the EC launched the Europe, A Common Heritage campaign, the contents of which included photography, Europe's oldest universities, handicraft industries, and the European musical tradition.

In 2006, the EC, together with the United Nations Educational, Scientific and Cultural Organization (UNESCO), established the European Cultural Heritage Report Award, aiming at encouraging European cultural reporters to improve the quality of cultural news and pay more attention to the cultural heritage of Europe. The organizers believed that cultural news reports were increasingly important in cultural heritage protection and in influencing private and social organizations and governments. In 2007, the EU launched new plans for cultural heritage protection. The Council of the EU adopted the plan that was submitted by the EC, which included Culture 2007, Media 2007 and the digitization of cultural heritage. The EC set up a new website to support the free flow of personal and museum collections, and to introduce more intercultural dialogues, so that people in Europe could have more contact with the cultural heritages of different countries.

7.3.2   Supporting Cultural Research and Cultural Industry

Film, audiovisual media, publishing, music, and other cultural industries, employing up to 7 million staff, were one of the major sources of jobs in many EU countries. They made contributions to the communication between different cultures. Therefore, the EU developed a supporting plan for the cultural industries, which included giving more capital and regulatory support, and therefore creating a sound environment for them.

7.3.2.1   Supporting Two Types of Cultural Industries

Supporting the European Audiovisual Industry
Since 1991, the EU had formulated in succession the Media Plan, Media Plan II, and Media Additional Plan to strengthen the European audiovisual industry. The EU, through supporting promotion campaigns, enabled the audiovisual industry to gain a foothold in the global market. The Media Plan was not meant to provide sponsorship for production, but to take measures to ensure stable production. Another objective was to promote the sales of European audiovisual products (including films, cartoons, and documentaries) in other countries. Through the implementation of

these plans, the European audiovisual industry fitted in with the economic changes. The EU paid special attention to countries with low production capacity and marginal languages. At the same time, training recognized by EU member states was carried out to help professionals adapt to changes in the industry by applying European and international standards in practice, and to promote their connections with training institutions.

Supporting the European Multi-Media Industry
Developing the Internet and electronic business was a global trend. To gain an advantage in economic, social, and cultural competitions, Europe had to produce, use, and disseminate digital resources of its own. In order to improve industrial competitiveness and promote the use of the Internet among Europeans, the EU formulated the European Global Network of Digital Contents, namely the E-Content Programme, in December 2000. This plan encouraged the use of digital technology in the information industry, especially in public sector and in the field of cultural diversity. It focused on sponsoring projects that could link manufacturers and public institutions. At the same time, language and cultural diversification, training and funds for small and medium enterprises, and legal issues of property rights were considered.

With the rapid development of Information Technology (IT), broadband, and 3G, the market of digital content changed. From 2005 to 2008, the EU injected up to 149 million Euro to stimulate innovation and the production of digital content, to strengthen communication and cooperation between member countries, and to create a clustering effect between practitioners with a common goal. Its strategic objective was to develop, use, and spread European digital information in the global network, to protect the diversity of network language and culture, and to provide network service for all citizens. In addition to English, other languages such as French, German, and Spanish were also employed, because some of these languages not only had a large number of speakers but also contained a lot of outstanding cultural essentials. Digital technology was especially required to preserve these languages.

7.3.2.2 Creating a Sound Competition Environment
Financial assistance from the EU was part of the support plan for cultural industry. Competition in the cultural industry not only demanded a fair legal and financial environment, but also the ability to create wonderful content. To provide a sound environment, the EU focused on the following.

Formulating Laws and Regulations for the Audiovisual Industry
In the policy framework for the audiovisual industry, the EU developed a series of European standards, which not only supported national specific policies but also considered the economic, cultural, and social standards of the industry. On October 3, 1989, Television without Frontiers was passed, becoming a milestone in the regulating of the audiovisual industry by the EC. The directive was first amended in 1997 and then again on December 13, 2005. After the implementation of this directive, satisfactory results were achieved: the number of TV stations increased, popular television programs spread beyond national borders, a reasonable time ratio was arranged for films and television programs from different member states, the free flow of television programs within the community was promoted, and cultural diversity and the interests of minor groups and consumers were protected.

On February 12, 2001, the Council of the EU stressed that the importance of providing state aid to film and audiovisual industry lay in the protection of cultural diversity and creating a European audiovisual market. The EC, the Council of the EU, the European Parliament, the European Economic and Social Committee, and the Committee of Regions jointly formulated the Regulation on Films and Audiovisual Works in September 2011. This described the general principles of providing state aid to films and television shows from the perspective of the EC. It specified the standards used to determine whether an aid plan was in compliance with EU treaties. The EU, with the additional protocols of the Amsterdam Treaty, pointed out that as long as the broadcasting company played a role in democracy, society, and cultural development, member states were required to provide funds. The Law of European Commission Communication, formulated in October 2001, provided rules for governmental aid to public broadcasters. As film and audiovisual industries failed to make full use of the internal market, the EC spotted the technical and regulatory barriers existing in film distribution and the protection of audiovisual heritage. Solutions were proposed, such as establishing common principles in Europe for intellectual property right registration, freeing the classification of audiovisual works from the media and other interference. The EU also protected cultural diversity in international trade. In the negotiations with the World Trade Organization, the EC and the member states stressed free development and the implementation of audiovisual public policy.

Promoting Digitalization

In 1999, the EC passed a law on principles and guidelines of audiovisual policy in the digital age, proposing the use of different rules for transmission facilities and audiovisual content. Agencies providing audiovisual content should be regulated according to its properties, not its transmission means. On May 24, 2005, the EC asked twenty-five EU member states to accelerate the process of digital broadcasting, to end analog transmission before 2012, and to realize complete digitalization. If the EU could achieve this goal as scheduled, it would be in the forefront of digital broadcasting.

Allowing Cultural Industry into the Capital Market

To support research and development into cultural industries, the European Investment Bank provided long-term loans for cultural investment projects. The EU proposed Innovation 2000, in which it suggested offering loans or venture capital for companies engaged in audiovisual and other cultural industries (including fiction, documentary, animation, and multi-media). The plan should co-ordinate with the EC's plan, to promote audiovisual content and research in the EU's most backward areas. The EU's business policy, in addition to emphasizing free competition, provided capital for small and medium-sized enterprises in cultural and tourism industries. In the Electronic Content Plan, the EU provided money for projects concerning training, building networks and services, strengthening the partnership between small and medium-sized enterprises and investors, and improving small and medium-sized enterprises' ability to do well in the capital market. The EU Media Plan mainly supported movie production and distribution; therefore, it was more easily accepted by the market. This measure made it easier for EU citizens to have the opportunity to appreciate the cultural products of other member states, which was also beneficial to maintaining EU cultural diversity.

Emphasizing Research and Innovation

The EU attached great importance to knowledge, research, and innovation, believing that knowledge was the best resource in Europe, an important guarantee for European economic growth, competitiveness, and jobs. Investment into research accounted for 3% of GDP. The EU created the Research Framework Program, which covered all fields associated with digital technology. The EU had formulated and implemented seven research framework programs. Cultural industry had benefited from these, for example by the use of research results and the implementation of the

Multimedia Content and Tools program, which advocated the idea of a user-friendly information society. The plan pushed the EU to adopt new methods in the management of cultural industry and to draw up new laws and regulations. Details included the management of the relationship between different types of content (image, video, music, and text), intellectual property rights, and manufacturers, the relationship between creation and publishing of digital content, and between users and content providers. Users were able to acquire cultural heritage data from online libraries, museums, and archives.

7.3.2.3 Developing Cultural Industry in Other Countries

The EU not only developed cultural industries within member states, but also paid attention to European non-member states and other countries. According to the agreement on co-operation with non-member states, the EU supported the development of technology, tourism, media, and the audiovisual industry. This kind of support was more prominent in partnership with nations in Africa and the Caribbean region, the Pacific, and the Mediterranean region.

In June 2000, the EU, in the economic capital of Benin, Cotonou, reached the Cotonou Agreement with seventy-seven countries from Africa, the Caribbean, and the Pacific region. This agreement prioritized cultural development, helped countries develop their own cultural characteristics, and promoted communication between different cultures. It also protected cultural heritages and finally gave their cultural products an opportunity to become available in a larger market. To support the development of the audiovisual industry in Mediterranean countries, the EU established the 2000–2004 Europe Audio-Visual Program with a budget of 20 million Euro. In 2005–2007, the budget of the Europe Audio-Visual Program II was 15 million Euro. In addition, the EU formulated the European Heritage Plan for the protection of cultural heritage and tourism industry in this area. The European Heritage Plan I with a budget of 17 million Euro started in 1998, and funded sixteen projects in six years. The European Heritage Plan II, started in 2001, was a seven-year plan, which emphasized the number of experts and the protection of intangible cultural heritage in the Mediterranean area. The plan sponsored eleven projects with a budget of 30 million Euro. The European Heritage Plan III began in 2004 and funded four projects.

The Audiovisual Eureka was an intergovernmental organization with thirty-five European countries as its members. Its main role was to boost co-operation and exchanges in the audiovisual industries of European regions (including Middle and Eastern European countries). The EC was a part of the European Audiovisual Observatory, which was founded in December 1992. With thirty-five countries and the EU as its members, it was a information collecting and disseminating center whose purpose was to provide professional information for the audiovisual industry. Under the current trend of digital technology and media convergence, the EU has followed two principles of cultural industry: one was to encourage free competition; the other macro-management. On the one hand, the cultural industry of the EU was a business entity, stressing the value of free competition in improving competitiveness. The EU has done a lot to improve the competitiveness of European cultural industry, such as the formulation of a series of laws and regulations, the elimination of barriers among EU countries, co-ordination of industrial policies to survive pressure from the American media industry, and provision of support in technical training, research, and innovation. On the other hand, the EU has deemed cultural industry to be the basic carrier of ideology, and has provided direct or indirect financial assistance to small and medium-sized enterprises and protected cultural diversity. On macro-management, the EU set a timetable and goals to speed up the development of cultural industry and to improve its standing in the world.

BIBLIOGRAPHY

Chen Chunchang. 2003. Cultural Diversity During the European Integration. *International Review* 1: 27–31.

Guo Lingfeng. 2007. EU Cultural Policies and Cultural Governance. *Chinese Journal of European Studies* 2: 64–76.

Luo Qing, and Lange, Andre. 2007. Establishing the System of 'Cultural Protectionism' Under the Mechanism of Market-Guidance—Reflection on the Mode of Public Funding for Film and Audiovisual Works in the EU. *Modern Communication* 2: 108–112.

Ma Shengli. 1997. Important Task in the European Integration. *Deutschland-Studien* 3: 50–54.

Wang Yu. 2000. On the Cultural Identity During the Contemporary European Integration—With Comments on EU Cultural Policies and the Intention. *The Journal of International Studies* 4: 120–126.

Wang Yamei. 2007. Analysis on Significance of Protecting and Developing the Cultural Industry to EU. *Deutschland-Studien* 22: 51–58.

Wang Yamei, and Tan, Xiaozhong. 2004. EU Cultural Polices Indicated in the Euro Patterns. *Social Science Research* 2: 155–159.

Yao Qinhua. 2002. The Political Function of National Cultures—A Perspective of Understanding the European Integration. *Journal of World Peoples Studies* 3: 21–28.

Zhang Ji, and Yan Lei. 2004. On the Influence of Cultural Factors on the European Integration. *Issues of Contemporary World Socialism* 1: 83–93.

Zhao, Boying. 1999. The Origin and Development as Well as the Historical Heritage of 'European Unity'. *Theory Front* 1: 16–17.

Zhou Hong. 1998. The Sources of European Civilization. *Chinese Journal of European Studies* 4: 18–26.

WEBSITES

http://ec.europa.eu/index_en.htm
http://www.cjcb.com.cn/news_SpecialTopicShow.asp?id=873
http://www.delchn.ec.europa.eu/index.php?=&l=cn
http://www.europe.sdu.edu.cn/ouzhouzhongxin/php/article.php/36
http://www.fmprc.gov.cn/ce/cebe/chn/default.htm

CHAPTER 8

Religious Culture

8.1   INTRODUCTION TO RELIGION

Religion is a strong spiritual and supportive force derived from a person's persistence in holding on to particular hopes. Religion is sometimes considered a social behavior consisting of a guiding ideology (religious faith), organizations (such as the Church), conduct (activities held within religious organizations, such as worship and ritual), and culture (architecture, paintings, music). A successful religion is one that is accepted by many people and exercises an influence on human social developments over a certain period of time.

Throughout human history, various schools of thinkers have defined religion in varied ways. James George Frazer defined religion as an ingratiation and reconciliation with supreme powers; Herbert Spencer defined religion as belief in a particular power that is beyond man's cognition; Francis Herbert Bradley regarded religion as people's pursuit of goodness; while others believed that religion was the connection between individuals and society and was a moral norm; and some considered religion as an attitude towards life. Marxist-Leninist religious views describe religion as a social phenomenon that comes into being when human society and men's thinking enters a certain developmental level. Religion, as an ideology, demonstrates convictions in a particular form. It is also a cultural phenomenon that contributes to human cultural, civil, and social progress. As an integral part of world civilization, religion develops as human civilization advances.

© The Author(s) 2018   199
G. Xu et al. (eds.), K. Chen et al. (trans.), *Understanding Western Culture*, https://doi.org/10.1007/978-981-10-8150-7_8

Religion is a common cultural phenomenon of human society. All countries in the world have their own distinctive religions, which in turn reflect different cultures, ethnic habits, legal systems, and political systems. Religion plays a special role in people's social lives and is an attribute that separates one ethnic group from another. Religions are generally divided into three types: primitive, ethnic, and world. Primitive religion covers an extensive range of beliefs in spirits and nature gods, totemism, and various forms of magic. Ethnic religion is diverse and includes Hinduism, Judaism, and Shintoism, among many others. World religion refers to Buddhism, Christianity, and Islam. In conclusion, religion is awe and respect for a divine providence and a behavioral rule. It is a social and historical phenomenon. The discipline that studies religion is called Religious Studies.

8.2   CHRISTIANITY

Christianity is a religion based on the belief that Jesus Christ is the savior of humanity. It has a number of divisions, the primary three being Roman Catholicism, Eastern Orthodoxy, and Protestantism. Christianity is the world's largest religion, with approximately 2.14 billion adherents, who are known as Christians, and it is growing most rapidly in Asia and Africa.

8.2.1   Origin and Development

Christianity, a religion that emerged in the Jewish community in Palestine in the first century, inherited some of the Jewish concepts including that of a Messiah as savior of the world, and recognized the Hebrew Bible as the Christian Old Testament.

The founder of Christianity, according to Christian scripture, is Jesus Christ, who began his ministry in Palestine at the age of thirty (AD 30). He proclaimed that he would not replace the commandments recorded in the Jewish scriptures but would fulfill them. When asked what the greatest commandment was, Jesus replied: "'Love the Lord your God with all your heart and with all your soul and with all your mind' … And the second is like it: 'Love your neighbor as yourself'" (Matthew 22:37–39). Jesus preached the gospel to all humanity, teaching people to rectify their behavior and refrain from sin.

8.2.2   Christian Doctrine

8.2.2.1   Shaping of Christian Doctrine

Christianity originated from Judaism. There were distinctions as well as aspects in common from the very beginning. As Christian theologians sought instruction from Jewish biblical scholars, Jewish mysticism exerted a constant influence on mystical Christian denominations. Christianity likewise drew on Greek culture from the second century. Some theologians hold that the concept of *Logos* in Greek philosophy is the Messiah, who was later revealed as Jesus Christ. Plato's idealist explanations about the world and Aristotle's theories about existence and knowledge were presented in Christian teachings. Some Christian worship rituals and liturgies can be traced back to Greco-Buddhism and mysterious philosophy. In the times when Christianity was regarded as the state religion of the Roman Empire, particularly in the late fourth century after Emperor Theodosius came to the throne, heresy was seen as a crime that was subject to legal punishment, and any objection to the Church was considered as betrayal of the Empire. Between the fourth and eighth century, bishops attending religious symposiums used to consider those who held different opinions as heretics and eliminated them as traitors. For the protection of orthodox doctrine, the Inquisition was established by the medieval Church and the Expurgatory Index (a list of proscribed books) was promulgated.

8.2.2.2   Common Beliefs

There are three primary divisions of Christianity, which however share the consistent basic creeds: creationism, original sin, heaven, and hell. The Bible, consisting of the Old Testament and the New Testament, is the sacred scripture of Christianity. The cross is a Christian symbol. Christians believe in the Trinity, the belief that God is three in one: God the Father, God the Son (Jesus), and God the Holy Spirit.

God: Christians believe in Father, Son, and Holy Spirit as one God, also known as the Trinity. The Father is unbegotten and the Creator of all beings; the Son was begotten of the Father; the Holy Spirit proceeds from the Father and operates within every living thing. That proceeding from the Son operates through the Church. Trinity does not imply three gods, nor that each member of the Trinity is one-third of an infinite God; Trinity is defined as one God or a Godhead in three persons.

Creation: Christianity believes that God created the universe (time and space) and all beings, including the first human beings, Adam and Eve.

Sin: Adam and Eve committed the original sin when they violated God's word of love in an attempt to gain wisdom without the help of God and ate the forbidden fruit in the Garden of Eden. Because of this they were forever estranged from the source of all life, and were bound to suffer from sin and the Devil and end up with diseases and death. Since men are the offspring of Adam and Eve, they are all born to commit the same sins, which finally lead to the end of mankind.

Redemption: The hope of mankind lies in the belief in Jesus as God, who made atonement on the cross for all the sins of men, and was resurrected three days after his death to forgive his believers, despite all the sins they committed and to give them eternal life that would overcome the Devil and death.

Soul and immortality: Most Christians believe that human beings experience divine judgment particular to the individual soul upon physical death, and that people who have faith in Jesus before death are rewarded with eternal life, whereas non-believers are rewarded with eternal damnation. There will be an end to the human world, but in the new world that God creates there is immortality.

Essential views concerning God in Christian teachings are as follows:

- God is one God with personhood.
- God is the creator of the universe.
- God dominates history/is the dominator of history.
- God saves men, forgives their sins, and makes them his sons and daughters.
- God judges men at the Last Judgment.

The Devil, Satan, is created by God as his opponent and enemy, who revolts against God's salvation plan.

Ever since the foundation of the Christian Church, there have been various conceptions of Jesus Christ. The Gospel of St Mark depicts that "In those days Jesus came from Nazareth in Galilee and was baptized by John in the Jordan. Immediately coming up out of the water, He saw the heavens opening, and the Spirit like a dove descending upon Him; and a voice came out of the heavens, 'You are My beloved Son, in You I am well-pleased.'" This view is followed by nearly all Antioch theologians in their studies of Christian theories. The Gospel of St. Mark, however, proclaims a different view, which describes Jesus as the incarnation of divine *Logos* through whom all things were made, as the object of veneration, a view to which most Alexandrian theologians adhere. Jesus proclaimed the coming of heaven and started to construct heaven. Believing in Jesus is to believe in heaven. Christian eschatology is related to God's pledge about the Messiah that is recorded in the Old Testament. Before the coming of Jesus, revolts under the name of the Messiah erupted one after another, but Jesus refused to be the Messiah in political terms, which disappointed those people who were longing for heaven on earth. Another kind of eschatology believes not in the Messiah in the human world but in heaven, building a heaven that is not of the earth.

The veneration of the Virgin Mary, or St. Mary, became pervasive after Constantine the Great declared Christianity to be the state religion of the Roman Empire. Nationalities inhabiting Mediterranean areas and the Near East felt it hard to comprehend the supreme authority of God the Father, and thus for thousands of years they had been worshiping a goddess, a holy virgin, the Virgin Mary; and this spread from Babylonian and Assyrian folk religion to Greek culture. Although Christian gospels expressed opposition to the reverence of this goddess, it was continued as the worship of St. Mary. It is believed that in the body of Mary the Holy Spirit, united with humanity, became Jesus Christ.

The Holy Spirit, according to Christian doctrine, is as free as the wind. The spirit of prophecy and the spirit of knowledge cannot be disposed by any prophets or wise men. The revelation of the Holy Spirit is presented through prophecy or in wise words, namely the Bible. The Holy Spirit is a renewing force that advances the Church and boosts creativity.

Humans, as expressed in Christian doctrine, are created in the image of God and thus play a crucial role in God's revelation. Since humans reflect the image of God, God inevitably needs man's cooperation to accomplish His plans. God and humans depend on each other so much that they exist for the sake of each other. Christian doctrines hold that the Church is a community composed of people chosen by God and blessed by the Holy Spirit. The Church is made up of Jesus' disciples, both Jews and non-Jewish people. All members of the Church are "new Israelis," the chosen people of God; the Church is the incarnation of Jesus Christ, and Church members are the "living stones" that construct the Church.

8.2.2.3 Doctrines of Major Denominations

The seven sacraments—Baptism, Confirmation, Holy Communion, Confession (the Mass), Marriage, Holy Orders, and the Anointing of the Sick—are the core of Catholic church life. Among them the Mass is broadly considered the most important. Chanting is also a ritual for Catholics as are prayers such as the Lord's Prayer, the Apostles' Creed and the Rosary.

Eastern Orthodox theology and its interpretation of Scripture are consistent with the beliefs that were passed on from the earliest days of Christianity. Great endeavors are made to continue and pass on that which Jesus Christ revealed to his twelve apostles, as well as the theology and beliefs that they imparted to the earliest churches. The Eastern Orthodox Church, in this sense, is the most conservative Christian denomination.

Protestant doctrines are distinctive from those of the Eastern Orthodox and Roman Catholic Churches. The doctrine of Justification by Faith says that justification requires no good deeds but faith. Everyone can be a priest because (1 Peter 2:9) "But you are a chosen race, a royal priesthood, a holy nation, a people for his own possession, that you may proclaim the excellencies of him who called you out of darkness into his marvelous light." The Bible is the supreme authority for the Protestant Church, which recognizes Baptism and the Eucharist as the only two sacraments: this represents a salient distinction from the Catholic and Orthodox traditions of sacraments.

8.2.3   The Bible

The Bible is the sacred book of Judaism and Christianity, a canonical collection of texts composed of the Old Testament and the New Testament. The Old Testament is the canonical book of Judaism and the New Testament is a collection that records the words, conduct, and stories about Jesus Christ and his disciples.

8.2.3.1 The Old Testament
The Roman Catholic Church and the Eastern Orthodox Church recognize forty-six books (fifty-one books with some combined) as the canonical Old Testament, including several that are considered uncanonical by other denominations. The Protestant Old Testament of today has a thirty-nine-book canon. The Hebrew Bible, which combined a number of scriptures with short chapters into one book, consists of twenty-four books, whose content is consistent with the Old Testament.

8.2.3.2 The New Testament

The Bible consists of sixty-six books, thirty-nine from the Old Testament and twenty-seven from the New Testament. The Old Testament was finished hundreds or even more than a thousand years prior to the birth of Jesus. For instance, the five books of Moses or the Torah (the biblical books of Genesis, Exodus, Leviticus, Numbers, and Deuteronomy) were written in 1400 BC and the book of Malachi in the late first century. Collectively it took over 1500 years to write the New Testament and the Old Testament.

There were approximately forty authors involved in the writing of the Bible; they were of diverse backgrounds and lived in many places. Isaiah was a prophet, Ezra was a priest, Matthew was a tax collector, John was a fisherman, Moses was a shepherd, and Luke was a physician. Despite such variety, the sixty-six books teach consistently and without contradiction on a wide range of issues. The authors each present a different perspective, yet they all proclaim the same God and the same singular path of salvation—Jesus Christ.

8.2.4   Church Government and Rites

The Orthodox Church and the Catholic Church implement episcopacy, which is government of the church by bishops. Despite religious reforms and strong opposition from puritans and independents in England, Episcopalian theories and practice have been inherited by the Anglican Church. The Swedish Lutheran Church also preserves this tradition. In Germany, however, the episcopacy of the Evangelical Church has been abolished. The Presbyterian Church in Scotland and North America as well as most puritan churches follow this tradition, which operates in a way similar to a democratic republic. Congregationalism is another system of church government in which each member church is self-governing in its conduct of missionary work, church services, administration, and so on.

Worship may differ among denominations, but personal prayer and family worship are commonly emphasized by all Christians. Family is the basis of the Christian community. The form and frequency of social worship activities vary among denominations.

8.2.5   *Dissemination of Christianity*

Christianity has spread around the world more widely than any other religion. Before Islam came to the Western world, churches in the East had vigorously engaged in missionary work. Eastern Christian churches, in particular the Nestorius Church, were introduced to China, Middle Asia and Mongolia in the third and fourth centuries. It also diffused into a variety of Slavic communities through Byzantium. Missionary work, civilization, and colonialism always go hand in hand. As a result, missionaries from advanced cultures often bring about significant changes to culturally backward regions. Protestant missionary work was from the beginning impacted by a Pietist theory that the "dark" heretic world had to be illuminated by the light of the Christian gospel. In the twentieth century European and American churches initiated Ecumenism, a movement promoting unity among Christian churches or denominations.

Christianity was introduced to China in 635 AD during the reign of Emperor Tai Zong (627–649) of the Tang Dynasty. Nestorius Christianity (known in China as Nestorianism at that time but today Maronite Christianity) was regarded as heretic and was prohibited in 845. Its second entry into China occurred in the Yuan Dynasty, in the name of Nestorianism and Catholicism, which came to an end after the fall of the Yuan Dynasty. In 1582, Ricci, a priest sent to China by the Catholic Church, was allowed to settle and preach Christianity in Zhaoqing, Guangdong Province. His missionary work earned the Catholic Church a foothold in China. The Eastern Orthodox Church started to spread in China in 1727 and in 1807 a Protestant priest, Robert Morrison, brought Protestant Christianity to China. Christianity embraced its rapid development in coastal trading ports in China. Hung Xiuquan, the leader of a peasant revolutionary war who founded the Taiping Heavenly Kingdom (1851–1864), called himself the younger brother of Jesus, and established the Society of God Worshipers in 1843.

The journal *Heavenly Wind* commenced publication in February 1945, published by the Association of Christian Publishers in Chengdu. It became the official publication of the National Christian Council after 1949. The number of Catholics in China was 2.7 million after the foundation of the Republic of China and reached 5 million in 2006.

8.3   JUDAISM

Judaism is the oldest religious belief and one of the three world religions. It embodies the belief and lifestyle of the Jewish people, as are described in the Torah, the first five books of the Hebrew Bible.

8.3.1   Origin and Formation

Judaism originated in the Middle East, around the valleys of the Euphrates and the Tigris, historically known as the cradle of human civilization. Sumerian culture flourished in 2300 BC but then declined around 1800 BC, the year when Abram left Ur, a city south of the valleys of the Euphrates and the Tigris, passed Babylon, Mari, and Haran, and traveled to Beersheba in Canaan (now Palestine). According to the Bible, the Lord told Abram to leave his country and kindred and go to a land that he would show him, promising to make a great nation, to bless him, to make his name great, bless them that bless him, and curse him that curses him (Genesis 12:1–3). When Abram was ninety-nine years of age, God declared Abram's new name to be Abraham, and that he was "a father of many nations" (Genesis 17:5). After this, Abraham begat a son, Isaac, and Isaac begat Jacob. Abraham, Isaac, and Jacob are the three patriarchs and progenitors of the Jewish people, and the founders of Judaism.

People in Abraham's hometown believed in Sabianism, a religion that worshiped the sun, the moon, and the stars, and observed the sun as their supreme God. But Abraham held a different opinion, claiming that God the Creator was greater than the Sun and should be venerated. For this, he was opposed by the majority of people and put into prison by the king, who also confiscated his properties and banished him to Haran, to prevent him from spreading ideas that would threaten polytheism. Later, Abraham left Haran and settled in Canaan, where he gave up polytheism and converted to a belief in one God, El. In the Semitic language El is a general word for the highest God. El has different names, for instance El Shaddai (God Almighty or God of Mountains), El Elyon (God Most High), El Roi (the God Who Sees), and El Bethel (The God of House). Among them El Shaddai is the most respected, for it is believed to be the name of the Lord used by Abraham's family, who instructed him, made a covenant with him, and blessed him, according to the Book of Genesis. This is why later generations of Israelis observe El Shaddai as the Lord who was worshiped by Abraham, Isaac and Jacob.

Despite the various names given to God in the early history of Judaism, Jews have always believed in a single god. Despite these different names Judaism was a monotheistic religion from the very beginning. If the transformation from polytheism to monotheism could be defined as a great leap forward in human history, it is because of the contribution of its Jewish progenitors.

Jacob had twelve biological sons, whose offspring became the twelve tribes of Israel, also known as the Israelites. In 1720 BC, the Israelites left Canaan for Egypt owing to a severe famine, hence starting a history of 430 years of slavery and misery in Egypt. In the fourteenth century BC, a great Jew was born whose name was Moses. Moses and his fellow Hebrews could not bear their mistreatment by the pharaoh, so they decided to leave Egypt and go back to the promised land, Canaan, the land where their ancestors had lived. In 1290 BC, Moses and his fellow Hebrews escaped from the pharaoh's army, went out of Israel, crossed the Red Sea, and entered the wilderness of Sinai. This was a milestone in Jewish history, and Moses is hence universally recognized as a great leader and a national hero for Israelites.

The Israelites did not go to the promised land of Canaan directly after the Exodus from Egypt but stayed on the Sinai Peninsula for forty years, where Moses received laws from the Lord on Mount Sinai. There are three versions of this in the Hebrew Bible, in Exodus 20:1–17, Deuteronomy 5:6–21, and Exodus 34:10–26. The descriptions may differ in detail, but they all convey the same truth that the laws that form the basis of Judaism were established through Moses, and thus Moses is the actual founder of Judaism. According to Exodus 20:1–17, the Lord descended upon Mount Sinai in a fire and spoke to the Israelites those words that included the Ten Commandments and a range of other laws. Afterwards, the Lord summoned Moses to Mount Sinai twice more, asking him to wait there for forty days and forty nights after which he would give him tablets of stone, with the laws and the commandments written on them.

After Moses descended the mountain, he followed the words of the Lord and made an ark of acacia wood, placed the tablets of stone in it, then put the ark in the tabernacle built in accordance with what the Lord had showed him. From then on, the Lord of the Israelites was with them, guiding them through the forty years of hardship in the wilderness and helping them to defeat the seven tribes in Canaan, before entering the "promised land" of milk and honey, where they established the Kingdom of Israel.

By receiving the laws from the Lord on Mount Sinai, the Israelites renewed the covenant they had made with the Lord. The Hebrews maintained that they had made a covenant with the Lord through Abraham: that Abraham shall worship the Lord as the only one God, and the Lord would make for him a great country, making him into the ancestor of a multitude of nations, giving to him the land of Canaan in perpetuity, and blessing his offspring (Genesis 12:2,17,22). However, over the course of time, particularly after over four hundred years of slavery in Egypt, the Israelites' awareness of the covenant gradually faded. After they had left Egypt, they had to adapt to harsh living conditions in the desert while they prepared to go back to Canaan. It was a time when they were in desperate need of a binding force and for confidence in their future. It was at such a crucial time that the Lord gave laws to the Israelites, through which their perpetual covenant with the Lord was made. According to the Bible, the Lord was the God of their ancestors, the God of Abraham, the God of Isaac, and the God of Jacob (Exodus 3:14–15): "Now therefore, if you obey my voice and keep my covenant, you shall be my treasured possession out of all the peoples. Indeed, the whole earth is mine, but you shall be for me a priestly kingdom and a holy nation" (Exodus, 19:5–6). All the people answered with one voice, and said, "All the words that the Lord has spoken we will do" (Exodus, 24:3). With the covenant made, the status of the Israelites as the chosen people of God was therefore set. The Israelites have since regarded themselves as the chosen people who have maintained a special relationship with God. The awareness of being the chosen, together with the laws given by the Lord, became a strong bonding force for the Jewish nation.

8.3.2   Sacred Texts and Commandments

8.3.2.1 Sacred Texts

There are three Jewish holy books. The first is the Old Testament, also known as the Tanakh or Hebrew Bible, which all Jews must observe faithfully. The first five books of the Old Testament are called the Torah or the Five Books of Moses, and they make up one of the most significant books of Judaism. The second Jewish sacred book is the Talmud, expounding on the "613 Principles" in the Torah and other Jewish texts. The third is the Mishnah. The Tanakh (also Tenak, Tanach) consists of three sections: the Torah, Nevi'im (the eight Books of the Prophets), and Ketuvim (eleven books, usually entitled "Writings" or "Hagiographa"). In total, there are twenty-four books, so the Tanakh is also referred to as the twenty-four-book canon. Tanakh is an acronym of the first Hebrew letter of each of these three divisions: Torah, Nevi'im, and Ketuvim—hence TaNaKh. It was written by a group of Jewish rabbis and writers who collected and edited traditional Jewish religious texts, laws, and ordinances. The Tanakh is the canon of the Hebrew Bible. The Talmud is another important canon of Judaism, second only to the Tanakh.

In 70 AD, the Temple in Jerusalem was burned down by the Roman emperor and the Jews were expelled from the land of Judah. Later, some Jewish scholars living in Israel began to compile the six books that were entitled Mishnah, a series of scriptures that conserved the ordinances, principles, and customs of Judaism. In the mid-fifth century, the series of books that became the Gemara added supplementary notes to the Mishnah, including notes and discussions that dated back to the times of Israel and Babylon, and the oral arguments between Jewish priests. This became the second part of the Talmud (oral scriptures). It set the basic norms and principles for the Jewish people to observe when learning about belief, concepts, laws, and ordinances.

8.3.2.2 Basic Teachings
At the core of Jewish teachings are the thirteen commandments summarized by the rabbi Maimonides:

- God exists, and is the creator.
- God is one and unique.
- God is not physical.
- God is eternal.
- Prayer is to be directed only to God.
- The words of the prophets are true.
- The prophecies of Moses are true; he was the greatest prophet.
- The Torah was given to Moses.
- There will be no other Torah.
- God knows the thoughts and deeds of all.
- God rewards the good and punishes the wicked.
- The Messiah will come.
- The dead will be resurrected.

The primary principle of Judaism is faith in one God, the God that is not physical but eternal. He blesses all, practices justice, gives mercy, and creates man in his own image. Therefore, all men have dignity and shall be treated respectfully.

The Jewish people observe the Lord by learning and praying, and by obeying the commandments of the Five Books of Moses. They believe that their covenant with the Lord is a call from God, and is thus their commitment and mission for the world. But they do not urge other nations to follow their beliefs or rituals because they are convinced that people will be judged on what they have done rather than what they have believed in, and that all righteous people will live together in the peaceful world to come. This is why Judaism is not a missionary religion. Those who convert to Judaism and are recognized by the Church shall abide by the principles set by the Jewish authorities, for conversion is much more than an act of self-identification.

8.3.2.3 Disciplines
Jewish canon law regards the Passover, Sukkot, and Pentecost as the three major festivals, and also recognizes a number of others, such as Hanukkah, Rosh Hashanah, Purim, Yom Kippur, and Shabbat.

Besides the Ten Commandments, there are a variety of rules and laws concerning almost every aspect of Jewish daily life, from social ethics to food. A person born to a Jewish mother is a Jew. Every Jewish male must be circumcised when he is eight days old, as a sign of the covenant with God. After death, the body must be cleaned with water and wrapped in white cloth before it is buried. There are also dietary rules and taboos. The symbol of Judaism in ancient times was the menorah (a nine-branched candelabrum), but after the medieval period the Star of David became identified with the Jews, and has long since been used as a symbol of Judaism.

Jewish religious activities are generally carried out at home. These usually consist of three prayers throughout the day, in the morning, afternoon, and evening. Group prayer is conducted in local synagogues, places for Jewish worship and learning. On Monday, Thursday, the Sabbath, and High Holy Days, people read the Torah and Prophets at the synagogue. Worship is normally hosted by a learned person from the congregation, or a cantor or rabbi, who are professional priests trained by the Jewish theological school Yeshiva. The responsibility of rabbis is to guide the people in daily and weekly learning, provide a counseling service, and explain how they can practice the Jewish commandments and traditions in everyday life. Rabbis help with interpersonal conflicts or disagreements, but more serious issues such as withdrawing from Judaism must be handled by higher authorities.

Traditional Jews follow the strict dietary laws recorded in Leviticus. Milk and meat shall not be eaten together. Animals shall be slaughtered in a humane fashion. Eating blood, pork, or fish without fins and scales is prohibited. These foods may be beneficial to physical health but are prohibited in order to train people in self-control, abstinence, and morality. One is expected to unconditionally obey the rules of the Torah even under the hardest circumstances. However, the observance of these dietary disciplines, laws, and traditions differ among the three Jewish denominations (Orthodox, Conservative, and Reform).

8.3.3   Development of Judaism

Between 2000 and 1800 BC, some pastoral tribes from the northeast of the Arabian Peninsula crossed the Euphrates and entered Canaan (in present-day southern Palestine). Known as the Hebrews, their offspring became twelve tribes, who later left Canaan during a severe famine and settled in Egypt. Around 1100 BC, the Israelites emancipated themselves from Egyptian slavery under the leadership of Moses and made a covenant with God on Mount Sinai, hence establishing Judaism as their national religion with unified teachings and rituals. After the Israelites settled in Canaan, they founded the Kingdom of Israel in 993 BC and built the Holy Temple in the capital of Jerusalem.

The kingdom was then divided into the Southern Kingdom of Judah and the Northern Kingdom of Israel. In 722 BC, the Kingdom of Israel was conquered by the Assyrian Empire and its ten tribes were exiled. In face of this severe national crisis and social conflicts, a group of prophets rose from the ordinary people, advocating admiration of the one true god, criticizing priestly religions that overemphasized outward rituals, and putting forward the idea of inner beliefs and moral disciplines. In 586 BC, when the Babylonians overran Jerusalem, the Temple in Jerusalem was burned down and many Jewish captives were put into prison. In the following decades of exile, the Jews reviewed their history and reflected on the commandments and laws given by God. In 538 BC, when the Persian Empire conquered Babylonians, the Jews, released from prison, returned to Jerusalem and built a second temple, to be destroyed by the Romans in 70 BC.

Once again the Jews were scattered across the country, subject to the rule of the Roman Empire and the Persian Empire. To adapt to the current conditions, the Jews found it necessary to redefine their religious laws and texts. The destruction of the Temple replaced the sacrificial rituals based around a temple with a tradition of studying and learning centered around local synagogues. These are led by religious teachers, the rabbis. Thus Judaism is also known as Rabbinic Judaism, and it emphasizes social ethics, religious rituals, and the learning of canon law, especially oral laws. Around 200 AD, Rabbi Judah ha-Nasi redacted and edited the Mishnah based on Jewish oral traditions and laws. This began to prevail in the early third century and was passed down for generations until the fifth century, when it was compiled into another redaction of oral laws, the Talmud, which became a set of standards for daily behavior and religious worship of the Jewish community, penetrating laws and social life alike.

After the rise of Islam, Jewish communities were rejuvenated, with Babylonia replacing Palestine as the center of Judaism. In the early eighth century, the Babylonian interpretation of laws was recognized by the Jews as their compulsory law. The yeshiva academies of Babylonia not only provided training courses for rabbis but also established legislation institutes that exercised governance over the Jewish community worldwide and applied common laws, traditions, and lifestyle to Jewish people everywhere. The late tenth century witnessed within the Jewish community a trend of reform, during which some Jews appealed to rationality and developed medieval Jewish theology and philosophy. One of the representative figures of this reform was Rabbi Maimonides, who compiled a compendium of laws in order to help the Jews break away from the constraint of complicated traditional doctrines and adapt to new situations. He summarized Jewish beliefs into thirteen commandments, which were widely accepted by the Jews as their basic teachings. Some Jews explored the spiritual world through mysterious beliefs that comprised a theosophical doctrinal system known as medieval Jewish mysticism, or Kabbalah (received tradition).

In the Middle Ages, the Jews were regarded as an inferior race in many European countries, suffering religious persecution, economical restrictions, and deprivation of political rights and freedom. Forced to live in ghettos, their spirit and soul allowed them to indulge in their traditional learning framework based on the Talmud. The ghettos separated them from the rest of the country and they were seen as "aliens" by the rest of the population. Nevertheless, circumstances changed after the French Revolution in 1789, after which Jews across Europe gradually obtained their civil rights and came to enjoy equal status, freedom, and dignity to other nationalities. This actualization of their centuries-old aspiration, also known in Jewish history as the Liberation, started an era of Jewish prosperity. In this sense, the French Revolution, as a famous Jewish scholar put it, marked the end of the Jewish medieval period.

In the late eighteenth century, Hasidic Judaism emerged among lower-class Jewish communities in Eastern Europe; this was known as the Hasidic Movement. Hasidic Judaism was opposed to the over-emphasis on confession. Instead, it put the religious laws in a secondary place and accepted rabbis as spiritual mentors. According to Kabbalah writings, it emphasized inner dimensions of mystical thought, internalization of Jewish mysticism, and continuous prayer to approach God. It required absolute belief in the goodwill of God and in the eventual coming of a future Messiah to save the Jews from misery.

Europe in the eighteenth century was dominated by rationalism. Nearly all kinds of ideologies including religion were subject to the judgment of rationality, Judaism being no exception. This trend in the Jewish community in Europe was known as the Haskalah or the Jewish Enlightenment, through which Jews integrated into European society and culture. It denied the traditional Jewish lifestyle and the authority of rabbis, promoting reform of the traditional education system focusing on the oral Torah, advocating science, and assimilating secular culture, all of which led to modernized Jewish community life. As a result, the Haskalah gained support from many Jewish merchants in Europe and evolved into the Zionism of capitalist nationalism. On the one hand, the Haskalah was aimed at breaking away from the restriction of the ghetto and transforming Jews into genuine Europeans; on the other, it tried to maintain the ethnicity of the Jewish nation. These two seemingly inconsistent goals gave birth to religious reform within the Germany Jewish community.

This reform resulted in the division of Judaism into Reform Judaism, Orthodox Judaism, and Conservative Judaism, which became Reconstructionist Judaism in the USA in the twentieth century. These denominations divided Jews into different groups and caused the division in the Jewish nation that continues today.

8.3.4   Doctrines of Major Denominations

Orthodox Judaism adheres to the laws and ethics of the Torah and rejects the reform of Judaism. It believes in the eternity of God and the Torah given by God. Any change to the laws and commandments in the Torah would be considered heresy by Orthodox Jews. They also believe in the eventual coming of the Messiah to rejuvenate the Jewish nation, rebuild the Temple, and restore Jewish sacrificial rituals. Orthodox Judaism is generally divided into Modern Orthodox Judaism, ultra-orthodox or Haredi Judaism, and Hasidic Judaism.

Haredi Jews stick to the traditional Jewish belief system and follow strict doctrines and customs, oppose modern science and culture, and indeed anything that is modern. They do not recognize the State of Israel (although many of them live there) or co-operate with other streams of Judaism. Modern Orthodoxy acknowledges the Hebrew Bible and the Talmud as the authoritative books of Jewish teaching. It observes Jewish festivals, customs, and traditional ethics, with flexibility.

Orthodox Jews pray in Hebrew at synagogue, with men and women seated separately and with the absence of music. They engage in modern scientific and cultural activities, and seek peaceful co-existence and co-operation with other streams of Judaism. Modern Orthodoxy in general places a high significance on the State of Israel, and engaged in institutions that are typically Zionist in orientation.

Hasidic Judaism originated in Eastern Europe in the eighteenth century as a school of Jewish mysticism. It deprecates rationalism and scientific knowledge but emphasizes human feelings as a means to connect with God through sincere prayer. It advocates prayer in a simple form anywhere at any time as long as it is directed to God. It encourages dance, singing, and other bodily movements to stimulate emotional feelings in prayer. Although Orthodox Jews account for only 6% of the total Jewish population of 6 million in the United States, they exert considerable influence in many European countries, such as France and the United Kingdom.

At the core of Reform Judaism is the rational view that Judaism, like other ideologies, should abandon irrational and outdated factors in order to adapt to the needs of modern life, and hence develop alongside changing times. Reform Judaism defines Judaism as a monotheistic religion that lives in harmony with science and rationalism. It promotes the cosmopolitanism ideal of world peace, justice, and equality. Many medieval customs were abandoned by Reform Jews. For instance, men and women are allowed to sit together when praying in the synagogue; Bible reading and learning are in the local language as well as Hebrew; and a choirs and pipe organs are introduced to the synagogue. It practices the principle of equality between men and women, giving women the right to become a rabbi (the first female rabbi was appointed in 1972). Prior to 1960, Classic

Reform Judaism was against Zionism, but it later changed its stance to become an important supporting force for Zionism and the State of Israel. The hub of Reform Judaism was Germany before the Second World War but this transferred to North America after the war. Reform Jews are 42% of the total Jewish population in the USA, being the largest and fastest-growing denomination of Judaism today.

Conservative Judaism is a stream of Judaism that observes a range of beliefs and practices more liberal than those affirmed by the Orthodox and more traditional than Reform Judaism. It has its roots in the school of thought known as Positive-Historical Judaism that developed in Germany. During the religious reform of the nineteenth century, some German Jews found that Orthodox Judaism placed too much value on traditions in order to be able to face realistic needs, while Reform Judaism put too much emphasis on reality to observe Jewish tradition. Conservative Jews, therefore, decided to adopt a neutral path that could link tradition with modern life. Conservative Judaism recognizes and supports Zionism. It used to be the largest Jewish denomination in the USA but today it comprises only 40% of the Jewish population there. It is parallel with Orthodox Judaism in terms of the conservation of Jewish laws and rituals, and overlaps with Reform Judaism in terms of its tolerance for the change and evolution of the Halakha. Hebrew is the language used in conservative synagogues, where men and women are seated separately. Conservative Judaism started to assign female rabbis in 1985, marking its recognition of equality between men and women.

Reconstructionist Judaism originated as a branch of Conservative Judaism in the USA, based on the ideas of Mordecai Kaplan, who held that Orthodox Judaism, Reform Judaism, and Conservative Judaism could not meet the needs of modern Jewish life and therefore should be reconstructed as a naturalistic and democratic religion. He viewed Judaism as a progressively evolving civilization, consisting of three equally important elements- the Lord God, the Torah, and Jews. He claimed that God was not personal or supernatural but a salvation force within all in the universe. Despite the similar religious rituals to Conservative Judaism, Reconstructionist Judaism is more radical than Reform Judaism, in that it encourages the free interpretation of Jewish tradition, democratic Jewish life centered around synagogues, and the construction of the State of Israel. As the smallest denomination of Judaism, Reconstructionist Judaism accounts for 2% of the Jewish population in the USA, but exerts an ideological influence on Jews.

8.3.5   Influence

Judaism is a religion limited to the Jewish nation with a modest population of followers. Nevertheless, as the origin of two of the world religions, Christianity and Islam, it greatly influences religious communities worldwide. Despite the limited Jewish population, even smaller than that of Sikhs or Shintos, Judaism is referred to in almost every commentary on religion for its profound influence on the world religious community.

As Jews have suffered persecution and disasters throughout history, the Jewish population has been scattered around the world, with their oral and written traditions separate from those around them. Under such circumstances, Judaism has been the only bond that has preserved the ethnicity of the Jewish nation. Traditional Jewish belief holds that the Messiah of Israel is yet to come, while Christians view the Messiah in the person of Jesus. The disparity between these two views has often led to persecution and discrimination by Christians. When Zionism arose in the nineteenth century, Jews around the world sought to return to Palestine via means such as land trading, and they finally built the State of Israel there, causing severe conflicts with the Arabs who had been living in Palestine for over 2000 years. Despite the difference between Islam and Judaism, both religions claim to arise from the patriarch Abraham, and are therefore considered Abrahamic religions by some religious scholars.

8.4   Islam

Islam, together with Judaism and Christianity, is one of the three world religions. It was referred to by multifarious names in ancient China, such as the Tianfang religion. Islam is the Arabic word for "obedience" and "peace," denoting the worship of and total obedience to Allah, the sovereign master of the universe, and his will in pursuit of peace and safety in this life and the afterlife. An adherent of Islam is called a Muslim (a word that means "conformist").

Muslims today (over 700 million in number) account for 18.54% of the world's population, residing in over forty Muslim-majority countries in Asia and Africa. Islam is the state religion of over thirty countries. Islamic countries and Muslims are playing an increasingly important role in international political life. All Muslims, regardless of their nationality, skin color, language, or residence, adhere to the same belief in the only one God Allah and to the teachings of the Qur'an.

8.4.1   History

Islam came into being as an inevitable outcome of the social, economic, political, and religious development of the Arabian Peninsula. Between the late sixth century and the early seventh century, the Arabian Peninsula was under a transitional period in which the primitive tribal society was being replaced by a class society. The social, economic, and political development was uneven, mainly owing to geographical differences. Foreign invasion and changes in Arabian commercial routes worsened the economic crisis and social conflict. The intensifying social crisis and constant foreign invasions pushed the Arabian nation to seek a way out. The nobility, who wanted to safeguard their reign, were trying to occupy new lands and control the commercial routes, while the vast lower-class majority were aspiring to peace and stability, freedom from economic exploitation and political persecution, and poverty alleviation. At this moment, Islam emerged as an ideology that spoke to people's aspiration for social, economic, and political reform. Muhammad created Islam and used it to lead a social reform campaign that finally realized the unification of the Arabian Peninsula.

Muhammad, the founder of Islam, is an eminent historical figure. Born into the Banu Hashim clan in about 570 AD in the Arabian city of Mecca, Muhammad was orphaned at an early age; he was raised by his paternal grandfather and paternal uncle. He dropped out of school and worked as a shepherd in his early childhood. At the age of twelve, he accompanied his uncle's trading caravan to Syria, Palestine, and the eastern coast of the Mediterranean Sea. During his career as a merchant there, Muhammad learned about the social circumstances of the Arabian Peninsula and Syria as well as the primitive religions, Judaism, and Christianity. This provided him the social and religious knowledge necessary to preach Islam later. At the age of twenty-five, he married Khadijah, the widow of his employer, and enjoyed a prosperous life and improved social status. Influenced by the thoughts of Hanif, he occasionally retreated to a cave in the mountains for seclusion and self-cultivation, to reflect on possible ways in which he could help the Arabian nation out of its troubles. It was said that in the year 610, during his meditations on Mount Hira near Mecca, the angel Gabriel appeared to him and commanded the forty-year-old Muhammad to recite verses that were revelations from God.

Henceforward, Muhammad proclaimed that he had received a mission from God and started preaching these revelations in Mecca privately among his close friends. In 612, he began to preach Islam publicly, telling people to worship Allah instead of idols or deities and that Allah was the creator of the universe and the only one true God. He criticized polytheism for bringing ignorance and moral failure to the Arabs, and preached on the concept of resurrection of the dead and the Day of Judgment, when polytheists would be punished and sent to hell while adherents of Allah would be rewarded with admission to heaven. He also advocated that all Muslims were brothers whatever clan they belonged to, and therefore should be united with the ending of all blood feuds. He proposed a set of ideas for social reforms: that usury should be forbidden, the wealthy should give relief to the poor, and orphans, widows, and slaves should be treated well or released. These ideas gained wide support among the vast lower classes, who gradually converted to Islam. As the teachings of Islam profoundly threatened the tradition of polytheistic faith in clan-patronized deities, as well as the religious privilege and economic interests of the nobles and merchants who were governing Kaaba, Muhammad met hostility and persecution from some tribes, which made it difficult for him and his followers to stay in Mecca.

To escape persecution, Muhammad and his followers migrated to Medina in September 622, marking the beginning of a new era for Islamic development. Muhammad led the Muslims as they carried out a series of political, economic, and religious reforms. He appealed to them to submit to Allah and his messenger. He also sent some of his disciples to preach Islam among the Arabian clans in Mecca, converting the majority of local residents to Muslims. He drafted a document known as the Constitution of Medina, specifying guidelines for both Muslims and Jews in handling civil affairs and foreign relations. He also reached certain agreements with the Jewish tribes concerning religious freedom, alliance, and peaceful coexistence. After he united the tribes under the Constitution of Medina, Muhammad replaced the governance by clan kinship with the common belief in Islam and under the slogan of "All Muslims are brothers" he united the muhājirūn and ansār into the Ummah (meaning "nation" or "community"), a political–religious governance system, establishing the Islamic faith system and various social systems in the name of revelations from God. At this point, Muhammad had become the highest leader in Medina in terms of religion, politics, the military, and jurisdiction, with Abu Bakr al-Siddiq, Umar, Uthman, and some other famous disciples constituting the supreme leadership regime. He articulated the Pillars of Islam, the five basic acts considered obligatory for all Muslims. He also built a jurisprudence system containing religious doctrines, civil laws, criminal laws, commercial laws, and military laws, thus establishing a set of social norms and morals centering on the core principle of forsaking evil and promoting goodness.

To consolidate his power in Medina, Muhammad built a Muslim army. In the name of Allah, he launched the battle of Ghazwah Badr, the battle of Ghazwah, and the battle of Ghazwah al-Khaildaq against the Meccan nobility during 624 and 627, which severely harmed the Meccan army, placing Muslims in an advantageous position. In 628, Muhammad led an army into the suburbs of Mecca, where he forced the Meccan nobles to sign the Agreement of Sulh al-Hudaybiyyah that provided for a ten-year ceasefire. He took advantage of this peaceful period to further preach Islam among Arabian clans in neighboring countries and the Peninsula, after sending envoys with letters of credence to kings and tribal chieftains. In the meantime, he sent punitive expeditions against the Jews inhabiting Khaybar and surrounding areas, to eliminate opposition to Islam.

In 630 Muhammad accused the Meccan nobility of violating the Agreement and gathered an army of around 10,000 Muslim converts to attack the city of Mecca. The attack went largely uncontested and Abu Sufyan, the head of Meccan nobles, was forced to surrender and recognize Muhammad as the prophet and Islam as the religion for all in Mecca. Muhammad destroyed all the pagan idols in the Kaaba except the Black Stone and renamed the Kaaba as the Mosque. Since then the Kaaba has been the center of prayers and pilgrimage for Muslims worldwide. By the end of 631, all clans of the Peninsula had converted to Islam and accepted the leadership of Muhammad, signifying the Peninsula's political unification. In March 632, Muhammad, accompanied by a group of 100,000 Muslims, went to Mecca for his last pilgrimage, known to history as the Farewell Pilgrimage. During this, he established a set of ordinances and rites of Hajj pilgrimage for all Muslims to follow. After completing the pilgrimage, Muhammad delivered a famous speech, known as the Farewell Sermon, at Mount Arafat, east of Mecca. He declared: "Today I have perfected your religion, and completed my favours for you and chosen Islam as a religion for you" (Qur'an 5:3). A few months after the Farewell Pilgrimage, on June 8, 632, Muhammad died in Medina. Before his death, most of the Arabian Peninsula had converted to Islam and Islam had become a spiritual bond for the whole Arabian nationality. This opened a new era in the history of Arabia.

8.4.2   *Basic Teachings*

The core tenet of Islam is the absolute belief in Allah (God) and Muhammad, the Messenger of God. "He is Allah, the One and Only; Allah, the Eternal, Absolute; He did not beget, nor is He begotten; And there is none like unto Him" (Qur'an, Chapter 112:1–4). The Qur'an teaches Muslims to obey Allah and Muhammad. Islam believes in angels. They were created by Allah to fulfill their mission and the responsibilities given by him. All the good and bad deeds of human beings are overseen and recorded by the angels. The Qur'an is the holy book of the revelations of Allah. Everything that occurs in the world has been preordained by God. Islam claims that Allah created all and controls all, both nature and human society. This is known as predestination. Although events are preordained, man possesses the faculty to choose between right and wrong, and is thus responsible for his own actions. Islam believes in the resurrection of the dead and the Day of Judgment. It holds that everyone has to go through this life and an afterlife, and that all in the world will disappear when the final day arrives. On this day, all that have ever lived will be resurrected to receive the judgment of Allah, who will send good men to heaven and sinful ones to hell. The present life is temporary but the afterlife is eternal, so man should take responsibility for both lives.

There are five articles of faith in Islam.

8.4.2.1 *Allah (God)*

Islam believes that Allah is the only one God, the Supreme God of the universe. According to the Qur'an, Allah has ninety-nine names and attributes, being unique, eternal, absolute. He knows all, controls all, and deposes all. Muslims believe that everything in the universe was brought into being by God's command and that the purpose of existence is to worship God. Monotheism is the most fundamental concept of Islam.

8.4.2.2 *Prophets*

The Qur'an mentions the names of numerous figures who are considered prophets in Islam, including Adam, Noah, Abraham, Moses, and Jesus, to name a few. Among them, Muhammad is seen by Muslims as the last prophet (Seal of the Prophets) sent by God to convey the divine message of Allah to the whole world, and thus all adherents of Allah shall defer to him.

8.4.2.3 Angels

Muslims believe that angels are made by Allah out of light and assigned by him to govern heaven and hell, to communicate revelations from Allah, and to record every person's actions. There are four primary archangels in the Qur'an: Jibra'il (Gabriel), Mikhail, Azral, and Israfil, respectively responsible for delivering messages from Allah to the prophets and revealing the Qur'an to Muhammad, bringing rain and thunder to Earth, parting the soul from the body at the time of death, and blowing a horn to signify the coming of Judgment Day.

8.4.2.4 Revelations

The Islamic holy books are the records which most Muslims believe were dictated by God to various prophets. The Qur'an is viewed by Muslims as a holy book of revelation and the literal word of God that all Muslims must observe and follow; it shall not be altered or vilified. Islam recognizes the previously revealed scriptures from Allah (such as the Bible), but maintains that all adherents must align their acts to the Qur'an.

8.4.2.5 Judgment Day and Resurrection

Muslims believe that the Day of Judgment connects this life and the afterlife, on which the world will come to an end and Allah will make his ultimate judgment on mankind's good and bad deeds.

8.4.3   Spread and Development of Islam

The growth of Islam, from a national religion limited to Arabia into an international one observed by multiple nations, is a process of the expansion, economic and commercial trade, cultural exchange, and active missionary activity on the part of Arabian Islamic countries with the rest of the world.

After the death of Muhammad in 632, Islam entered the era of Four Rashidun Caliphs. With the continuous expansion of the Arab Empire, Islam was widely spread beyond the Peninsula, known to history as the Expansion of Islam. The year 661 marked the beginning of the era of the Arab Empire, spanning the Umayyads Dynasty and the Abbasids Dynasty. This period is known as the Golden Age of Islam, and it lasted until the Arab Empire collapsed in the mid-thirteenth century because of foreign invasions that gave rise to declarations of independence by dynasties in the east and west of the Empire. In the late Middle Ages there were three empires—the Ottoman Empire, the Safavid Empire, and the Mogul Empire. Among them the Ottoman Empire was the largest and most powerful. This period of time is known as the Third Expansion of Islam. Western colonist countries started their invasion into the Islamic world in the mid-eighteenth century, many Islamic countries becoming colonies or semi-colonies. The Islamic states, in the name of "holy war" and religious movements, launched numerous anti-colonial battles that caused heavy blows to the colonist countries. After the Second World War many Islamic states declared independence, which formed the international Islamic landscape that exists today. The spread and development of Islam demonstrates features peculiar to specific historical periods.

8.4.3.1 Caliphate

After Muhammad's death in 632, he was succeeded by four of his disciples in succession—Abu Bakr, Umar, Uthman, and Ali, called the four rightly guided caliphs (meaning "successor of messenger of Allah"), who made great contributions to the spread and growth of Islam during their thirty years of their reign. Abu Bakr crushed the apostasy led by the self-proclaimed prophet Musaylimah in southern Yemen, Yamama, eastern Bahrain, and the Mahra region, thus consolidating the unity of the Arabian Peninsula and his rule in Medina.

When Umar took office as the second caliph following Abu Bakr, the Persian Empire and the Byzantine Empire had been at war for years. He took the opportunity to conquer Syria, Palestine, Iraq, Persia, Egypt, and surrounding areas. He made a tremendous contribution to the growth of Islam into a multi-national religion with his efforts to convert the local residents of the conquered states to Islam by implementing a policy that freed Islamic converters from paying the poll tax. He established the administrative system, judicial system, military system, land system, and distribution system for the country. He also established the Islamic calendar and set 622 as the first year of the calendar, in honor of the hijra (migration) of Muhammad from Mecca to Medina.

After Uthman assumed the office of caliph, succeeding Umar, he conquered Armenia in the east and North Africa in the west, taking Bourke, Tripoli, and Carthage. He suppressed a rebellion in Persia and Khorasan with his expeditionary army that later arrived in Kabul, and converted many of the local residents to Islam. Uthman obtained the complete manuscript of the Qur'an compiled by the first caliph, Abu Bakr, and summoned the leading compiling authority to conduct research and investigation, proofread, and redact a standard version, the Uthman Version of the Qur'an, which was accepted by the Muslim community as an authoritative sacred book that spread Islam and the Arabic language to the rest of the world.

During the reign of Ali, the fourth Rashidun caliph, conflicts within the leadership regime of the Islamic community led to the first Islamic civil war. The Battle of the Camel, the Battle of Siffin, and the Battle of Nahrawan, coupled with disputes over religious ideas and political leadership, gave rise to schisms in the Muslim community. When Ali was assassinated in 661, the era of the Rashidun Caliphate (or the Rightly Guided Caliphs) came to an end. Mu'awiyah came to power and began the Umayyad Dynasty.

8.4.3.2 The Umayyad Dynasty
The Umayyad Dynasty was founded by Mu'awiyah (600–680) in 661, with Damascus as its capital. After stabilizing the social turbulence and suppressing the revolts against the Umayyad regime, the Umayyads continued Muslim conquests in the mid-seventh century. By the mid-eighth century, the realm of the Umayyad Empire had reached the Indus Valley in the east, the Atlantic Ocean in the west, the Aral Sea in the north, and the Nile in the south, crossing Asia, Africa, and Europe. It was the largest empire the world had ever seen.

8.4.3.3 The Abbasid Dynasty
The Abbasid Dynasty was founded by Abu al-Abbas (722–754) after taking over leadership of the Muslim empire from the Umayyads in 750. The caliph proclaimed himself as the "reflection of Allah on earth." He implemented a policy that integrated religion with secular life, and inherited an administrative system from Persia which emphasized the centralization of authority with the caliph as the highest leader. The Abbasid caliphate established religious schools, libraries, observatories, and hospitals across the country, contributing to the nation's academic and cultural development. The House of Wisdom was founded in Baghdad, where both Muslim and non-Muslim scholars sought to gather, preserve, study, and translate the classic literature of Greece, Persia, and India into Arabic. Islam became the dominant religion of the empire that penetrated into political, economic, and cultural fields, being a social lifestyle for all Muslims.

The Sunni and Shi'ite sects had evolved from political parties into Islamic branches, having their own distinctive teachings and theological views. Mu'tazilism, another branch of Islam, flourished during the reign of the Abbasid Caliph al-Ma'mun (833). Ash'arism (or the Ash'arite school of Islam) gradually became a dominant theological school of Islam in the tenth century. Sufism was introduced into the Islamic belief system by theologians, Al-Ghazali in particular, and became a form of Islamic philosophy. In 1055 the Seljuq Turks took hold of Baghdad, and the caliph was reduced to a political puppet under the control of the Seljuq king. The conquest by Hulagu Khan's Mongols in 1258 brought an end to the Abbasid Dynasty.

8.4.3.4 *The Ottoman Empire*

Decades after the Ottoman Turks came to prominence in the early thirteenth century in central Asia, the Ottoman Empire was founded in 1299 when the tribal chieftain, Osman I, proclaimed himself as the sultan. In 1453, the Ottomans, under Mehmed II, defeated the Byzantine Empire and captured its capital, Constantinople, which was renamed Istanbul and thereafter served as the Ottoman capital. By the end of the fifteenth century, the Ottomans had conquered the entirety of Asia Minor and the Balkan Peninsula and brought Islam to southwestern Europe. The sixteenth century witnessed the zenith of the Ottoman Empire, its realm having expanded to countries and regions including Armenia, Georgia, Syria, Egypt, Baghdad, Mesopotamia, Tripoli, Algeria, Hijaz, and Yemen. It also controlled the sacred Islamic cities Mecca, Medina, and Jerusalem. Occupying most of the territory of the Byzantine Empire and the Arab Empire, the Ottoman Empire became a powerful multi-national Islamic empire stretching over Asia, Africa, and Europe.

At the end of the thirteenth century, the descendants of Mongols who had settled down in central Asia converted to Islam. Islam was introduced by Sufi preachers to Kazakhstan in central Asia and Bengali in the subcontinent of southern Asia in the fourteenth century. It was also brought to China in the mid-seventh century through the Silk Road by Muslim merchants and scholars from Arabia, Persia, and central Asia. In the late fourteenth century, Muslim merchants in Gujarat, western India, introduced the Islamic religion to the Indonesia Archipelago, and it grew into the major religion there and in the Malay Peninsula in the seventeenth century. Islam was brought to the southern Philippines by merchants and priests during the fourteenth and fifteenth centuries. It was preached in Western Europe and north America by Islamic migrants, businessmen, and scholars in the twentieth century, and has been growing rapidly ever since.

BIBLIOGRAPHY

Bulgakov. 2001. *The Orthodox Church*. Beijing: The Commercial Press.
Jin Yijiu. 1987. *An Introduction to Islam*. Xi'ning: Qinghai People's Publishing House.
Lü Daji. 1998. *New General Theory of Religion*. Beijing: China Social Sciences Press.
Sha Zongping. 1995. *Islamic Philosophy*. Beijing: China Social Sciences Press.
Sun Shangyang. 1996. *Christianity and Confucianism in Late Ming Dynasty*. Taipei: The Eastern Publishing Co., Ltd.
———. 2001. *The Sociology of Religion*. Beijing: Peking University Press.
Walker, Williston. 1991. *A History of the Christian Church*. Beijing: China Social Sciences Press.
Zhang Zhigang. 1995. *A Path to Holiness—Issues and Approaches of Modern Religious Studies*. Beijing: People's Publishing House.
Zhang Baichun. 2000. *Contemporary Theology of the Orthodox Churches*. Shanghai: SDX Joint Publishing Company.
Zhang Zhigang. 2002. *What Is Religious Studies*. Beijing: Peiking University Press.
Zhao Dunhua. 1994. *Christian Philosophy in 1500 Years*. Beijing: People's Publishing House.

CPSIA information can be obtained
at www.ICGtesting.com
Printed in the USA
LVOW13*2012020418

571979LV00013B/305/P